Microsoft®

Step by Step

Microsoft®
Windows® 2000
Professional

Built on **NT** Technology

/ActiveEducation™

PUBLISHED BY
Microsoft Press
A Division of Microsoft Corporation
One Microsoft Way
Redmond, Washington 98052-6399

Library of Congress Cataloging-in-Publication Data
Microsoft Windows 2000 Professional Step by Step / ActiveEducation.
        p. cm.
    Includes index.
    ISBN 1-57231-847-3
    1. Microsoft Windows (Compuer file)   2. Operating systems (Computers) I.
ActiveEducation (Firm)

QA76.76.O63 M5241325   1999
005.4'4769--dc21   99-045608

Printed and bound in the United States of America.

3 4 5 6 7 8 9   WCWC   5 4 3 2 1 0

Distributed in Canada by Penguin Books Canada Limited.

A CIP catalogue record for this book is available from the British Library.

Microsoft Press books are available through booksellers and distributors worldwide. For further information about international editions, contact your local Microsoft Corporation office or contact Microsoft Press International directly at fax (425) 936-7329. Visit our Web site at mspress.microsoft.com.

For ActiveEducation:
Managing Editor: Ron Pronk
Series Editor: Kate Dawson
Project Editor: Lisa Probasco
Writer: Marianne Krcma
Production/Layout: Nicole French
Technical Editors: Leif Fedje, Linda Savell
Proofreaders: Holly Freeman, Jennifer Jordan,
 Nicole French
Indexer: Maria Townsley
Production Assistant: Carrice L. Cudworth

For Microsoft Press:
Acquisitions Editor: Susanne M. Forderer
Project Editor: Anne Taussig

Contents

*Quick*Look Guide

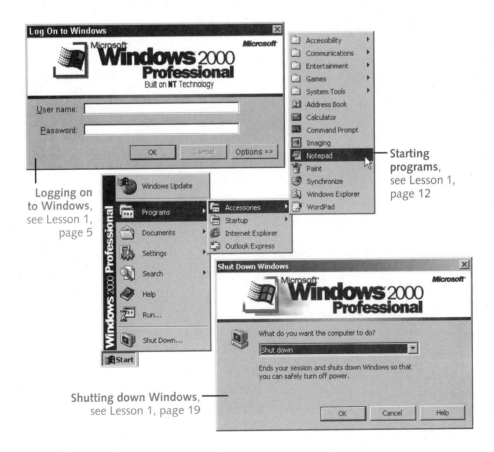

Logging on to Windows, see Lesson 1, page 5

Starting programs, see Lesson 1, page 12

Shutting down Windows, see Lesson 1, page 19

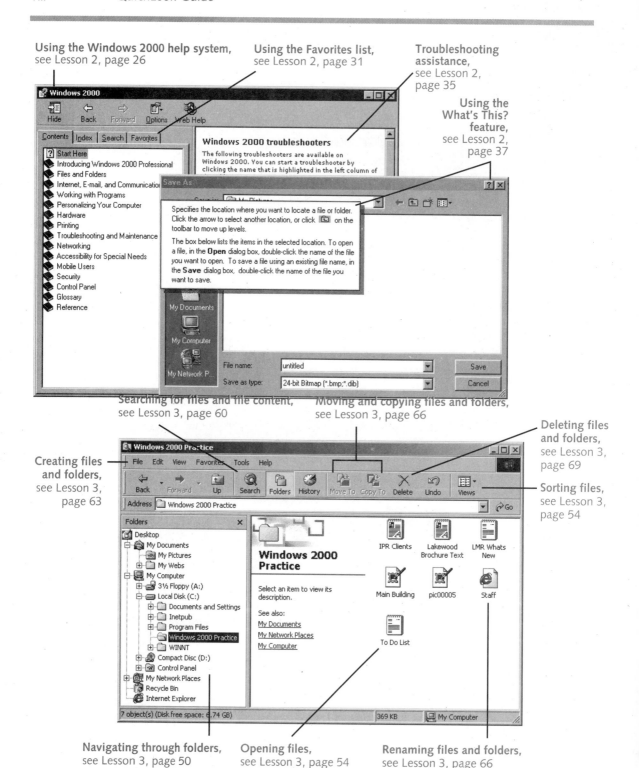

Using the Windows 2000 help system, see Lesson 2, page 26

Using the Favorites list, see Lesson 2, page 31

Troubleshooting assistance, see Lesson 2, page 35

Using the What's This? feature, see Lesson 2, page 37

Searching for files and file content, see Lesson 3, page 60

Moving and copying files and folders, see Lesson 3, page 66

Deleting files and folders, see Lesson 3, page 69

Creating files and folders, see Lesson 3, page 63

Sorting files, see Lesson 3, page 54

Navigating through folders, see Lesson 3, page 50

Opening files, see Lesson 3, page 54

Renaming files and folders, see Lesson 3, page 66

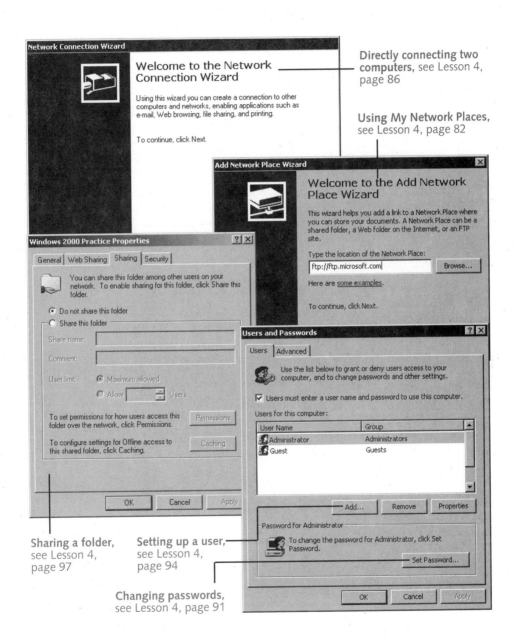

Directly connecting two computers, see Lesson 4, page 86

Using My Network Places, see Lesson 4, page 82

Sharing a folder, see Lesson 4, page 97

Setting up a user, see Lesson 4, page 94

Changing passwords, see Lesson 4, page 91

Connecting to the Internet,
see Lesson 5, page 108

**Finding what you
need on the Web,**
see Lesson 5, page 117

Keeping track of Web sites,
see Lesson 5, page 118

**Navigating
the Web,**
see Lesson 5,
page 113

Using
Windows
Update,
see Lesson 2,
page 41

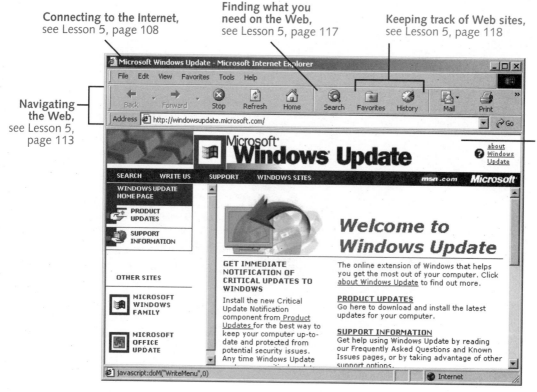

Managing e-mail messages
with Outlook Express,
see Lesson 6, page 132

Organizing your messages,
see Lesson 6, page 139

Keeping track of contacts,
see Lesson 6, page 136

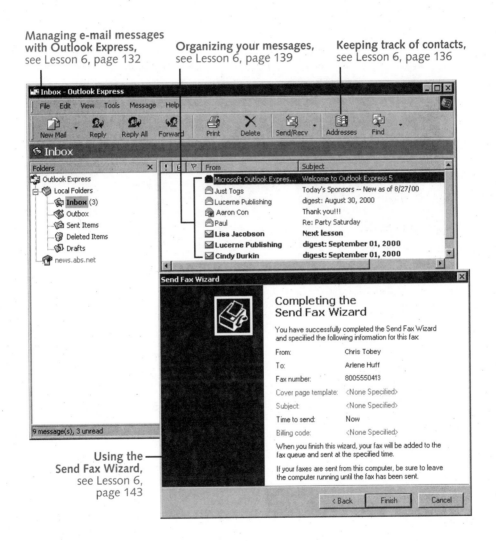

Using the
Send Fax Wizard,
see Lesson 6,
page 143

Adding Active Desktop items,
see Lesson 7, page 168

Changing the appearance of the desktop,
see Lesson 7, page 164

Arranging icons on the desktop,
see Lesson 7, page 162

Creating shortcut icons on the desktop,
see Lesson 7, page 158

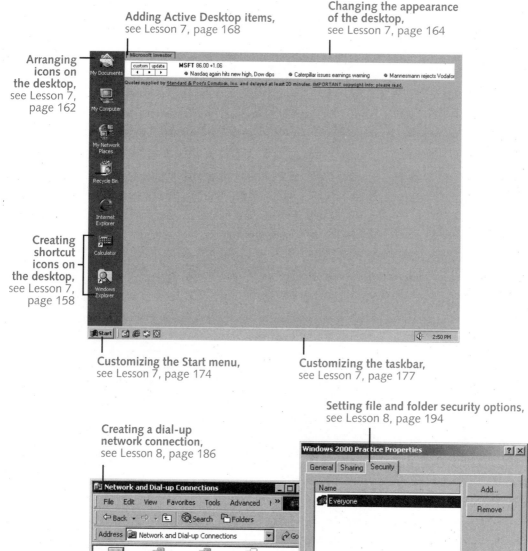

Customizing the Start menu,
see Lesson 7, page 174

Customizing the taskbar,
see Lesson 7, page 177

Setting file and folder security options,
see Lesson 8, page 194

Creating a dial-up network connection,
see Lesson 8, page 186

Using Web files offline,
see Lesson 8, page 191

Removing software,
see Lesson 9,
page 209

Installing software,
see Lesson 9,
page 205

Configuring Windows components,
see Lesson 9,
page 202

Installing Plug and Play hardware,
see Lesson 9,
page 215

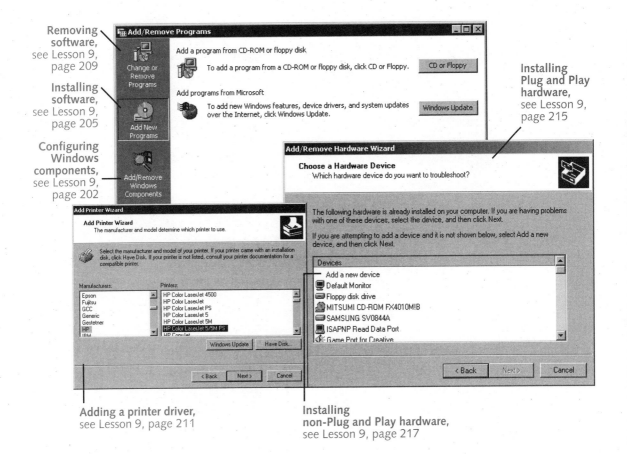

Adding a printer driver,
see Lesson 9, page 211

Installing non-Plug and Play hardware,
see Lesson 9, page 217

Defragmenting a disk,
see Lesson 10, page 230

Scheduling maintenance,
see Lesson 10, page 241

Backing up data,
see Lesson 10, page 233

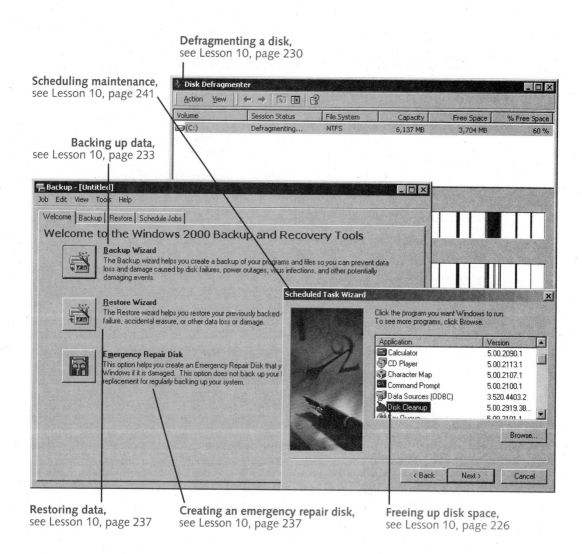

Restoring data,
see Lesson 10, page 237

Creating an emergency repair disk,
see Lesson 10, page 237

Freeing up disk space,
see Lesson 10, page 226

Finding Your Best Starting Point

Microsoft Windows 2000 Professional is the newest version of the Windows operating system. Windows 2000 is built on Windows NT technology, but it includes much of the appearance and feature set of Microsoft Windows 98. Windows 2000 offers many new features and enhancements, including easier networking and Internet connectivity and enhanced file and folder security. Windows 2000 Professional runs equally well on networked computers or on a standalone personal computer. Also, Windows 2000 is compatible with most programs designed for Windows 95 and Windows 98, so you probably won't need to upgrade your programs when you install Windows 2000 on your computer.

Finding Your Best Starting Point in This Book

This book is organized for beginning Windows users, as well as readers who are switching or upgrading their operating systems to Windows 2000. If you have not yet installed Windows 2000, read Appendix B, "Installing Windows 2000," before proceeding. Then use the following table to find your best starting point in this book.

If you are	Follow these steps
New	
To computers or Windows	1 Install the practice files as described in "Using the Microsoft Windows 2000 Professional Step by Step CD-ROM."
To graphical (as opposed to text-only) computer programs	2 Work through Lessons 1 through 10 chronologically.

If you are	Follow these steps
Switching From OS/2	1 Install the practice files as described in "Using the Microsoft Windows 2000 Professional Step by Step CD-ROM." 2 Learn basic skills for using Windows by working through Lesson 1. Then you can work through Lessons 2 through 10.

If you are	Follow these steps
Upgrading From Windows 98	1 Install the practice files as described in "Using the Microsoft Windows 2000 Professional Step by Step CD-ROM." 2 Complete the lessons that cover the topics you need. You can use the Table of Contents and the *Quick*Look Guide to locate information about general topics. You can use the index to find information about a specific topic or feature.

If you are	Follow these steps
Upgrading From Windows NT	1 Learn about the features of Windows 2000 that are covered in this book by reading through the following section, "New Features in Windows 2000." 2 Install the practice files as described in "Using the Microsoft Windows 2000 Professional Step by Step CD-ROM." 3 Complete the lessons that cover the topics you need. You can use the Table of Contents and the *Quick*Look Guide to locate information about general topics. You can use the index to find information about a specific topic or feature.

If you are	Follow these steps
Referencing This book after working through the lessons	1 Use the index to locate information about specific topics, and use the Table of Contents to locate information about general topics. 2 Read the Quick Reference at the end of each lesson for a brief review of the major topics in the lesson. The Quick Reference topics are presented in the same order as they are presented in the lesson.

New Features in Windows 2000

The following table lists the major new features of Windows 2000 covered in this book and the lesson in which you can learn how to use each feature. You can also use the index to find specific information about a feature or about a task you want to perform.

The New! 2000 icon appears in the margin throughout this book to indicate the features in Windows 2000 that are new over Windows NT.

To learn about	See
The Quick Launch bar	Lesson 1
Personalized menus	Lesson 1
The window resize area	Lesson 1
The Shut Down Windows dialog box	Lesson 1
The two-pane help window	Lesson 2
The Favorites tab in the help window	Lesson 2
Windows Update	Lesson 2
The Standard Buttons toolbar	Lesson 3
The Folders pane	Lesson 3
Typing a Web address in the Windows Explorer Address bar	Lesson 3
The Open With command	Lesson 3
Thumbnails view	Lesson 3
The renamed Find command	Lesson 3
The Restore button in the Recycle Bin	Lesson 3
My Network Places	Lesson 4
The Network Connection Wizard	Lesson 4
The Windows password controlling the My Documents folder	Lesson 4
The Windows Security dialog box	Lesson 4
The Users And Passwords icon	Lesson 4
The Map Network Drive dialog box	Lesson 4
The Customize This Folder command	Lesson 7
Additional background pictures to choose	Lesson 7
Active Desktop	Lesson 7
The option to single-click or double-click an item	Lesson 7
Additional toolbars to display on the taskbar	Lesson 7
File and folder encryption	Lesson 8
The Windows Components Wizard	Lesson 9
The Administrative Tools window	Lesson 9
The pie chart representing used and free disk space	Lesson 10
Disk cleanup and drive compression	Lesson 10

Using the Microsoft Windows 2000 Professional Step by Step CD-ROM

The CD-ROM inside the back cover of this book contains the practice files that you'll use as you perform the exercises in the book and multimedia files that demonstrate 11 of the exercises. By using the practice files, you won't waste time creating the samples used in the lessons, and you can concentrate on learning how to use Microsoft Windows 2000 Professional. With the files and the step by step instructions in the lessons, you'll also learn by doing, which is an easy and effective way to acquire and remember skills.

important

Microsoft Windows 2000 Professional is not included with this book. Before you break the seal on the Microsoft Windows 2000 Professional Step by Step CD-ROM package, be sure that this book matches your version of the software. This book is designed for use with Microsoft Windows 2000 Professional. If your product is not compatible with this book, a Step by Step book matching your software is probably available. Please visit our World Wide Web site at *mspress.microsoft.com* or call 1-800-MSPRESS (1-800-677-7377) for more information.

Hardware Requirements

If you're unsure whether Windows 2000 is installed on your computer, try the "Starting Windows 2000" exercise in Lesson 1, "Touring Microsoft Windows 2000 Professional." If you see screens similar to those shown in the exercise, Windows 2000 is installed.

To install and run Windows 2000, your computer must have:

- A processor (also called a CPU) that runs at 233 MHz or faster.
- At least 64 MB (megabytes) of RAM (memory).
- At least 650 MB of free space on your primary hard disk (the one that the operating system accesses each time you start your computer).
- A monitor that supports a resolution of VGA or better. (If you have purchased your monitor within the past five years, your monitor probably meets this requirement.)
- A CD-ROM drive (unless you are installing from a network, in which case you will need access to the Windows setup folder on the network).
- A mouse (or other pointing device) and a keyboard.

To find out whether your computer meets these requirements, check the documentation that came with it or check with your technical support contact or network administrator.

Additional Hardware to Use This Book

In addition to the computer itself, you will need one or more of the following devices to perform one or more of the exercises. (Hardware requirements for completing lesson exercises are described at the beginning of each lesson.)

- A network interface card for connecting your computer to your organization's network.
- A modem for connecting to the Internet.
- A sound card and speakers.
- A printer.
- Other hardware for entering information into your computer or getting output from it, such as a scanner, a digital camera, or a backup drive.

Network Requirements

If you will be using Windows 2000 to access your organization's network, your user name and password must match those set up on the network server. If you haven't been set up as a user on the network, you might be able to view other computers connected to the network, but you won't be able to open any files or folders stored on other computers or use any shared resources on other computers.

Installing the Practice Files

Follow these steps to install the practice files on your computer's hard disk so that you can use them with the exercises in this book.

1 If your computer isn't on, turn it on now.

If you are connected to a network, you will see the Log On To Windows dialog box.

2 If you're connected to a network, you will see a dialog box asking for your user name and password.

3 Type your user name and password in the appropriate boxes, and click OK. If you see the Welcome dialog box, click the Close button.

4 Remove the CD-ROM from the package inside the back cover of this book.

5 Insert the CD-ROM in the CD-ROM drive of your computer.

If a menu screen does not appear, double-click StartCD.exe in the root of the CD.

6 Click the Install Practice Files option, and follow the prompts that appear on your screen.

7 When the files have been installed, remove the CD-ROM from your CD-ROM drive, and replace it in the package inside the back cover of the book.

A folder called Windows 2000 Practice has been created on your hard disk, and the practice files have been placed in that folder.

If your computer is set up to connect to the Internet, you can double-click the Microsoft Press Welcome shortcut to visit the Microsoft Press Web site. You can also connect to this Web site directly at *mspress.microsoft.com*.

Using the Practice Files

Each lesson in this book explains when and how to use any practice files for that lesson. The lessons are built around scenarios drawn from two fictitious companies: Impact Public Relations and one of its clients, Lakewood Mountains Resort, so you can easily apply the skills you learn to your own work.

The practice files used in the lessons are as follows.

Filename	Description
IPR Clients.rtf	File used in Lessons 3 and 7
Lakewood Brochure Text.rtf	File used in Lesson 3
LMR Whats New.txt	File used in Lesson 3
Main Building.jpg	File used in Lesson 3
Pic00005.jpg	File used in Lesson 3

Filename	Description
Staff.htm	File used in Lesson 3
To Do List.txt	File used in Lesson 3
pandemo.exe	File used in Lesson 9

Using the Multimedia Files

Throughout this book, you will see icons for multimedia files for particular exercises. Follow these steps to play the multimedia files.

If a menu screen does not appear, double-click startCD.exe in the root of the CD.

1   Insert the Microsoft Windows 2000 Professional Step by Step CD-ROM in your CD-ROM drive.

2   Click the Browse CD option.

3   In the right pane, double-click the Multimedia folder.

   The Multimedia folder opens.

4   In the right pane, double-click the multimedia file that you want to view.

   Windows Media Player shows the video of the exercise.

5   After the video is finished, click the Close button in the top-right corner of the Media Player window.

   Media Player closes, and Windows Explorer reappears.

6   Close Windows Explorer, and return to the exercise in the book.

Uninstalling the Practice Files

Use the following steps when you want to delete the practice files added to your hard disk by the Step by Step setup program.

1   On the Windows taskbar, click the Start button, point to Settings, and then click Control Panel.

2   Double-click the Add/Remove icon.

3   Click Windows 2000 Practice in the list, and then click Remove.

4   Click Yes when the confirmation dialog box appears.

Corrections, Comments, and Help

Every effort has been made to ensure the accuracy of this book and the contents of the Microsoft Windows 2000 Professional Step by Step CD-ROM. Microsoft Press provides corrections and additional content for its books through the World Wide Web at *mspress.microsoft.com/support*

If you have comments, questions, or ideas regarding this book or the CD-ROM, please send them to us.

Send e-mail to:

>   mspinput@microsoft.com

Or send postal mail to:

>   Microsoft Press
>
>   Attn: Step by Step Editor
>
>   One Microsoft Way
>
>   Redmond, WA 98052-6399

Please note that support for the Microsoft Windows 2000 Professional software product itself is not offered through the above addresses. For help using Windows 2000 Professional, you can call Windows 2000 Technical Support at (425) 635-7070 on weekdays between 6 A.M. and 6 P.M. Pacific Time.

Visit Our World Wide Web Site

We invite you to visit the Microsoft Press World Wide Web site. You can visit us at the following location:

>   *mspress.microsoft.com*

You'll find descriptions of all of our books, information about ordering titles, notices of special features and events, additional content for Microsoft Press books, and much more.

You can also find out the latest in software developments and news from Microsoft Corporation by visiting the following World Wide Web site:

>   *microsoft.com*

We look forward to your visit on the Web!

Conventions and Features in This Book

You can save time when you use this book by understanding, before you start the lessons, how instructions, keys to press, and so on are shown in the book. Please take a moment to read the following list, which points out helpful features of the book that you might want to use.

Conventions

- Hands-on exercises for you to follow are given in numbered lists of steps (1, 2, and so on). A round bullet (●) indicates an exercise that has only one step.

- Text that you are to type and glossary terms that are defined at the end of the lesson appear in **bold**.

- The icons below identify certain types of exercise features:

Icon	Identifies
	Skills that are demonstrated in multimedia files available on the Microsoft Windows 2000 Professional Step by Step CD-ROM.
	New features in Windows 2000.

Other Features of This Book

- You can get a quick reminder of how to perform the tasks you learned by reading the Quick Reference at the end of each lesson.

- You can practice the major skills presented in the lessons by working through the Review & Practice section at the end of each unit.

- You can see a multimedia demonstration of some of the exercises in the book by following the instructions in the "Using the Multimedia Files" procedure in the "Using the Microsoft Windows 2000 Professional Step by Step CD-ROM" section of this book.

UNIT 1

Getting Started with Microsoft Windows 2000 Professional

1

Touring Microsoft Windows 2000 Professional

After completing this lesson, you will be able to:

✔ *Start Windows.*
✔ *Recognize the components of Windows 2000 Professional.*
✔ *Start programs.*
✔ *Move, resize, and close windows.*
✔ *Make windows active.*
✔ *Shut down Windows.*

ESTIMATED TIME
20 min.

Microsoft Windows 2000 Professional, referred to here as simply Windows, is the newest version of the Windows **operating system**. An operating system is a collection of programs that controls the way a computer's hardware devices work and the way programs interact with hardware and the computer's user. Whenever you work with your computer, you are using Windows—either directly or indirectly through another program like Microsoft Word.

Windows plays an important role in helping you complete your work successfully and efficiently, so you'll want to become familiar with it as quickly as possible. That's where this book comes in: it explains in simple, straightforward language how to use the features of Windows, and it offers many opportunities to practice what you learn. To help you understand concepts, the lessons in this book frequently use example scenarios drawn from two fictitious companies: Impact Public Relations and one of its clients, Lakewood Mountains Resort.

This book is designed to allow you to choose the topics you want to learn. You can work through the entire book, or you can focus on only the lessons you want, as you want them. For instance, you might not want to learn about installing a hardware device now. But if you purchase a modem or monitor, you might want to work through the relevant lessons at that time.

In this lesson, you will be introduced to the major components of Windows 2000. You will also learn how to find what you need on your computer.

Starting Windows 2000

Each time you start your computer, it goes through a **boot process** (from the phrase "pull yourself up by your bootstraps"). The boot process checks that all the necessary parts of the computer are plugged in and functioning properly. As soon as the computer finishes booting, it turns control over to Windows. From then until the time you shut down your computer, Windows is in charge.

Programs that you work with—such as Microsoft Word or Microsoft Excel—are actually controlled by Windows. This approach to the control of programs allows you to have several programs running on your computer at the same time. For instance, when you use the keyboard to type a memo in Word or use the mouse to choose menu commands, Windows evaluates the keystrokes and mouse clicks to determine which program should receive your input. Windows also manages all of the hardware connected to your computer. For example, when you print a memo from your computer, Windows handles, among other things, the communication between the computer and the printer. When you are finished with the memo, Windows makes sure it is filed properly on your hard disk, ready for use again.

Starting Windows is a simple procedure: you turn the computer on and wait for the boot process to be completed. At your workplace, your computer might also be connected to other computers to form a **network**, which lets computers share and exchange information. If your computer is connected to a network, you will need to **log on** after the boot process is complete. That is, you will be prompted to provide a **user name** and **password** to identify yourself to Windows and the network. Typically, your user name will have been created for you by a network administrator within your organization, and it will appear on the screen automatically. However, each time you start your computer on a network, you must supply a password. The password works much like a personal identification number (PIN) on an ATM. Passwords prevent unauthorized individuals from accessing information on your computer and on the network.

Touring Windows 2000

The first time you start your computer after Windows has been installed, Windows will guide you through the password set-up process. Or, if your network administrator has already gone through the password process and assigned you a password, you will need to type the password when prompted.

In this exercise, you start Windows so you can begin exploring it.

1   Turn on your computer, your monitor (if it is not turned on automatically when you turn on your computer), and any other hardware that you want to use, such as speakers or a printer.

2   If you have Windows 2000 and another version of Windows (such as Windows 95 or Windows 98) available on your computer, you will be prompted to start the one you want. If necessary, press the Up arrow key or Down arrow key until Microsoft Windows 2000 Professional is selected, and press Enter.

If the Welcome To Windows dialog box appears, follow the instructions before logging on.

There will be a pause while Windows starts. You will see the Windows 2000 startup screen and then the main Windows 2000 display. If you are connected to a network, you will see the Log On To Windows **dialog box**, similar to the following.

If you prefer, you can press Enter instead of clicking OK.

3   In the Log On To Windows dialog box, type your user name and password in the areas provided. (Click in the appropriate box or press Tab to move from one box to the next.) After you are finished entering logon information, click OK.

The Getting Started With Windows 2000 dialog box appears.

If you don't want to see the Getting Started With Windows 2000 dialog box each time you start Windows, clear the Show This Screen At Startup check box before you click Exit.

4   Click the Exit button in the bottom-right corner of the Getting Started With Windows 2000 dialog box to close it.

The Getting Started With Windows 2000 dialog box closes.

Understanding Windows 2000 Components

When you start Windows for the first time, your screen should look similar to the one shown below. As you install programs and customize Windows to suit the way you work, you will see additions and changes to this screen, but the same basic components will still be displayed. If you installed Windows 2000 over a previous version of Windows, your desktop will also include any icons that were placed on the desktop while you were using the previous version of Windows.

Quick Launch bar

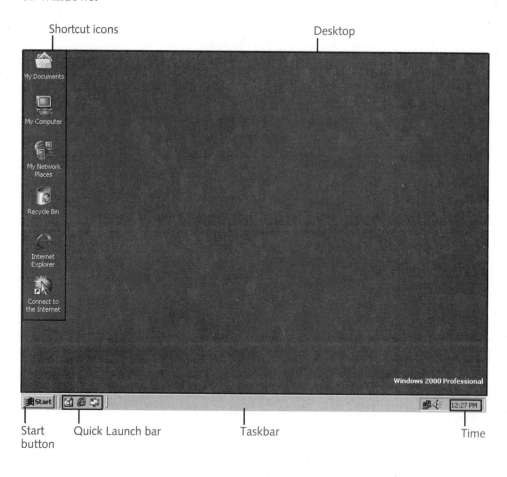

tip

Throughout this book, instructions like **click** and **drag** always refer to the primary mouse button. (Unless the buttons are swapped for left-handed use, the primary mouse button is on the left.) **Double-click** means to quickly tap the left mouse button twice. If you need to use the right, or secondary, mouse button to complete an instruction, the instruction will say so. For example, **right-click** the file. The term *drag* means to click an object on the screen, hold down the left mouse button, and then move the mouse toward you, away from you, left, or right. Release the mouse button when the object is placed in the desired location. If the mouse has a middle button or another control, you can ignore it for now.

It's helpful to know the correct names of the basic Windows components and the ways that you can use the mouse to interact with them. The following list describes the basic Windows components.

- **Desktop** The desktop comprises all the contents of your computer screen after Windows has been started. Items on the desktop include icons for frequently used programs and other utilities.

- **Window** A portion of the screen that displays a program or a document. Several windows can be displayed on the screen at one time, either side by side, top to bottom, or overlapping.

- **Shortcut** A type of icon that offers quick access to files, folders, or programs. For example, you might have a spreadsheet to which you refer several times a week. The spreadsheet might be stored within several layers of folders, and you might open the file by opening each folder in sequence and double-clicking the file's icon. To avoid such a time-consuming process, you can create a shortcut that appears on the desktop and provides faster access to the same file. You use shortcuts in the same way you use other icons, double-clicking them to open a file, folder, or program. Shortcuts look similar to other icons except each has a small, curved arrow in its bottom-left corner. You might think of shortcuts as placeholders for other icons. You can create, copy, move, and delete shortcuts without affecting the file, folder, or program itself.

■ **Taskbar** The taskbar is the strip along the bottom of the screen. It typically shows, from left to right, the Start button, the Quick Launch bar, icons for certain utilities, such as the volume control for the computer's sound system, and the time. Also, programs that are running appear as buttons on the taskbar. Click a program's button on the taskbar to display its window.

■ **Start button** The Start button is located near the left edge of the taskbar and is the most important component on the Windows desktop. It is the launching point for every program and window on your computer. Click the Start button to open a series of menus for starting programs, finding files, setting options, getting help, adding hardware and software, and shutting down the computer.

■ **Quick Launch bar** The Quick Launch bar is the first set of buttons on the taskbar, to the right of the Start button. These buttons let you start programs with a single click. The Quick Launch bar also includes the **Show Desktop button**, which you can click to reduce all windows to buttons on the taskbar.

Show Desktop

■ **Time** The time is displayed near the right edge of the taskbar. This area of the taskbar can also be used to display a calendar. Position the mouse pointer on the time to view a pop-up description showing the day and date. Double-click the time to open the Date/Time Properties dialog box, which displays a calendar and lets you change the date, time, or time zone Windows recognizes.

Anatomy of a Dialog Box

A dialog box appears on your screen when you need to communicate with a program. It provides a way for you to make decisions and select from available options.

Typical components of a dialog box include text boxes, options, check boxes, and menus. You will have an opportunity to use many dialog boxes as you work through the lessons in this book.

(continued)

continued

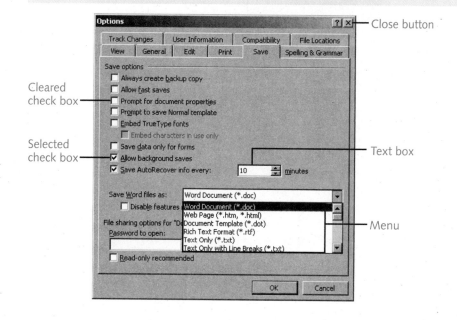
Close

In the top-right corner of every dialog box is a **Close button**. At the bottom of most dialog boxes is an OK button and a **Cancel button**.

Click OK when you are ready to have Windows execute the options you've specified in the dialog box. Click the Cancel button or the Close button in the top-right corner to close the dialog box without making any changes.

In this exercise, you practice common mouse pointing and navigation techniques while touring Windows.

1   Click the Start button on the taskbar.

The Start menu appears.

2   Click a blank area on the desktop.

The Start menu closes.

You can also close a menu by clicking the same button or menu name that you used to open it.

3   Point to the time in the bottom-right corner of the screen.

The date appears in a **pop-up description**.

If a pop-up description does not appear when it should, try taking your hand off the mouse for a few seconds.

4   Move the mouse slightly, in any direction.

The pop-up description disappears.

tip
Even if you don't move your mouse, a pop-up description disappears after a few seconds so it doesn't block your view. To see the pop-up description again, move your mouse away from the Windows component, and then back to it.

5   Double-click the time.

The Date/Time Properties dialog box appears.

6   Click the Cancel button in the Date/Time Properties dialog box.

The dialog box closes. No changes were made.

7   Click the My Computer icon.

The icon appears darker to show that it's selected.

8   Drag the My Computer icon down a little so that it slightly overlaps the icon below it. Release the mouse button when you're done.

9   Right-click a blank area on the desktop.

A shortcut menu, offering choices for organizing the desktop, appears.

10   On the shortcut menu, click Line Up Icons.

The My Computer icon returns to its previous position.

> **tip**
> The Line Up Icons command arranges the icons in rows and columns across the desktop, but it doesn't place them in any particular order. If Line Up Icons doesn't return My Computer to its original position, drag the icon back into position.

Starting Programs

A **program,** also called an application, is a tool that helps you perform a set of tasks. For example, the WordPad program allows you to create documents and edit and format text, and the Calculator program helps you make calculations. You can start a program in Windows from the Start menu. Sometimes, however, you have to open several menus to get to the program you want. For programs you use frequently, therefore, double-clicking a shortcut icon on the desktop might be more convenient than opening the Start menu. (You will learn about creating shortcut icons in Lesson 7, "Customizing Your Desktop.")

*Personalized
Menus*

tip

Windows customizes itself to the way you work by temporarily hiding menu commands you rarely use. You can display all menu commands by clicking the double arrows at the bottom of a personalized menu. Throughout this book, menus are shown as they would appear before any personalization.

In this exercise, you start Notepad (a word processing program that saves text in text-only format) using the Start menu.

1   Click the Start button.

The Start menu appears.

2   On the Start menu, point to Programs.

The Programs submenu appears.

3   On the Programs submenu, point to Accessories.

The Accessories submenu appears.

*Submenus,
or **cascading
menus**, are dis-
played when
the mouse
pointer is
positioned
over commands
with right-
pointing arrows.*

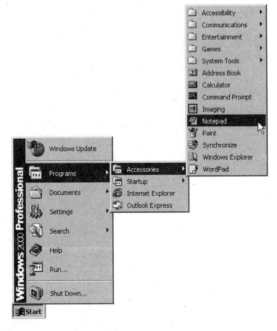

4   On the Accessories submenu, click Notepad.

The Notepad program starts, and its window opens.

Moving, Resizing, and Closing Windows

The space on your desktop is limited, so you should manage it carefully. Sometimes, that means moving a window to another part of the desktop or shrinking it so that it appears as only a button on the taskbar. Other times, "managing your desktop" means resizing a window so you can simultaneously view another window on your desktop.

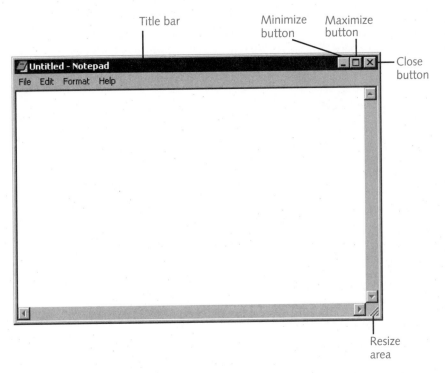

You can use the following buttons and components to manage your windows:

- **Title bar** In addition to telling you the name of the program and (usually) the name of the document you are working on, this bar is used to reposition the program window on the screen. To move a window, drag its title bar.

Minimize

- **Minimize button** This button shrinks a window so that the window appears as only a button on the taskbar.

Maximize

- **Maximize button** This button expands a window so that the window fills the entire desktop (except for the taskbar).

Restore Down

Restore Down button When a window is maximized, the Maximize button is replaced by the Restore Down button, which returns the window to its previous size so that part of the desktop (or another window) is visible. You can also maximize or restore a window by double-clicking its title bar.

Close

Close button This button closes a program, removing it from the computer's temporary storage (memory). Clicking this button is like removing a file from your desk and returning it to a filing cabinet.

Resize area

Resize area This area appears as three diagonal lines in the bottom-right corner of a window. You can drag the resize area to change the height and width of a program window.

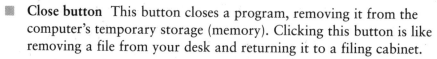

important

Minimizing a program is not the same as closing it. A minimized program is still running. If you don't remember whether you closed a program, check the taskbar before starting it. Otherwise, you might end up with two versions, also called instances, of the same program running at the same time. There's nothing wrong with this as far as Windows is concerned, but it can be confusing to get warning messages about files already being open. If you accidentally run two instances of a program at once, close the one with the fewest changes.

In this exercise, you start WordPad. Then you move and resize the Notepad and WordPad windows.

1   Click the Start button.

The Start menu appears.

2   Point to Programs, and point to Accessories.

The Accessories submenu appears.

3   On the Accessories submenu, click WordPad.

The WordPad program starts, and its window opens.

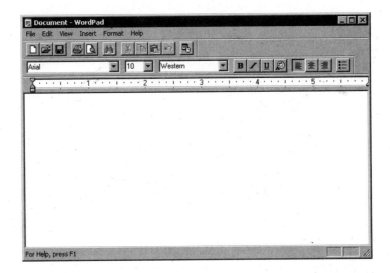

Touring Windows 2000

When WordPad starts, it should not be maximized. If it is, click its Restore Down button.

4 Drag the title bar in the WordPad window several inches down and to the right.

The Notepad window is now at least partially visible.

Minimize

5 Click the Minimize button in the top-right corner of the Notepad window.

The Notepad window no longer appears on the desktop. It's displayed as only a button on the taskbar. Notepad is still running; you've just done the equivalent of pushing it to a corner of your desk to make room for other things.

Maximize

6 Click the Maximize button in the top-right corner of the WordPad window.

The WordPad window expands to cover the desktop. Note that the Restore Down button replaces the Maximize button in the top-right corner of the WordPad window.

Restore Down

7 Click the Restore Down button in the top-right corner of the WordPad window.

The WordPad window returns to its previous size and shape.

Minimize

8 Click the Minimize button in the top-right corner of the WordPad window.

The WordPad window no longer appears on the desktop, but its button is still displayed on the taskbar.

9 Click the Untitled – Notepad button on the taskbar.

The Notepad window reappears on the desktop.

Making Windows Active

It's very common in Windows to have more than one window open at the same time. You can move and resize windows according to your needs. When two or more windows are on the screen at once, the one with the blue or brightly colored title bar is the **active window**, or the one currently in use. The inactive window usually has a gray or lightly colored title bar. For example, look at the following two windows.

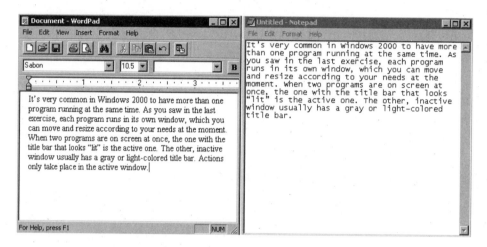

WordPad is the active window, so if you were to start typing with these two windows on screen, the text would appear in the WordPad window.

To switch between windows when you can see more than one of them on the screen, just click anywhere in a blank area of the window you want to make active. The title bar is also a good place to click.

If any window is maximized, though, you can't see any part of any other window. In that case, you can make a different window active by clicking its button on the taskbar. To quickly minimize all windows, click the Show Desktop button on the Quick Launch bar.

Show Desktop

tip

To switch from one program to another using the keyboard, press and hold down the Alt key while you tap the Tab key quickly. A dialog box appears, displaying icons of all programs that are running. Keep holding down Alt and tapping Tab until the program you want is selected. When you release Alt and Tab, the selected program will be the active one.

In this exercise, you practice changing the active window when more than one window is open, and then you display the desktop.

1   Click the Document – WordPad button on the taskbar.

The WordPad window becomes active. Note the color of its title bar.

2   Click the Notepad title bar.

The Notepad window becomes active.

Maximize

3   Click the Maximize button in the top-right corner of the Notepad window.

The Notepad window expands to fill the entire screen. The insertion point is placed at the beginning of the document.

4   Type **My typing affects the active window.**

The text appears in the Notepad document.

5   Click the Document – WordPad button on the taskbar.

The WordPad window becomes active.

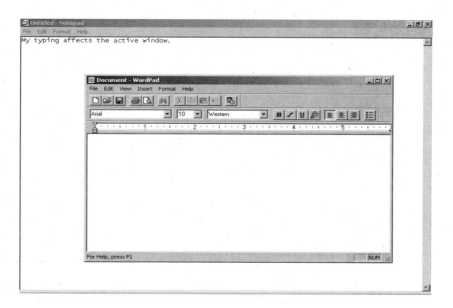

Maximize

6   Click the Maximize button in the top-right corner of the WordPad window.

Now you have two maximized windows on the desktop, but only the active window appears.

Show Desktop

7   Click the Show Desktop button on the Quick Launch bar.

Both program windows are minimized, and the desktop appears.

Shutting Down Windows 2000

When you finish using your computer, you should always **shut down** Windows before you turn off your computer. During the shut-down process, Windows logs you off the network (if you were logged on to one), deletes any temporary files that Windows created to help you work with programs, closes any programs that are still running, and prompts you to save any changes that you haven't saved already.

You might prefer to close each program before you shut down Windows. This lets you see exactly what you were doing in each program and more easily decide whether to save any unsaved work.

The list in the Shut Down Windows dialog box can have up to three other options in addition to Shut Down. The options you see depend on the power-saving features that are available for your computer.

Alternatives to Shutting Down

Log Off This command disconnects your computer from the network and closes any programs that are still running. Use Log Off when you want to allow someone with a different user name and password to work on your computer.

Restart This command disconnects your computer from the network, closes any programs that are still running, and restarts the computer. Adding hardware or software to your computer often requires restarting Windows.

2000
New!

Stand By and Hibernate

Stand By This command is used to reduce power consumption when the computer is idle. Devices (such as the monitor) turn off, and your computer uses less power. This feature is particularly helpful for saving the battery charge on **laptop computers** (small, portable personal computers). You will learn to use Stand By in Lesson 8, "Using Windows on the Go."

Hibernate This feature is available on computers that support Windows 2000 Power Options and have the Enable Hibernation Support feature turned on. Hibernate is similar to Shut Down, but it can be scheduled to shut down at a specified time, whereas Shut Down can't. This feature saves everything in memory on disk, turns off the monitor and hard disk, and then turns off the computer. When you restart the computer, the desktop is restored exactly as you left it.

In this exercise, you shut down Windows. You close WordPad but leave Notepad running so that you can see what happens when you shut down Windows without closing all programs.

1.   Click the Document – WordPad button on the taskbar.

The WordPad window reappears on the desktop.

Close

2   Click the Close button in the top-right corner of the WordPad window.

The WordPad window closes.

tip
If a program is minimized, you can close it without restoring it. Right-click its button on the taskbar, and click Close on the shortcut menu that appears.

3   Click the Start button.

The Start menu appears.

4   At the bottom of the Start menu, click Shut Down.

The Shut Down Windows dialog box appears.

Shut Down Windows dialog box

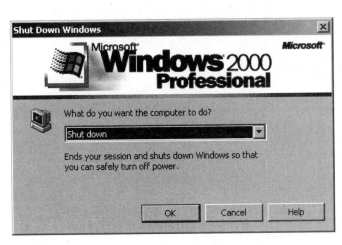

5   If necessary, click the arrow, and click Shut Down in the list. Then click OK.

Windows starts the shut-down process by first checking what programs are running. An alert box for Notepad appears, asking if you want to save changes to your document.

> **tip**
> If you don't respond to the alert box within a few seconds, another alert box replaces it. The second alert box prompts you to either close the program or cancel the shut-down process. If the second alert box appears, click the End Now button.

6   Click the No button.

The document is not saved, and Windows continues shutting down the system. After the shut-down process is complete, you see a blank screen or a message that it's safe to turn off the computer.

7   Turn off the computer and everything connected to it.

Lesson Wrap-Up

In this lesson, you learned how to start Windows and became familiar with the basic Windows components. You also learned how to start programs, resize and move windows, and make windows active. Finally, you learned how to shut down Windows.

If you are continuing to other lessons:

1   Turn on the computer and any other hardware.

2   If necessary, log on to a network.

Glossary

active window The window that is affected by cursor movement, text entry, and other actions.

boot process A procedure a computer follows immediately after you turn it on. The computer checks whether all necessary parts are connected and functioning properly.

Cancel button A button found in many dialog boxes. Clicking the Cancel button closes the dialog box without making any changes.

cascading menu A list of commands that appears when the mouse pointer is positioned over a menu command that has a right-pointing arrow.

clicking Tapping the left mouse button once.

Close button A button used to close a program, removing it from the computer's temporary storage (memory).

Glossary

desktop The contents of your computer screen after Windows has been started. Items on the desktop typically include shortcut icons and open windows.

dialog box A screen element that appears when you need to communicate with a program. A dialog box provides a way for you to make decisions and select options.

double-clicking Quickly tapping the left mouse button twice.

dragging Moving an item on the screen using the mouse pointer. To drag an item, move the mouse pointer over it, hold down the left mouse button, move the mouse until the item is in the desired location, and then release the mouse button.

Hibernate A feature that is similar to Shut Down, but it can be scheduled to shut down at a specified time, whereas Shut Down can't. This feature saves everything in memory on disk, turns off the monitor and hard disk, and then turns off the computer. When you restart the computer, the desktop is restored exactly as you left it.

icon A small picture that appears on the screen and represents a program or document.

laptop computer A small, portable personal computer.

Log Off A command that disconnects your computer from the network and closes any programs that are running.

log on To gain access to the network by entering identification information.

Maximize button A button used to expand a window so that it fills the entire desktop (except for the taskbar).

Minimize button A button used to shrink a window so that it appears as a button on the taskbar.

mouse pointer An icon that moves to reflect the position of the mouse.

My Computer A window that displays the resources on your computer.

network A group of computers and associated devices that are connected by cables, phone lines, or other pieces of transmission equipment.

operating system A collection of programs that controls the way a computer's hardware devices work and the way programs interact with you and the hardware.

Glossary

password A string of letters and/or numbers that you enter when logging on to gain access to network resources. Requiring a password prevents unauthorized individuals from accessing information on your computer or on a network.

pop-up description A brief message that appears when you position your mouse pointer over a screen element. The message explains what the element does.

program A set of instructions that a computer follows to help you perform tasks.

Quick Launch bar The first set of buttons on the taskbar, to the right of the Start button. These buttons provide a way for you to start frequently-used programs with a single click.

resize area Three diagonal lines in the bottom-right corner of a window. Drag the resize area to make a window larger or smaller.

Restart A command that disconnects your computer from the network, closes any programs that are running, and then restarts the computer.

Restore Down button A button that appears when a window is maximized. When you click the Restore Down button, the window returns to its previous size so that part of the desktop (or another window) is visible.

right-clicking Tapping the right mouse button once.

shortcut A type of icon that offers quick access to files, folders, or programs.

Show Desktop button A button located on the Quick Launch bar on the taskbar. Clicking this button minimizes all open windows so that only the desktop is displayed on screen.

shut down To log off the network, delete any temporary files, and close all open programs. This process should always precede shutting off the computer.

Stand By A command used to reduce power consumption when the computer is idle. Devices, such as the monitor, turn off, and your computer uses less power. This feature is particularly helpful for saving the battery charge on laptop computers.

Start button A button located at the left edge of the taskbar. It is the launching point for every program and window on a computer.

Glossary

taskbar The strip along the bottom of the screen. It typically shows, from left to right, the Start button, the Quick Launch bar, icons for certain utilities, such as the Volume Control for the computer's sound system, and the time. Also, programs that are running appear as buttons on the taskbar.

time An area on the taskbar, near its right edge, that displays the hour of the day. This area can also be used to display a calendar. Position the mouse pointer on the time to view a pop-up description showing the day and date. Double-click the time to open the Date/Time Properties dialog box, which displays a calendar and lets you change the date, time, or time zone Windows recognizes.

title bar The strip across the top of a window that displays the name of the program and (usually) the name of the document you are working on. You can move windows around the screen by dragging their title bars.

user name A sequence of characters that, in combination with the password, identifies you to Windows and provides you with access to network resources.

window A portion of the screen that displays a program or a document.

Quick Reference

To start Windows 2000

● Turn on your computer. If necessary, enter logon information, and click OK.

To start a program

● Double-click the program's icon on the desktop, or click the Start button, point to Programs, navigate to the desired program, and click it.

To change the size and shape of a window

● Drag the resize area, or click the Minimize, Maximize, or Restore Down button.

To move a window

● Drag the title bar until the window is in the desired location.

Touring Windows 2000

Quick Reference

To make a window active

- Click anywhere in a blank area of the desired window.

To close a program

- Click the Close button in the top-right corner of the program window.

To restore a minimized program

- Click the program's button on the taskbar.

To quickly minimize all windows

- Click the Show Desktop button on the Quick Launch bar.

To shut down Windows

- Click the Start button, and click Shut Down on the Start menu. If necessary, click the arrow, and click Shut Down in the list. Then click OK.

LESSON

2

Getting Help When You Need It

ESTIMATED TIME
30 min.

After completing this lesson, you will be able to:

✔ *Use the Windows help system.*

✔ *Create complex searches.*

✔ *Keep track of favorite help topics.*

✔ *Diagnose computer problems.*

✔ *Use the "What's This?" feature.*

✔ *Get updates to Windows.*

Microsoft Windows 2000 Professional offers an extensive help system, which features reference guides, context-sensitive help, interactive troubleshooters, and Web-based support. You can use these resources to find out about virtually anything in Windows, from what the Notepad program does to why your CD-ROM drive isn't working.

In this lesson, you will discover how to use Windows itself to answer your questions about Windows, and you will learn how to store the answers you find in the Favorites list for quick reference. You will also learn how to get help within a Windows-based program. Finally, you will examine the Windows Update feature so that you can keep Windows running smoothly.

Using the Help System

To fix a Windows problem or find out about a Windows component, click Help on the Start menu. You will see a window similar to the following.

The two-pane help window

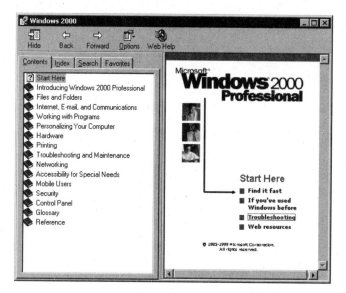

If you have upgraded to Windows 2000 from Windows NT, you will probably notice that the Windows 2000 help window looks different. The new look is designed to integrate with a Web browser such as Microsoft Internet Explorer to provide online support.

As in previous versions of Windows, the help system in Windows 2000 provides three approaches to help you find what you're looking for. These approaches are set up as **tabs** in the Windows 2000 help window, like folders in a filing cabinet. Click the tab with which you want to work.

- **Contents tab** This tab is like the table of contents in a book. The "book" is divided into the equivalent of chapters, which contain overview pages and topics. Click a chapter title, indicated by a book icon, to display a list of its contents. Click an overview or topic heading under the chapter title to display that overview or topic.

- **Index tab** This tab is like the index in the back of a book. As you start typing a word or phrase, the index displays the first entry that begins with the letters you type. Double-click an entry or a subentry to display the topic that discusses it. (If more than one topic relates to your query, choose a topic from the list that appears.)

■ **Search tab** This tab is similar to the Index tab, but it provides more flexibility. Instead of looking for only index keywords, Search examines the entire help system for the word or phrase you type. You can fine-tune your search by using words called **operators**. An operator refines the search by including or excluding topics that contain certain words. The operators that Windows recognizes are *and*, *or*, *near*, and *not*. You can also specify words that must appear together in sequence by typing the phrase you are looking for in quotation marks.

A fourth tab, Favorites, provides a place for you to keep track of help topics to which you would like to return. The Favorites tab is discussed in more detail later in this lesson.

Creating Complex Searches

If you type more than one word in the Search tab, the help system finds all topics that contain all of the words you typed, in any order. To change the focus of your search, include one or more of the following operators in your search phrase:

■ *Or* finds any topic containing any of the words you typed. This is the most general way to search. For example, searching for *fax or modem* locates 141 topics.

■ *Not* finds all topics that contain all of the words, but it excludes topics that contain words you precede with *not*. Searching for *fax not modem* reduces the number of topics found from 141 to 21. This method finds topics that discuss faxes but excludes topics that mention modems.

■ *And* is the default. It is implied if you search for more than one word, and it requires topics to contain all words you specify. Typing *fax modem* and typing *fax and modem* yield the same 14 topics. Although you don't need *and* in simple searches, it can be helpful if you combine it with other operators. For example, *fax not modem and printer* locates 12 topics.

■ *Near* can be useful if the words you're looking for tend to be part of the same thought but might have other words between them. Searching for *fax near modem* locates nine topics.

■ *Quotation marks* specify that the words must occur together and in the order you typed them. This is the narrowest type of search; *"fax modem"* finds just five topics.

*For help start-
ing Windows,
see Lesson 1,
"Touring
Microsoft
Windows 2000
Professional."*

In this exercise, you use the Contents tab in the Windows 2000 help window to find general information on a broad topic, and you use the Search tab to quickly locate information on a specific issue.

1   If necessary, turn on your computer and any other hardware, and log on.

The Windows desktop appears.

2   Click the Start button, and on the Start menu, click Help.

The Windows 2000 help window appears. The Start Here topic appears in the right pane of the window, and the Contents tab appears in the left.

*If the Contents
tab is not
displayed, click
Contents to
make it the
active tab.*

3   On the Contents tab, click Files And Folders.

An overview link and topics related to files and folders are listed under the chapter title.

4   Click the Open A File Or Folder topic.

The steps to open a file or folder are listed in the right pane of the Windows 2000 help window, along with a link to related topics.

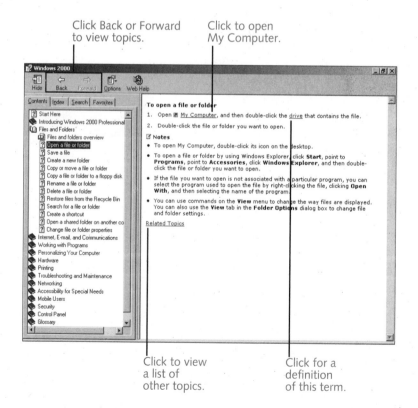

Click Back or Forward to view topics.

Click to open My Computer.

Click to view a list of other topics.

Click for a definition of this term.

5   Click the link to My Computer in the right pane of the window.

The My Computer window opens so that you can perform the steps while you read them.

![Close]

Close

6   Click the Close button in the top-right corner of the My Computer window.

The My Computer window closes, and the Windows 2000 help window becomes active again.

7   Click the link to Related Topics in the right pane of the window (near the end of the topic).

A menu lists other topics about files and folders.

You will learn about working with files and folders in Lesson 3, "Managing Files and Folders."

tip

After you find a topic that interests you, you can close the left pane in the Windows 2000 help window by clicking the Hide button on the Standard Buttons toolbar. This makes the screen less cluttered. To display even more of the topic, you can maximize the Windows 2000 help window. If you need the left pane again, click the Show button on the Standard Buttons toolbar.

8   On the Related Topics menu, click Open A Recently Used File.

The topic you clicked replaces the Open A File Or Folder topic in the right pane of the window.

Clicking the Back and Forward buttons is like flipping back and forth through pages in a book.

9   Click the Back button on the Standard Buttons toolbar.

The Open A File Or Folder topic reappears.

10   In the left pane of the window, click the Search tab.

The Search tab appears, and the insertion point is positioned in the Type In The Keyword To Find box.

11   Type **networking infrared**, and click the List Topics button.

Thirteen topics contain both of these words.

12   Click to the left of the word *infrared*, and type the word **near**, followed by a space. Then click the List Topics button again.

This time, nine topics are listed.

You can double-click a listed topic instead of clicking the topic and then clicking the Display button.

13   In the list of topics, click Connect With An Infrared Network Connection, and click the Display button in the bottom-right corner of the left pane.

The topic appears in the right pane.

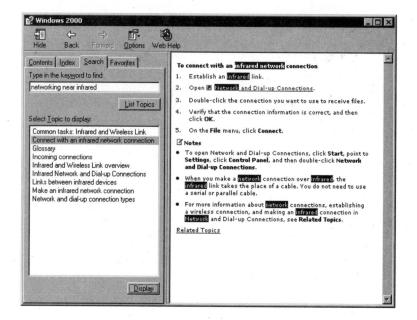

14   Keep the Windows 2000 help window open for the next exercise.

tip

When a topic is displayed as a result of a search, every occurrence of any of the words you searched for is highlighted in the topic. To turn off the highlighting until your next search, click the Options button on the Standard Buttons toolbar, and then click Refresh on the Options menu. To remove highlighting permanently (or until you explicitly turn it back on), click Search Highlight Off on the Options menu, and then click the Display button.

Creating a List of Favorite Help Topics

Favorites tab

Whenever you learn a skill or work on a large project—from studying a foreign language to remodeling a room—it's helpful to keep a "cheat sheet" handy. The notes on it might not mean a lot to anyone else, but they are invaluable to you. The **Favorites tab** in the Windows 2000 help window is an electronic version of a cheat sheet. Here, you can store the topics you find most useful as you discover them, and you can quickly retrieve them later.

Consider, for example, the conference coordinator at Lakewood Mountains Resort; she needs to quickly set up computers to accommodate the different needs of conference participants. Her Favorites list might look like the following.

tip

If you use a Web browser such as Internet Explorer, working with the Windows 2000 help window probably feels familiar to you. Internet Explorer uses many of the same concepts as the Windows 2000 help window: clicking links, moving back and forward through pages, and maintaining a Favorites list. In fact, the Windows 2000 help window is based on **HTML** (Hypertext Markup Language), the same language that is used to create Web pages.

In this exercise, you add the topic you searched for in the last exercise to the Favorites list, and you use the Index tab to find information about shortcut keys. You also add the topic from the Index to your Favorites list.

1   Click the Favorites tab in the left pane of the Windows 2000 help window.

The Favorites tab appears. In the Current Topic box (near the bottom of the tab), the topic *Connect with an infrared network connection* appears.

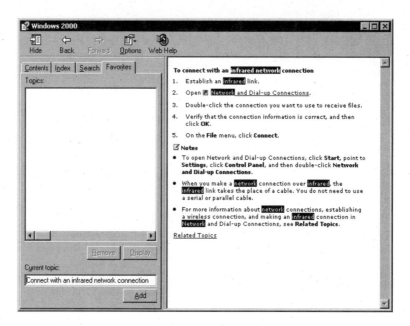

2   On the Favorites tab, click the Add button.

The Connect with an infrared network connection topic is added to the Favorites list.

3   Click the Index tab in the left pane, and in the Type In The Keyword To Find box, type **short**.

These few letters are enough for the help system to find entries related to shortcuts.

You can double-click an index entry or subentry instead of clicking it and then clicking the Display button.

4   Click the For Windows Explorer subentry under the Shortcut Keys entry, and click the Display button.

The topic for this subentry appears in the right pane of the Windows 2000 help window.

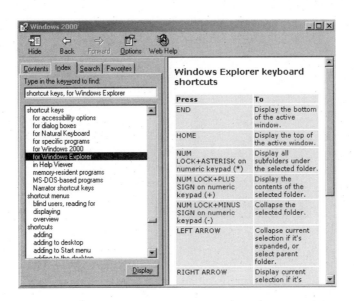

tip

If an index entry has subentries, you must click one of the subentries to display the information. Clicking the entry itself will not work.

5   Click the Favorites tab, and in its bottom-right corner, click the Add button.

The Windows 2000 Keyboard Shortcuts topic is added to the Favorites list.

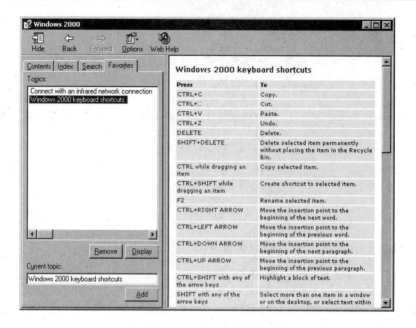

Close

6   Click the Close button in the top-right corner of the Windows 2000 help window.

The Windows 2000 help window closes.

7   Click the Start button, and click Help on the Start menu.

The Windows 2000 help window reopens with the Favorites tab displayed.

To delete a topic from the Favorites list, click the topic in the Topics list, and click the Remove button.

8   In the Topics list, double-click Windows 2000 Keyboard Shortcuts.

The shortcut topic replaces the Start Here topic in the right pane of the window.

tip

To print a help system topic, display it in the right pane. Click the Options button on the Standard Buttons toolbar, and on the Options menu, click Print. The Print dialog box appears. Make any necessary changes to the printing options, and click the Print button.

Troubleshooting

In an ideal world, your computer would work exactly the way you want it to, all the time. In reality, your computer is a combination of hardware and software with an almost infinite number of variations—and the combinations can change as your needs change. You might buy a new scanner, switch from one printer to another, add new programs and remove others, or connect to different networks at different times. In such a complex system, problems can sometimes occur. Fortunately, Windows provides interactive **troubleshooters** to help you diagnose and solve problems.

The troubleshooters are part of the help system. They're called interactive because they rely on your answers to a series of questions to identify a solution for your particular problem. Based on the information you supply, the troubleshooters provide step-by-step instructions for diagnosing and fixing the problem.

In this exercise, you use an interactive troubleshooter to determine what is wrong with a monitor that is not displaying properly. Although your monitor is probably working properly, you work through this exercise to learn how troubleshooters work.

1   If necessary, open the Windows 2000 help window.

2   Click the Contents tab in the left pane of the Windows 2000 help window, and click the first topic—Start Here.

You can also get to the Start Here topic by clicking Home on the Options menu.

The Start Here topic appears in the right pane of the Windows 2000 help window.

3   In the right pane, click the link to Troubleshooting.

A list of troubleshooter links appears.

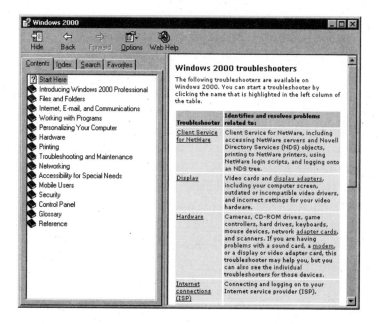

4   In the right pane, click the Display link.

The troubleshooter prompts you to click an option explaining the problem. The My Display Flickers Or Is Garbled option is selected.

5   Click the Next button.

The troubleshooter displays information about changing display settings. You are asked if changing your display settings solves the problem.

6   Click the No, I Still Have A Problem option, and click the Next button.

The troubleshooter displays information about finding out if Windows 2000 supports your display adapter. The Yes, Windows 2000 Supports My Display Adapter option is selected.

7   Click the Next button.

The troubleshooter displays information about finding out if your display adapter driver works. The Yes, Reinstalling My Display Adapter Driver Solves The Problem option is selected.

8   Click the Next button.

The troubleshooter thanks you for using it.

Close

9   Click the Close button in the top-right corner of the Windows 2000 help window.

The window closes, and the desktop appears.

Other Sources for Help

Windows retains the size and shape settings of the help window when you close it.

Context-sensitive help is information that you can display while using a particular feature—you don't have to open the Windows 2000 help window. Lesson 1, "Touring Microsoft Windows 2000 Professional," described one type of context-sensitive help: **pop-up descriptions**. A pop-up description appears when you point to a Windows element for a few seconds. Pop-up descriptions, although helpful, are necessarily brief. For a more complete description of an element, use the **What's This?** feature. This feature is available in dialog boxes and toolbars throughout Windows, and it provides a more complete description than a pop-up description.

To find out whether What's This? is available in a particular dialog box, look for the Help button in the top-right corner of the dialog box, to the left of the Close button.

In the Multimedia folder on the Windows 2000 Professional Step by Step CD-ROM, double-click the What's This icon for a demonstration of how to use the What's This? feature.

Help button

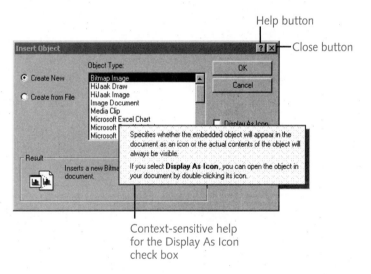

Close button

Context-sensitive help for the Display As Icon check box

important

To close any context-sensitive help that was displayed when you used the What's This? feature, click inside the **pop-up window**. Do not click the dialog box itself or you could accidentally click a button that starts an unwanted action.

Another source of help is available from a program's menu bar. In Windows programs, the Help menu is the last item on the menu bar. Options on the Help menu will vary from program to program. However, most Help menus include an option to display the topics in the program's help system. Most help menus also have an About option that provides information about the program itself, including copyright and licensing information.

Programs that are based on versions of Windows other than Windows 2000 have help systems that look different from those discussed here, but they work similarly.

Menu bar ——

In this exercise, you use the Paint program (a drawing program that is included with Windows 2000) to explore various ways to get help within a program.

1   Click the Start button.

    The Start menu appears.

2   On the Start menu, point to Programs, point to Accessories, and then click Paint.

    The Paint window appears.

Maximize

3   Click the Maximize button in the top-right corner of the Paint window, if necessary.

In Paint, the mouse pointer looks like a pencil when it is in the picture area, but it returns to its normal arrowhead shape outside that area.

4   Point to one of the drawing tools in the Tool Box in the left side of the window.

    A pop-up description of the tool appears. Additional information about the tool is displayed on the **Status bar** in the bottom-left corner of the Paint window.

Many programs display context-sensitive information on the Status bar.

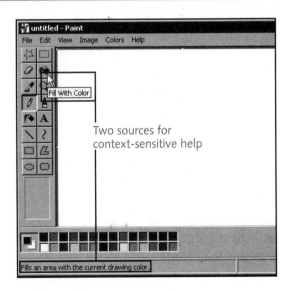

You can also start a program's help system by pressing the F1 key.

5   Click Help on the menu bar.

The Help menu in this program lists two commands: Help Topics and About Paint.

6   Click Help Topics.

The Paint help window appears. It should look familiar—it's designed like the Windows 2000 help window.

7   On the Contents tab in the left pane of the Paint help window, click Create Pictures.

The help topics related to creating pictures are listed.

8   Click Draw A Free-Form Line.

The topic appears in the right pane of the Paint help window.

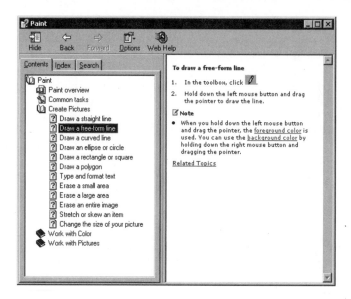

Close

9   Click the Close button in the top-right corner of the Paint help window.

The Paint help window closes. The Paint window becomes active again.

10   On the File menu, click Save As.

The Save As dialog box appears.

Help

Help pointer

Instead of clicking the Help button, you can point to an element in a dialog box and press Shift+F1.

11   Click the Help button in the top-right corner of the Save As dialog box.

The mouse pointer changes to an arrow with a question mark.

12   Click inside the Save In box.

A pop-up window appears, describing what the Save In box is used for.

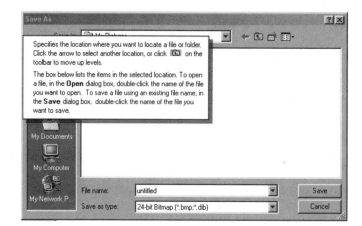

13   Click anywhere inside the pop-up window.

The pop-up window closes.

tip

Some Windows dialog boxes display a Troubleshoot button for context-sensitive troubleshooting. For instance, dialog boxes that relate to hardware usually offer this feature. Click the Troubleshoot button, and the interactive troubleshooter related to the dialog box appears.

Close

14   Click the Close button in the top-right corner of the Save As dialog box, and click the Close button in the top-right corner of the Paint window.

The Save As dialog box closes, and the Paint window closes.

Using Windows Update

2000 New!

Windows Update

Windows Update does not send any information about your system to Microsoft.

Imagine that you take your car to a service station and the mechanic recommends an engine tune-up, new tires, and an upgraded alarm system—for free. That's the kind of service Microsoft **Windows Update** provides to help you keep Windows running smoothly.

Windows Update links you to specific pages in Microsoft's Web site and lets you add Windows features and upgrades as they become available. The first time you use Windows Update to look for features and upgrades, Windows Update adds a small piece of software called a **control** to your system. The control determines what components of Windows you might want to add or update on your computer. Using that information, Windows Update displays a "shopping list" of files. When you have selected the items you want from the list, click the Download button. Windows Update transfers, or **downloads**, the items you selected from the Web site to your computer, and then Windows Update sets them up for you.

important

If your computer is connected to your organization's network, check with your network administrator before running Windows Update.

*For more
information
on setting up
an Internet
connection, see
Lesson 5,
"Accessing
and Browsing
the Internet."*

In this exercise, you use Windows Update to find out about its "Picks Of The Month," which are components for Windows that have recently been added or improved. Before you start this exercise, you must be connected to the Internet.

1   Click the Start button, and click Windows Update near the top of the menu.

The Windows Update home page appears in Internet Explorer.

*The Support
Information
link on the
Windows
Update home
page provides
additional
details about
the update
process. It
also includes
links to
other sources
of help.*

Maximize

Restore Down

2   Click the Maximize button in the top-right corner of the Internet Explorer window.

The window expands to fill the screen, and the Restore Down button replaces the Maximize button.

3   Click the Product Updates link.

Unless you have used Windows Update before, the Security Warning dialog box appears.

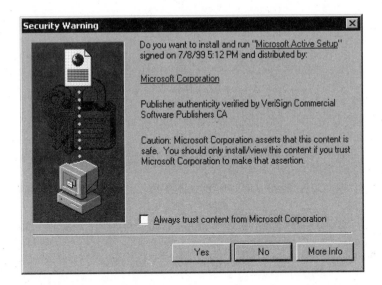

4   In the Security Warning dialog box, click Yes.

Windows Update lists new and updated software choices on the Select Software page.

The Select Software page is frequently updated. The page you see will differ from the one shown here.

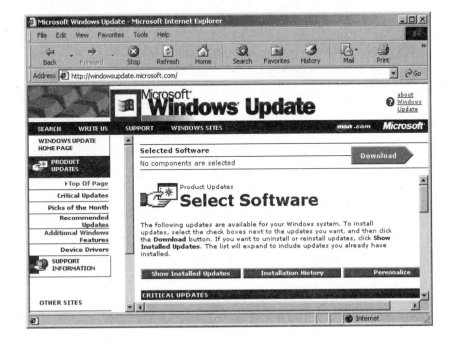

5   In the left pane of the window, click the Picks Of The Month link.

The Picks Of The Month appear in the right pane of the window.

Repeat steps 6
through 8 for
other updates
in the list until
you have
selected all of
the desired
software.

6   Click the Read This First link for the first update listed in Picks Of The Month.

A new window appears, containing information about the update: what it is, how to download and install it, how to use it, and how to uninstall it.

7   Click one of the Back To Product Updates links (near either the top or bottom of the page).

The window for the first update closes.

8   Select the check box for the update you just read, and click the Download button.

Windows Update provides a Download Checklist summarizing what you've selected so far and what you still have to do to finish the update process.

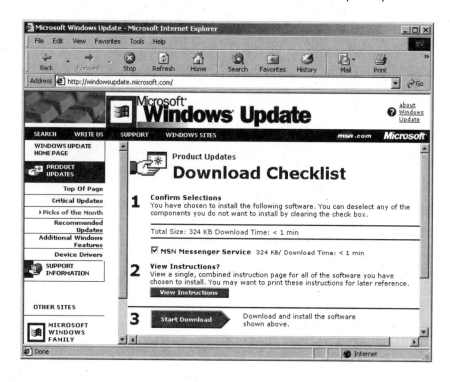

important

If you were to start the download, you would see a dialog box containing a licensing agreement. After you clicked Yes to accept the agreement, Windows Update would download and install your software. You might be prompted to restart your computer or supply other information. When the process finished, a "Download and Installation Successful" message would appear in the right pane of the Windows Update window.

Close

9   Click the Close button in the top-right corner of the Internet Explorer window.

The Internet Explorer window closes, and the desktop appears.

10   If necessary, disconnect from the Internet.

tip

For another source of Windows help on the Internet, click Help on the Start menu, and click the Web Help button on the Standard Buttons toolbar. Links for online support and information appear in the right pane. Click the desired link. Internet Explorer starts and connects to the appropriate Microsoft Web site.

Lesson Wrap-Up

In this lesson, you learned how to use the Contents, Index, Search, and Favorites tabs in the Windows 2000 help window. You also learned to use interactive troubleshooters. You then learned how to use the Help menu and the What's This? feature in a Windows-based program. Finally, you learned how to keep your Windows components current using Windows Update.

If you are continuing to other lessons:

●   Close all open windows. The desktop should be displayed.

If you are not continuing to other lessons:

1   Close all open windows, and click the Start button on the taskbar.

2   Click Shut Down on the Start menu. If necessary, click the arrow in the Windows Shut Down dialog box, and click Shut Down in the list. Then click OK.

3   After Windows has shut down, turn off the computer and, if necessary, all other hardware devices.

Glossary

Contents A tab in the Windows 2000 help window. The Contents tab is like the table of contents in a book. Windows topics are divided into the equivalent of chapters, overview pages, and topics. Click a chapter title, indicated by a book icon, to get a list of its contents.

context-sensitive help Information that can be displayed while you are using a particular feature, rather than what you find by opening the Windows 2000 help window.

control A program added to your computer by Windows Update that determines what components of Windows might need to be added or updated on your computer.

download To transfer information from an outside source—such as a file from a Web site—to your computer.

Favorites A tab in the Windows 2000 help window. The Favorites tab is an electronic version of a cheat sheet. On this tab, you can store the topics you find most useful and quickly retrieve them later.

HTML (Hypertext Markup Language) A collection of formatting and document-definition tags used to create pages that can be viewed in a Web browser.

Index A tab in the Windows 2000 help window. The Index tab is like the index at the back of a book. As you start typing a word or phrase, the index displays the first topic in the list that most closely matches the letters you are typing.

operator A word that instructs Windows to limit a search by including or excluding certain words or specific content in the help system. The available operators are *and*, *or*, *near*, and *not*. You can also specify a string of words that must appear together by typing the phrase you are looking for in quotation marks.

pop-up description A brief message that appears when you position your mouse pointer over an icon. The message explains what the icon does or where it's located.

pop-up window A message that appears when you click the Help button and then click an element on a toolbar or in a dialog box. Although similar to a pop-up description, a pop-up window provides a more detailed description of the chosen element.

Glossary

Search A tab in the Windows 2000 help window. The Search tab is similar to the Index tab but provides more flexibility. Instead of looking only for words in the index, Search looks through the entire help system for the word or phrase you've typed.

Status bar A bar located at the bottom of many program windows that displays a brief text message about the present state of the program.

tab A screen element that looks much like a tabbed file folder in a filing cabinet and that you can click to display different types of options in a dialog box.

troubleshooter An interactive part of the help system that provides step-by-step instructions for diagnosing, and then fixing, problems that you describe.

What's This? A feature available in dialog boxes and toolbars that provides a definition of an option or component when you point to it.

Windows Update Pages on Microsoft's Web site that let you add Windows features and upgrades as they become available.

Quick Reference

To start the help system

● On the Start menu, click Help.

To find general information

1 In the left pane of the Windows 2000 help window, click the Contents tab.

2 Click the desired topic.

To find a help topic by keyword

1 In the left pane of the Windows 2000 help window, click the Index tab, and then type the first few letters of the keyword.

2 Click an entry or a subentry, and click the Display button.

Quick Reference

To search the Windows 2000 help system for a word or phrase

1   In the left pane of the Windows 2000 help window, click the Search tab, and then type the desired word or phrase.

2   Click the List Topics button, click the desired topic, and then click the Display button.

To add a help topic to the Favorites list

1   In the right pane of the Windows 2000 help window, display the desired topic.

2   In the left pane, click the Favorites tab, and then click the Add button.

To diagnose a computer problem

1   In the Start Here topic in the right pane of the Windows 2000 help window, click Troubleshooting.

2   Click the desired troubleshooter.

3   Click the appropriate answers to its questions, and follow the steps provided until the "Thank you for using..." message appears.

To get help in a program

●   Click Help on the menu bar, and click an option.

To get help in a dialog box

●   In the top-right corner of the dialog box, click the Help button, and then click the element you want to learn about.

To update Windows

1   Connect to the Internet, and click Windows Update on the Start menu.

2   Click the Product Updates link, and click Yes in the Security Warning dialog box, if necessary.

3   Select the check boxes for the updates you want to add, and click the Download button.

4   Follow the steps in the Download Checklist.

3

Managing Files and Folders

**ESTIMATED
TIME
50 min.**

After completing this lesson, you will be able to:

✔ *Navigate through folders.*

✔ *Open and sort files.*

✔ *Print files.*

✔ *Search for files.*

✔ *Create, move, copy, rename, and delete files and folders.*

Files are perhaps the most important type of resource you will use in Microsoft Windows 2000 Professional. Every document, picture, or sound you work with is a file. Programs (such as Microsoft Word or Microsoft Excel) are actually collections of files. Windows itself is a collection of hundreds of files, each with its own purpose. For example, one file contains the sound Windows plays when it starts, and another contains the sound Windows plays when it shuts down. There are even files that specify the appearance of the mouse pointer by changing its shape or by changing the way clicking works. (Lesson 7, "Customizing Your Desktop," discusses customizing the appearance of the mouse pointer.)

To keep track of all your files, you need to group them in some logical way. In Windows, you do this by creating **folders**. A folder stores files that are related in some way. Think of a folder like a kitchen cabinet. Different cabinets store different types of kitchen hardware: utensils, glassware, and so forth. One cabinet might store food, while another stores dishes. In Windows, one folder might store documents (such as a memo in Word or a workbook in Excel), while another might store pictures you create or find on the Internet.

You might also divide each cabinet: a shelf for glassware, another for plates, and so forth. If you have lots of plates, you might divide a shelf: good chinaware on the left and daily-use plates on the right. Similarly, in Windows you can have folders within folders to provide additional levels of organization.

In this lesson, you will be introduced to ways to view and manage your files and folders. You will learn how to open and close them, how to add and remove them, and how to organize and print them. In addition, you will learn how to search for files and file content.

Sample files for the lesson ➡

For additional information on installing practice files, see the "Using the Microsoft Windows Professional 2000 Step by Step CD-ROM" section at the beginning of this book.

To complete the exercises in this lesson, you will need to use the Windows 2000 Practice folder and the files it contains: IPR Clients, Lakewood Brochure Text, LMR Whats New, Main Building, Pic00005, Staff, and To Do List. Before you can work with any of these exercise files, you must install them from the Microsoft Windows 2000 Professional Step by Step CD-ROM to your hard disk.

Navigating Through Folders

The two most popular ways to navigate through folders is to use either **My Computer** or **Windows Explorer**. My Computer displays all of the available resources for your computer including all disk drives and the network (if one is available). Windows Explorer displays all files and folders that are available on your computer and, if applicable, on the network.

2000 New!

Standard Buttons toolbar

Windows key

In Windows 2000, the My Computer and Windows Explorer windows are almost identical. The major difference is that the Folders pane appears by default in Windows Explorer and not in My Computer. However, you can add the Folders pane to the My Computer window by clicking the Folders button on the Standard Buttons toolbar. You can open the My Computer window by double-clicking the My Computer icon on the desktop. You can open Windows Explorer by holding down the Windows key (located between Ctrl and Alt on the keyboard) and pressing E. When you open Windows Explorer using this key combination, Windows Explorer opens with the My Computer resources displayed in the right pane of the window. It's a matter of personal preference whether to use My Computer or Windows Explorer to view files, folders, and other resources.

The left side of the Windows Explorer window displays the Folders pane when you first open it. The right side of the window displays the contents of the folder that is selected in the Folders pane. By default, the My Documents folder is selected when you first open Windows Explorer.

> ## tip
>
> **My Documents** is the **default** folder for the files you create in Windows programs. That is, unless you specify a different folder when you save a newly created document, Windows will place it in the My Documents folder.

The specific contents of your My Documents window will differ from those shown here. You might have many more icons.

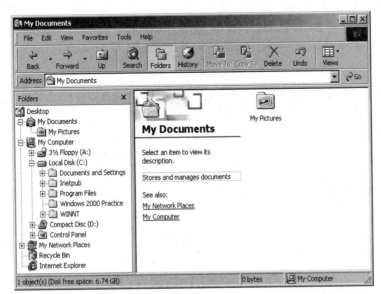

To open a folder, double-click it in the Folders pane. When you double-click a folder, its contents replace those of the previous folder in the right pane. If the new folder contains **subfolders** (lower-level folders), you can double-click one of them and continue navigating through these lower-level folders until you find the one you're looking for. To open a higher-level folder, click the Up button on the Standard Buttons toolbar. To open other folders you opened previously, click the Back button on the Standard Buttons toolbar.

The structure of folders and subfolders might be quite extensive, but you see only the top level of folders when you first open the Folders pane. Click the plus sign to the left of a folder icon to view all of its subfolders. When a folder is expanded, the plus sign changes to a minus sign. Click the minus sign to collapse the list of subfolders so that only the higher-level folder appears.

Folder Types

As you examine folders in Windows Explorer, you might notice that some of them look like plain manila folders, while others have a symbol super-imposed on them. In many cases, a folder with a symbol superimposed on it represents a Windows component, such as Control Panel. However, three other common folder types have special meaning.

Icon	Meaning
	An open folder with a sheet of paper sticking out of it and a cable connection beneath the folder represents a **network folder**. A network folder represents a location on another computer on the network. (Lesson 4, "Using Windows on a Network," explains network folders in more depth.)
	A hand holding a folder represents a **shared folder** on your computer, which means you have made the folder available to other users on the network. (Sharing folders and files is also discussed in detail in Lesson 4, "Using Windows on a Network.")
	A folder with an up arrow and a down arrow in its bottom-left corner represents a **synchronized folder**. A synchronized folder mirrors the contents of another folder on another computer, so both are always up-to-date. For example, if you have a laptop and a desktop computer, you can syn-chronize their My Documents folders so you never have to worry whether the computer you're working on has the most current version of the documents you need. (Synchroni-zation is discussed in detail in Lesson 8, "Using Windows on the Go.")

In this exercise, you navigate through folders in Windows Explorer and access the Windows 2000 Practice folder.

1   Hold down the Windows key, and press E.

Windows key

The Windows Explorer window appears. My Computer is expanded in the Folders pane, and all the devices (such as disk drives and CD-ROM drives) attached to your computer, as well as Control Panel, are displayed in the right pane of the window.

2   In the Folders pane, click the plus sign to the left of Local Disk. (If you have more than one local disk, click the plus sign next to the one labeled drive C.)

   You probably have many folders on this branch because it is your primary storage device.

3   Scroll down the Folders pane until you see the Windows 2000 Practice folder.

4   In the Folders pane, double-click the Windows 2000 Practice folder.

   The Windows 2000 Practice files appear in the right pane of the window.

The Folders pane can now be opened or closed with a click of a button.

5   Click the Back button on the Standard Buttons toolbar.

   The My Documents folder reappears because it was the folder displayed before you double-clicked the Windows 2000 Practice folder.

6   In the Folders pane, click the minus sign to the left of My Documents, and then click the minus sign to the left of My Computer.

   The My Documents and the My Computer folders collapse.

Opening Files

After you have found a file by navigating through the folders in Windows Explorer or My Computer, you can double-click the file to open it, and then you can modify it as desired. For example, you can edit the text in a document or change the colors in a picture. A file is associated with the program that you use to read it. (File association means that Windows uses the file extension to determine which program should be used to open the file.) So if you double-click a file that was created in Notepad, the Notepad program starts and displays the file. If you want to start a program other than the one with which the file is associated, right-click the file, and then click Open With on the shortcut menu.

The icon that is displayed with a file name in Windows Explorer indicates the program that is associated with that type of file. The following are examples of different icons and the programs with which they are associated.

Imaging Preview   Internet Explorer picture   Internet Explorer text   Notepad   Paint   WordPad   Unknown filetype

File and Folder Names

File and folder names can be any combination of up to 255 letters, numbers, and spaces. Some special characters, such as dashes and commas, are allowed in names, while others, such as colons, slashes, and question marks, are not. To avoid having to remember which special characters are allowed, use only letters, numbers, and spaces when you name files and folders.

Files are associated with programs based on their **extensions**. An extension is a period followed by one to three characters at the end of a file name. For example, a file that ends in .txt, such as To Do.txt, is a Notepad file. By default, extensions are not visible in Windows. To see extensions, click Tools on the Windows Explorer menu bar, click Folder Options on the Tools menu, and then click the View tab in the Folder Options dialog box. Finally, clear the Hide File Extensions For Known File Types check box, and then click OK.

In this exercise, you open a file using the default program associated with it. Then you choose a program to use when opening a file.

1   If necessary, open Windows Explorer, maximize it, and then open the Windows 2000 Practice folder.

You can also open a selected file by clicking Open or Open With on the File menu.

2   Double-click the Staff file.

This is an HTML file, so your default browser starts, and the Staff file appears in the browser window.

New!
The ability to type a Web address directly into the My Computer or Windows Explorer Address bar.

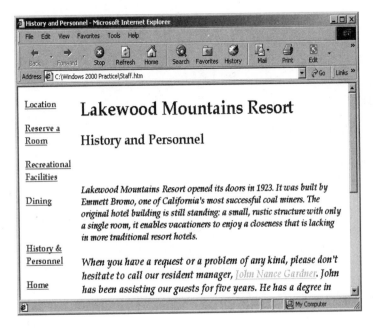

Close

3   Click the Close button in the top-right corner in the browser window.

The browser window closes.

4   In Windows Explorer, right-click the file named To Do List.

A shortcut menu appears.

5   On the shortcut menu, click Open With.

The Open With dialog box appears.

Open With
command

tip

Windows personalizes the Open With command on the shortcut menu. The next time you click Open With, a submenu will appear, displaying names of programs you've used before in conjunction with this command. You can click one of these program names, or you can click Choose Program to open the Open With dialog box.

To permanently associate the selected file type with a program in the Open With dialog box, select the Always Use This Program To Open These Files check box.

6 Scroll down the Choose The Program You Want To Use list, click WordPad, and then click OK.

The file named *To Do List* opens in WordPad, and the insertion point is placed at the beginning of the document.

7 Type **Things**, and press the Spacebar.

The title in the document now reads *Things To Do*.

8 Click the Close button in the top-right corner of the WordPad window.

Close

An alert box appears, prompting you to save your changes.

9 Click Yes to save the changes.

Another alert box appears, warning you that the file will be saved in a text-only format that will remove all formatting.

10 Click Yes to confirm the decision.

WordPad closes.

tip

Windows keeps track of the previous 15 files you opened, so you don't have to navigate through folders again to reopen a file you recently modified. To quickly reopen a file, click the Start button, point to Documents on the Start menu, and then click the desired file name on the Documents menu.

Printing a File

You can also print a selected file by clicking File on the menu bar and clicking Print on the File menu.

You can print a file directly from Windows Explorer without opening the file first. This can be a great timesaver if you have several documents that don't need to be changed—just printed using the default print settings.

To print from Windows Explorer, open the folder that contains the file you want to print, right-click the desired file, and then click Print on the shortcut menu. Windows will open the file using the program that created it, print the file, and then close the program and the file. You can also select multiple documents for printing from Windows Explorer. Hold down Ctrl, and click each file that you want to print.

In this exercise, you print a document from the Windows 2000 Practice folder.

important

A printer must be attached to your computer, either directly or to a computer that you can use on a network, before you can complete this exercise. To learn how to set up a printer, see Lesson 9, "Working with Software and Hardware."

1   If necessary, turn on your printer, and open the Windows 2000 Practice folder in Windows Explorer.

2   Right-click the LMR Whats New file.

     A shortcut menu appears.

3   On the shortcut menu, click Print.

The Notepad window appears briefly, and it disappears when printing starts.

Sorting Files

As the number of files you work with grows, you'll need to be able to find the file you want quickly and efficiently. One way to find a file easily is to sort the contents of a folder according to a certain characteristic, like date. Then, if you know the date when you most recently saved the file and the folder in which you saved it, you can find the file with minimum effort.

Windows Explorer can display files in one of several ways—as large or small icons, in a list of file names, in a list with file details (such as when each file was last modified), or as file names with their **thumbnails** (small representations of pictures). When you sort files, it's a good idea to display them in Details view. Details view lists each file on a line by itself, with columns for the name of the file, the amount of storage space it takes, the type of file it is, and the date when it was last saved. In Details view, you can click a column heading to sort files by that column.

Column headings

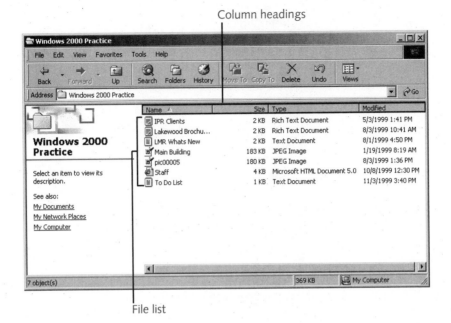

File list

In this exercise, you view files in Details view and sort them by size and modified date.

1 If necessary, open the Windows 2000 Practice folder in Windows Explorer.

2 Click the Folders button on the Standard Buttons toolbar to close the Folders pane.

The Folders pane closes. (You don't need the Folders pane displayed right now because you'll be working only with the files in the Windows 2000 Practice folder.)

3 Click the Views button on the Standard Buttons toolbar.

The Views menu appears. The default view, Large Icons, is selected.

Views

Thumbnails view

4 On the Views menu, click Details.

Each file, including the information pertaining to it, is listed in its own row. The files are sorted alphabetically by name.

5 Click the Size column heading.

The files are sorted by size, largest to smallest.

6 Click the Size column heading again.

The files are sorted by size in reverse order, smallest to largest.

Move pointer

tip

To resize a column in the Details view, position your mouse pointer over the vertical line to the right of a column heading. The mouse pointer changes to a double-headed arrow with a line through it. Drag to the right to make the column wider or to the left to make the column narrower. Double-click to automatically size the column to accommodate the widest item in it.

7 Click the Modified column heading.

The files are sorted by date, oldest to newest.

tip

In Details view, you can choose to display many other columns of information besides the default Name, Size, Type, and Modified columns. Click View on the menu bar, and click Choose Columns on the View menu. The Column Settings dialog box is displayed. In the Column Settings dialog box, select the check boxes for the columns you want to add, and then click OK.

Views

8 Click the Views button on the Standard Buttons toolbar.

The Views menu appears.

9 Click Large Icons.

The folder returns to its default view.

2000 New! Searching For Files and File Content

Sorting the contents of a folder, as discussed in the previous section, is great for finding a file in a folder with many other files. But what if you don't know the name of the folder in which it was saved? In cases like this, the Windows Search Assistant can help. The Windows Search Assistant pinpoints files that contain a certain word or phrase.

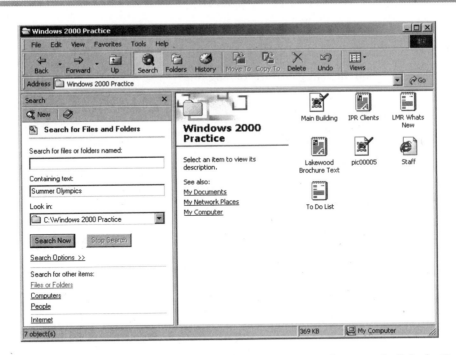

To display the Search Assistant, open Windows Explorer, and click the Search button on the Standard Buttons toolbar. The Search Assistant appears in a pane in the left side of the window.

In this exercise, you use the Search Assistant to find the file that mentions Lakewood Mountains Resort's "Summer Olympics" sports program.

1   If necessary, open the Windows 2000 Practice folder in Windows Explorer, and click the Maximize button in the top-right corner of the window.

2   Click the Search button on the Standard Buttons toolbar.

    The Search Assistant appears in a pane in the left side of the window.

3   Click in the Containing Text box.

    The insertion point is positioned in the Containing Text box.

4   Type **Summer Olympics**. (Be sure to capitalize the S and O because the Search Assistant is case-sensitive.)

5   Verify that Windows 2000 Practice appears in the Look In box.

tip
Regardless of the folder that's open in the right pane of Windows Explorer, the Search Assistant looks for the file in the disk drive or folder specified by Look In.

6   Click the Search Now button.

The Search Results appear in the right pane of the window. Only one file had the text you were looking for.

The Search Assistant lists results in Details view by default, but you can change the view by using the Views button on the Standard Buttons toolbar.

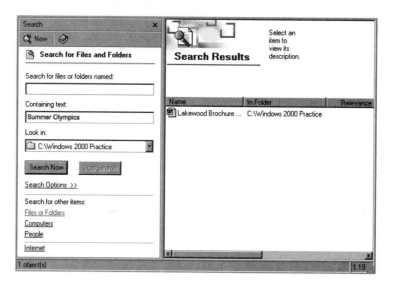

7   Double-click the file name (Lakewood Brochure Text) in the Search Results pane.

The Lakewood Brochure Text file is opened in WordPad or Word, if you have it installed. The second line of text contains a reference to *Summer Olympics*.

8   Click the Close button in the top-right corner of the WordPad (or Word) window.

The program window closes.

Close

9   In Windows Explorer, click the Back button on the Standard Buttons toolbar.

The contents of the Windows 2000 Practice folder reappear in the right pane of the window.

10   Click the Close button in the top-right corner of the Search pane.

The Search Assistant closes.

Close

Advanced Searches

A link to Search Options is located under the Search Now button in the Search pane. When you click this link, the area under it expands to show four check boxes:

- The *Date* check box lets you search for files that were created or modified on a certain date or a range of dates.
- The *Type* check box lets you search for files that have a particular extension.
- The *Size* check box lets you search for files of a particular size.
- The *Advanced Options* check box lets you search for subfolders and case-sensitive file names.

Select the desired check boxes to display options to refine your search. Using a combination of these options, you can create very sophisticated searches. For example, you could search for all e-mail messages created in the last month that include the word "BUDGET" in upper case only.

Creating Files and Folders

Folders are easy to create in Windows Explorer, and there's no limit to the number you can have. So it's a good idea to think about how you want to organize your folders. You might create a folder for each major client, project, or month of the year—it depends on how you prefer to organize your storage space. For example, the marketing director at Impact Public Relations created a folder for Lakewood Mountains Resort. That folder contains a subfolder for graphics and another for Web pages.

You can also create files in Windows Explorer. When you do so, you create a placeholder for a particular type of content, like a graphic or text file, by giving it a name. Then you fill in the content later. This process is the opposite of the more typical way to create files, which involves starting a program like Notepad, entering data, and then saving the data as a file.

Creating a file in Windows Explorer has certain benefits over creating a file in a program: it's faster, because you don't have to run the program, and it creates structure for the file by predetermining its name and the program that will be used to work with it.

A few months ago, the marketing director at Impact Public Relations hired a contractor to write some advertising copy. Before the contractor started the project, the marketing director created the necessary files so that she wouldn't have to search for them after the contractor completed his job. The few minutes she spent to create the files beforehand saved her valuable time later in the project.

In this exercise, you create two folders, one for Lakewood Mountains Resort and one for a freelance copywriter. In the copywriter's directory, you create shells of the files he is to write.

1   If necessary, open the Windows 2000 Practice folder in Windows Explorer.

2   On the File menu, point to New.

The New submenu appears.

3   On the New submenu, click Folder.

A new folder named New Folder appears in the window.

4   Type **Lakewood Mountains Resort**, and press Enter.

The new folder is renamed.

5   Repeat steps 1 through 4 to create a folder named **Freelance Copy**.

The window should look similar to the following.

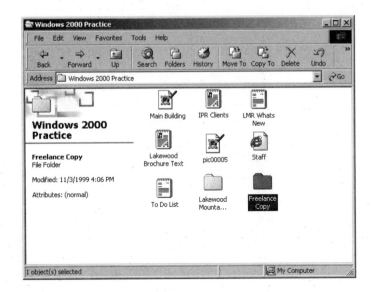

6 Double-click the Freelance Copy folder.

The folder is empty.

7 On the File menu, point to New, and then click Text Document.

A new file named New Text Document appears in the window.

8 Type **Lakewood Mystery Weekends**, and press Enter.

The new file is renamed.

9 Repeat steps 7 and 8 to create another text document file named **Fall Canoe Trips**.

The folder now has two empty text files in it.

10 Double-click the Fall Canoe Trips file.

The document is opened in Notepad, and the insertion point is located at the beginning of the document.

11 Type **Watch for our schedule of upcoming guided canoe trips**.

12 Click the Close button in the top-right corner of the Notepad window, and click Yes to save the changes to the file.

The Notepad window closes.

13 Click the Up button on the Standard Buttons toolbar in the Freelance Copy window.

The contents of the Windows 2000 Practice folder, the "parent" folder of Freelance Copy, reappear.

Close

Up

Moving, Copying, and Renaming Folders and Files

Just as you occasionally reorganize the space in your closets and drawers, you'll find that you want to reorganize your folders and files at some point. You might, for example, want to move files to a new folder you've made. Or you might want to copy a folder and its contents so that you have original versions and duplicates to experiment with. You might also want to rename a folder or file to better reflect its contents.

Move To

Copy To

You can move and copy folders or files using the Move To and Copy To buttons on the Standard Buttons toolbar in Windows Explorer. You can also simply drag a file or folder from one place to another. If you drag a file or folder from place to place on the same disk drive, Windows moves the item. If you drag a file or folder from one disk drive to another disk drive, Windows copies the item.

To rename a file or folder, right-click it, and click Rename on the shortcut menu. The name of the file is selected. Type the new name, and press Enter. The file is renamed.

In the Multimedia folder on the Microsoft Windows 2000 Professional Step-by-Step CD-ROM, double-click the Drag and Drop icon for a demonstration of how to move and copy files.

tip

To be able to choose whether to copy or move a file or folder that you drag, drag the file or folder holding down the right mouse button. When you release the mouse button to drop the item, a shortcut menu will be displayed. On the shortcut menu, click either Copy Here or Move Here.

In this exercise, you drag a file to the Lakewood Mountains Resort folder you created in the previous exercise. Then you copy a file to the folder using the Copy To button on the Standard Buttons toolbar. Finally, you change a file's name to better describe its content. You must have completed the previous exercise before you can begin this one.

1   In the Windows 2000 Practice folder, click the Lakewood Brochure Text file, and drag it on top of the Lakewood Mountains Resort folder.

The file disappears from the Windows 2000 Practice folder.

2   Double-click the Lakewood Mountains Resort folder.

The Lakewood Brochure Text file appears.

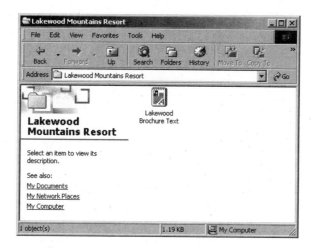

3   Click the Back button on the Standard Buttons toolbar.

The Windows 2000 Practice folder appears.

4   Click the Main Building file.

A thumbnail of the file appears in the left side of the window.

*Dragging the
Main Building
file within a
disk would
move the
file instead
of copying it;
that's why you
use the Copy
To button.*

5   Click the Copy To button on the Standard Buttons toolbar.

The Browse For Folder dialog box appears. The Windows 2000 Practice folder is selected.

6   Click the plus sign to the left of Windows 2000 Practice, click the Lakewood Mountains Resort folder, and then click OK.

The Browse For Folder dialog box closes. Because you copied the file, there is no change in the Windows 2000 Practice folder.

7   Double-click the Lakewood Mountains Resort folder.

The Lakewood Mountains Resort folder now contains two files.

8   Click the Back button on the Standard Buttons toolbar.

The Windows 2000 Practice folder reappears.

9   Right-click the Pic00005 file, and on the shortcut menu, click Rename.

The file name is selected.

10   Type **Fall Countryside**, and press Enter.

The file is renamed.

---

tip

If you change your mind about renaming a file while you are renaming it (before you press Enter or click anywhere else), press Esc. The file name will return to its original name. If you change your mind about renaming immediately after the new name takes effect, click Undo Rename on the Edit menu.

Selecting Multiple Files

You learned earlier in this lesson that you can select a single file by clicking it. Sometimes, though, you'll want to select more than one file at a time. For example, you might need to move a group of files or print several files at once. There are two ways to select multiple files:

- **Shift and Click** If the files you want to select are listed one after another, click the first file in the group, hold down Shift, and then click the last file in the group.

- **Ctrl and Click** If the files you want to select are not listed together, hold down Ctrl while you click each file. If you select a file that you don't want to include in the group, hold down Ctrl, and click the file again to deselect it.

Deleting Files and Folders

Although storage space on disk drives has become remarkably cheap, it's still a finite quantity. As with any other finite resource, you need to delete unnecessary files and folders to conserve space.

Deleting a file or folder does not really erase it from the disk the way an eraser removes pencil marks. It's more like tossing something into a junk drawer. Eventually, the drawer gets full, and you empty it. Sometimes, things get tossed into the drawer by mistake, and you need to take them out and put them back where they belong.

In Windows, this junk drawer is called the Recycle Bin. To send a file or folder to the Recycle Bin, select the file or folder, and click the Delete button on the Standard Buttons toolbar. Click Yes to confirm the deletion. To view the contents of the Recycle Bin, double-click its icon on the desktop. To remove an item from the Recycle Bin (undelete it), click the item, and click the Restore button in the left pane of the Recycle Bin window. To permanently delete an item from the Recycle Bin, click the item, and then click the Delete button on the Standard Buttons toolbar. Click Yes to confirm the deletion. To permanently delete everything in the Recycle Bin, click the Empty Recycle Bin button in the left pane of the Recycle Bin window.

important

Emptying the Recycle Bin cannot be undone. The items are permanently deleted. Use caution, therefore, when you empty the Recycle Bin. Also, if you are connected to a network and you delete a file or folder from a networked computer, the file or folder is not placed in the Recycle Bin. Instead, it is permanently deleted. Files and folders deleted from a floppy disk are also permanently deleted.

In this exercise, you delete a file and a folder, and you restore the deleted items from the Recycle Bin to their original folders.

1   If necessary, open the Windows 2000 Practice folder in Windows Explorer.

2   Click the file named To Do List, and click the Delete button on the Standard Buttons toolbar.

The Confirm File Delete dialog box appears.

Delete

3   Click Yes to confirm the deletion.

The file is deleted from the Windows 2000 Practice folder.

4   Click the Freelance Copy folder, click the Delete button on the Standard Buttons toolbar, and then click Yes to confirm the deletion.

The Freelance Copy folder is deleted from the Windows 2000 Practice folder.

Show Desktop

5   Click the Show Desktop icon on the Quick Launch bar.

The desktop appears.

6   On the desktop, double-click the Recycle Bin icon.

The Recycle Bin window opens.

7   Click the Freelance Copy folder.

The folder is selected, and information about it appears in the left side of the Recycle Bin window.

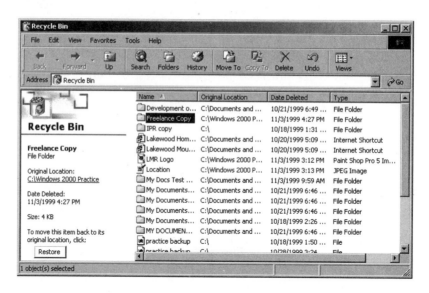

2000
New!

You can use the new Restore button in the Recycle Bin to move a deleted item back to its original location.

8   In the left side of the window, click the Restore button.

The Freelance Copy folder disappears from the Recycle Bin window.

9   Repeat steps 7 and 8 for the To Do List.

After a brief pause, the To Do List file disappears from the Recycle Bin.

10   Click the Close button in the top-right corner of the Recycle Bin window.

Close

The Recycle Bin window closes.

11   Click the Windows 2000 Practice button on the taskbar.

The Windows 2000 Practice window reappears, and the Freelance Copy folder and the To Do List file are restored.

12   Double-click the Freelance Copy folder.

The files in the folder, which were deleted along with it, have also been restored intact.

13   Click the Close button in the top-right corner of the window.

The Windows Explorer window closes, and the desktop reappears.

Close

Lesson Wrap-Up

In this lesson, you learned how to manage files and folders. You learned about Windows Explorer and My Computer. You found out how to retrieve a particular file, either by browsing through the Folders pane or by using the Search Assistant, and how to print a file without opening it. You also learned how to create, move, copy, and rename files and folders. Finally, you learned how to use the Recycle Bin to remove files and folders that you no longer need.

If you are continuing to other lessons:

● Close all open windows. The desktop should be displayed.

If you are not continuing to other lessons:

1   Close all open windows, and click the Start button on the taskbar.

2   Click Shut Down on the Start menu. If necessary, click the arrow in the Windows Shut Down dialog box, and click Shut Down in the list. Then click OK.

3   After Windows has shut down, turn off the computer and, if necessary, all other hardware devices.

Glossary

default A setting in a window, dialog box, or menu that is established when Windows is installed but that can be changed by the user.

extension A period followed by one to three characters at the end of a file name. An extension is typically used to identify the program that can open the file.

file Any document, picture, sound, or video that can be stored separately on a hard disk or other resource. Programs (such as Microsoft Word or Microsoft Excel) are actually collections of files; Windows itself is a collection of hundreds of files, each with its own purpose.

folder A container that stores files that are related in some way. In Windows, a folder can also contain other folders, called subfolders.

Glossary

My Computer A window that displays icons for all the available resources for your computer, including all your disk drives, the network (if your computer is connected to one), and Control Panel.

My Documents The default folder on your hard disk for storing documents that you create.

network folder A location on another computer to which your computer is connected.

shared folder A folder on your computer that you've set up to be accessible to other users on a network.

subfolder A folder within a folder.

synchronized folder A folder whose contents are automatically updated to match those of another folder.

thumbnail A small representation of a picture, Web page (HTML file), or video that displays in the Image Preview area of the My Computer or Windows Explorer window when you click the name of a graphic, Web page, or video.

Windows Explorer A window that you can use to navigate through folders and copy, move, delete, and open files.

Quick Reference

To navigate through folders

1   Hold down the Windows key, and click E.

2   In the Folders pane, click the plus and minus signs to expand and collapse folders and to navigate to the desired folder or file.

To open a file

● Double-click the file, or right-click the file, click Open With on the shortcut menu, and click the desired program name in the Open With dialog box.

To print a file

● Right-click the file, and click Print on the shortcut menu.

Quick Reference

To sort files

● Click Details on the View menu, and click the desired column heading in the right pane of the window.

To search for a file based on its content

1 In the Windows Explorer window, click the Search button.

2 In the Containing Text box, type the words to search for. In the Look In drop-down list, specify the folders to search.

3 Click the Search Now button.

To create a folder

1 On the Windows Explorer menu bar, click File.

2 On the File menu, point to New, and then click Folder.

3 Type a name for the new folder, and press Enter.

To create a file

1 On the Windows Explorer menu bar, click File.

2 On the File menu, point to New, and then click the type of file to create.

3 Type a name for the new file, and press Enter.

To move a file or folder within a disk drive

● Drag the file or folder to a different folder.

To move a file or folder to a different disk drive

1 Click the file or folder, and click the Move To button on the Standard Buttons toolbar.

2 In the Browse For Folder dialog box, select the desired folder, and then click OK.

To copy a file or folder within a disk drive

1 Click the file or folder, and click the Copy To button on the Standard Buttons toolbar.

2 In the Browse For Folder dialog box, select the desired folder, and then click OK.

Quick Reference

To copy a file or folder to a different disk drive

●   Drag the file or folder to the target folder on the other disk drive.

To rename a file or folder

1   Right-click the file or folder.
2   On the shortcut menu, click Rename.
3   Type the new name, and press Enter.

To undo a change

1   On the Windows Explorer menu bar, click Edit.
2   On the Edit menu, click Undo.

To delete a file or folder

1   Click the file or folder to be deleted.
2   On the Standard Buttons toolbar, click the Delete button.
3   Click Yes in the alert box to confirm the deletion.

To restore a deleted file or folder

1   Double-click the Recycle Bin icon on the desktop.
2   Click the appropriate file or folder, and click the Restore button.

1

Review & Practice

Review & Practice

**ESTIMATED
TIME
20 min.**

You will review and practice how to:

✔ *Open, close, resize, and move windows.*

✔ *Use the Windows 2000 help system.*

✔ *Open folders and files.*

✔ *Create a folder.*

✔ *Copy and move files to a folder.*

✔ *Delete a file and a folder.*

✔ *Restore the folder from the Recycle Bin.*

Before you move on to Unit 2, you can reinforce the skills you've learned so far by working through this Review & Practice. In this section, you will manage windows and programs on the desktop. Then you will search the Windows 2000 help system for a particular topic and add that topic to the Favorites list. Next you will navigate through folders, sort and open files, create a folder, and copy and move files to the new folder. Finally, you will delete and restore the new folder.

Scenario

The marketing director at Impact Public Relations has hired a graphic artist who is new to Windows. She needs a quick tour of Windows to learn about windows, programs, folders, and files. Also, because she is left handed, she wants to know how to switch mouse buttons.

Step 1: Open, Close, Resize, and Move Windows

Start the tour on the desktop, using My Computer to examine how to manipulate a window. Then move to the Start button to start the Paint and Calculator programs. Finally, restart Windows to demonstrate how to log on.

1   Open the My Computer window.

2   Maximize the My Computer window, and restore it.

3   Move the My Computer window to the top-left corner of the screen, and then move it to the bottom-right corner.

4   Increase the width of the My Computer window by a few inches.

5   Minimize the My Computer window.

6   Start Calculator (on the Accessories submenu from the Programs submenu), and minimize it.

7   Start Paint.

8   Make the Calculator window the active window.

9   Switch back to the Paint window, and close it.

10   Close the Calculator and My Computer windows.

11   Restart Windows 2000, and log on.

For more information about	See
Using desktop icons	Lesson 1
The Minimize, Maximize, and Restore Down buttons	Lesson 1
Resizing and moving a window	Lesson 1
Using the Start menu	Lesson 1
Making windows active	Lesson 1
Closing a window	Lesson 1
Shutting down Windows	Lesson 1
Starting Windows	Lesson 1

Step 2: Use the Windows 2000 Help System

Use the Windows 2000 help system to search for instructions on swapping mouse buttons for use in the left hand. Add the instructions to the Favorites list so they are easy to find.

1   Start the Windows 2000 help system.

2   Search for help about *left-handed mouse*.

3   Add the *Reverse Your Mouse Buttons* topic to the Favorites list.

4   Open the Mouse Properties dialog box using the Mouse link on the *Reverse Your Mouse Buttons* topic.

5   Use the What's This? button on the Mouse Properties dialog box to display information about the Test Area.

6   Close the Mouse Properties dialog box, and then close the Windows 2000 help window.

For more information about	See
Starting programs	Lesson 1
Searching the Windows 2000 help system	Lesson 2
Using the Favorites list	Lesson 2
Using a link in a help topic	Lesson 2
Using the What's This? feature	Lesson 2
Closing a dialog box	Lesson 1

Step 3: Open Folders and Files

Show the new graphic artist how to navigate through folders and sort and open files.

1   Open the Windows Explorer window.

2   Navigate to the Windows 2000 Practice folder.

3   Sort the files in the Windows 2000 Practice folder by type.

4   Open the LMR Whats New file.

For more information about	See
Opening folders	Lesson 3
Navigating through folders	Lesson 3
Sorting files	Lesson 3
Opening files	Lesson 3

Step 4: Manage Files and Folders

The graphic artist would like a copy of the Main Building picture so that she can experiment with it. She plans to acquire more art like this one, and she wants to store the files in a folder named LMR Art.

1   Create a subfolder named LMR Art within the Windows 2000 Practice folder.

2   Copy the Main Building file from the Windows 2000 Practice folder to the LMR Art folder.

3   Move the Fall Countryside file from the Windows 2000 Practice folder to the LMR Art folder.

For more information about	See
Creating folders	Lesson 3
Copying files	Lesson 3
Moving files	Lesson 3

Step 5: Use the Recycle Bin

Because picture files tend to consume storage space, the graphic artist needs to know the importance of deleting unneeded files and folders. She's concerned, however, that she might accidentally delete files that she needs. So you decide to show her how to use the Recycle Bin.

1   Open the LMR Art folder.

2   Delete the Main Building file.

3   Open the Windows 2000 Practice folder.

4   Delete the LMR Art folder.

5   Restore the LMR Art folder.

6   Verify that the LMR Art folder has been restored to the Windows 2000 Practice folder.

For more information about	See
Navigating through folders	Lesson 3
Deleting files and folders	Lesson 3
Using the Recycle Bin	Lesson 3
Restoring a deleted folder	Lesson 3

Finish the Review & Practice

1   Move the Fall Countryside file back to the Windows 2000 Practice folder.

2   Delete the LMR Art folder.

3   Close all open windows.

UNIT 2

Getting Connected

LESSON 4

Using Windows on a Network

ESTIMATED TIME
50 min.

After completing this lesson, you will be able to:

✔ *Use network resources.*

✔ *Connect two computers.*

✔ *Change your Windows password.*

✔ *Create a user account.*

✔ *Share a folder with others on the network.*

✔ *Map a network drive.*

When computers are connected so that they can exchange information, they are networked. A computer network might be composed of hundreds of computers or just two. The most common type of network is the **local area network** (LAN), in which computers in a building or several buildings in close proximity (such as a university campus or an office complex) are connected using cables. You can also connect to a network through a dial-up connection, in which your computer uses a number to dial in to a computer that is directly connected to a network. In this case, your computer connects to the network through phone lines, and other computers on the network are connected through cables.

In this lesson, you will learn about direct network connections, such as those over a LAN. (Dial-up connections are discussed in Lesson 5, "Accessing and Browsing the Internet," and Lesson 8, "Using Windows on the Go.") You will use My Network Places to examine the way your network is set up, and you will add a new connection to My Network Places. Then you will learn how to create a direct network connection between two computers. Because networks invite sharing files and folders with others, you will learn how to make selected folders available to others on the network. You will also learn how to change your Windows password so that you can protect sensitive information. Finally, you will learn to treat a folder on a network as if it were a disk on your own computer.

Your computer will need to be connected to a network for you to perform most of the exercises in this lesson. In addition, you must have Administrator privileges to complete the Setting Up A User exercise in this lesson. You will know that you aren't logged on with Administrator privileges if you see a message on screen telling you that you aren't authorized to perform the specified actions. If you see this message, you need to log off Windows and log back on, typing *Administrator* in the User Name box and typing *password* in the Password box. Your **password**, together with your user name, identifies you to Windows, and it authorizes you to open and modify certain files. The Administrator account was created and the password was set when Windows was installed on your computer. The password for the Administrator account is *password* unless whoever installed Windows specified a different password, or the password has since been changed. If a network administrator set up Windows on your system, you need to ask him or her for the Administrator password.

Using My Network Places

My Network Places

There are several ways to examine the contents of your network, but the most straightforward approach is to use the My Network Places icon on the desktop. My Network Places is a window that displays all resources—such as computers, hard disks, files, and folders—available to you on the network. When you open the My Network Places window in Windows Explorer, you will see at least three icons:

- *Add Network Place* Double-clicking this icon starts the Add Network Place Wizard, which you can use to create shortcuts to network locations—such as specific disks or folders. These shortcuts appear in the My Network Places folder.

- *Entire Network* Double-clicking this icon displays a list of all the computers on the network to which you have access.

■ *Computers Near Me* Double-clicking this icon displays the computers in your workgroup or domain. A workgroup is a collection of networked computers for users who frequently share files and folders with each other, such as a department within an organization. Similar to a workgroup, a domain usually identifies a larger set of computers, perhaps those located in one geographical place. A large corporation might have one domain for its headquarters and other domains in other areas of the country or other countries. (Do not confuse a network domain with an Internet domain. The two terms have different meanings.) All of these domains are connected to form one **wide area network** (WAN). Your workgroup or domain determines the computers on the network that you are most likely to need because they have something in common with the way you work and the specific files and folders you use. Only users who have a valid user name and password can access the domain.

After you've clicked the desired icon, you can navigate through the computers and folders that appear, as though they were folders on your own computer. However, depending on the access rights your network administrator has assigned you, you might not be able to delete or change network folders and files as you can on your own computer.

In this exercise, you use My Network Places to find a folder on another computer in your workgroup. Then you add a connection to an Internet folder to My Network Places.

Depending on the level of access you have to a folder on the network, you can examine its contents, move or copy files to and from it, or even delete it.

1 On the desktop, double-click the My Network Places icon.

The My Network Places window opens.

2 Double-click the Computers Near Me icon.

The names of the networked computers in your workgroup or domain appear.

3 Double-click one of the computer names.

The folders that you are allowed to access on that computer appear. The window should look similar to the following, although the name of the computer and the specific folders will be different.

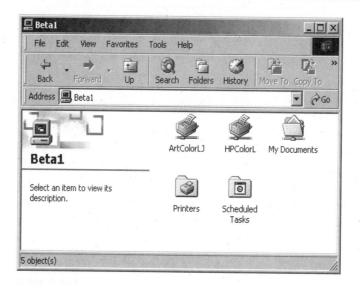

4   On the Standard Buttons toolbar, click the Up button twice.

The My Network Places window reappears.

5   Double-click the Add Network Place icon.

The Add Network Place Wizard appears.

FTP stands for "File Transfer Protocol," a collection of networking rules that computers use to send and receive files to and from servers on the Internet.

6   In the Type The Location Of The Network Place box, type **ftp://ftp.microsoft.com**.

The wizard should look similar to the following.

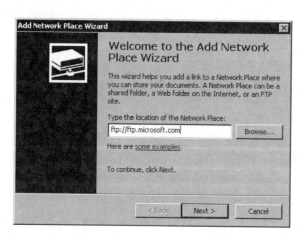

7   Click the Next button.

You are asked if you would like to log on anonymously. The Log On Anonymously check box is already selected.

8   Click the Next button.

You are prompted to name the network place. By default, the address of the network place is used as its name.

Lesson 5, "Accessing and Browsing the Internet," discusses how to set up an Internet connection.

9   In the Enter A Name For This Network Place box, type **Microsoft Files**.
If you do not have an Internet connection, click the Cancel button, and continue to the next section in this lesson. Otherwise, click the Finish button.

If you click the Cancel button, no change is made to My Network Places. If you click the Finish button, you are prompted to connect to the FTP site.

10   If necessary, click the Connect button.

When you are connected, the browser window opens to the Microsoft FTP site.

In this example, Internet Explorer is the default browser. Your screen will look different if you have a different default browser.

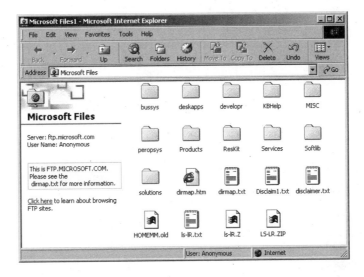

11   Click the Close button in the top-right corner of the browser window.

Close

The browser window closes.

12   If necessary, disconnect from the Internet by double-clicking the Internet icon on the taskbar (to the left of the time) and clicking the Disconnect button.

Internet

An icon for the connection to Microsoft Files appears in My Network Places.

Keep My Network Places open for the next exercise.

4

Using a Network

Directly Connecting Two Computers

Network Connection Wizard

Network administrators usually manage file sharing on networks within organizations. If you want to connect only two computers, however, you can do it yourself using the networking features built into Windows. This kind of network is referred to as **direct** or **peer-to-peer** because no server is used to control access to files or to the networked computers. Instead, the computers are connected directly to each other with cables.

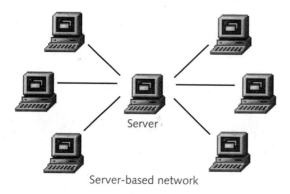

Server-based network

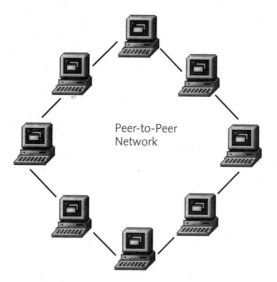

The most common way to connect computers is by adding a **network interface card** (NIC) to each computer and connecting a cable to each NIC. An NIC is a circuit board that you can insert into one of the internal slots on the main circuit board of your computer. The NIC controls communication between one computer and all the other computers on the network.

It's also possible to create a network connection by attaching a cable to a **port** on the back of each computer you want to network. A port is a connector, usually containing a series of pins or a series of openings, where pins from a cable can be inserted. A port connects a cable to the main circuit board of your computer. Different types of ports on your computer can be used for different types of devices. You can connect two computers using either **parallel** or **serial ports**. A parallel port allows two-way communication simultaneously. A serial port allows two-way communication, but data can travel in only one direction at a time. On some computers, you can also connect via infrared ports, which let you connect computers using beams of infrared light instead of a cable.

tip

To directly connect computers through a parallel port, you need a parallel cable that is especially made for connecting two computers, not the kind of cable that is commonly used to connect a printer to a computer. One brand of cable that you can use to connect two Windows computers is called *DirectParallel*. For more information on this cable and for information about ordering it, search the Windows 2000 help system for the name *DirectParallel*.

In this exercise, you directly connect two computers through their serial ports using a serial cable. To complete this exercise, you need two computers with Windows 2000 installed. Both computers should be turned off at the begining of the exercise. You also need a serial cable that matches the serial ports on your computers. (The serial port on the back of each computer can be either male or female. A male port contains pins. A female port contains openings for pins. As you might realize, the connectors on a serial cable can also be either male or female. You need to make sure you match the male/female computer ports with the male/female connectors on each end of the cable.) You'll also need an available serial port on each computer—in other words, a serial port that doesn't already have a cable connected to it. If you do not have this equipment, you can still work through steps 2 through 9 of the exercise. If you have a parallel cable, you can also connect the two computers by using their available parallel ports. However, you must make sure you are using a parallel cable that supports communication between two computers (such as a DirectParallel cable).

Male serial ports

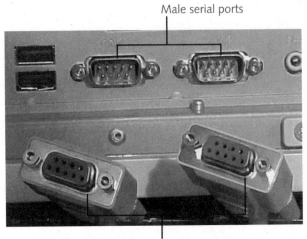

Female serial cables

1   Shut down both computers.

2   Connect the two computers by attaching an end of the serial cable to each computer's serial port, and start both computers.

The two computers are physically connected, but they aren't networked with one another yet.

You can also start the Network Connection Wizard by clicking the Start button, pointing to Settings, pointing to Network And Dial-Up Connections, and then clicking Make New Connection.

3   On one of the computers, double-click the My Network Places icon.

The My Network Places window opens.

4   In the left side of the My Network Places window, click the Network And Dial-Up Connections link.

The Network And Dial-Up Connections window appears.

5   Double-click the Make New Connection icon.

The Network Connection Wizard appears.

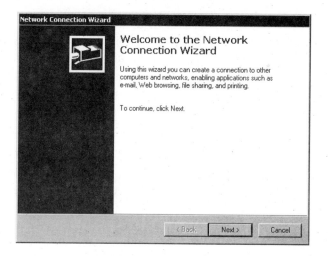

6 Click the Next button.

The Wizard prompts you for the type of connection you want to create.

7 Click the Connect Directly To Another Computer option, and click the Next button.

The wizard prompts you to specify the role for this computer: host or guest.

8 Verify that the Host option is selected, and click the Next button.

You are prompted to choose the device you want to use to make the connection.

9 If necessary, click the Device For This Connection arrow, and click Communications Port. (If you're using a DirectParallel cable, verify that DirectParallel Cable appears in the Device For This Connection box.) Then click the Next button.

The Allowed Users screen appears; none of the check boxes is selected.

10 Click the Next button.

The final screen appears, and the connection for the host computer is automatically named *Incoming Connections*.

11 Click the Finish button.

12 Repeat steps 2 through 6 on the other computer.

The wizard prompts you to specify the role for this computer: host or guest.

13 Click the Guest option, and click the Next button.

You are prompted to specify the port through which the computers are connected on the guest side.

*You might have
a number other
than 1 after
COM, such as
COM2. It
depends on the
ports that are
available on
your computer.*

14   If necessary, click the Select A Device arrow, and click Communications Cable Between Two Computers (COM1). (If you're using a DirectParallel cable, click the Select A Device arrow, and click DirectParallel Cable.) Then click the Next button.

You are prompted to specify the connection availability.

15   Click the Only For Myself option, and click the Next button.

You are prompted to name the connection.

16   In the Type The Name You Want To Use For This Connection box, type **Networking Practice**, and then click the Finish button.

You are prompted to connect to the other computer.

17   Click in the Password box, type your password for logging on to Windows, and then click the Connect button.

Windows "dials" the host computer. After the connection has been established, the Connection Complete message appears.

tip

If you receive an error message when you try to connect, you might need to fine-tune the connection by experimenting with the network properties. Right-click either the Incoming Connection icon on the host computer or the Networking Practice icon on the guest computer, and click Properties on the shortcut menu. Check each tab of the Properties dialog box for settings that might conflict. In particular, check the Internet Protocol (TCP/IP) properties on the host's Networking tab, and make sure all check boxes are selected.

18   Click OK.

The computers are now networked with one another. On the host computer, the name of the Incoming Connections icon might change to Unauthenticated User.

19   Click the Disconnect button.

The two computers are no longer connected.

20   Click the Close button in the top-right corner of the Network And Dial-Up Connections window.

The Network And Dial-Up Connections window closes.

Changing Passwords

You probably use many identification systems in your day-to-day routine: a personal identification number (PIN) to get money from an ATM, an identification card to gain entry into your office building, a code to disable your car alarm, and so on. When your computer is connected to a network, you must use a password to gain access to Windows.

From an authorization standpoint, anyone who correctly enters your password and user name is you. Therefore, it's a good idea to change your password periodically. In fact, many organizations have rules that require you to change your password every 60 days. Some organizations also have specific rules about the length and content of your password.

Guideline	Weak Password	Better Password
Choose a password that is easy for you to remember but hard for others to guess.	Your spouse's name	The name of your best friend from elementary school
Remember that longer passwords are safer than shorter ones.	mine	candelabra
Mix letters with numbers and/or punctuation. For example, substitute the numeral 1 for the letter *l*, and the numeral 0 for the letter *o*.	trolls	tr0l1s
Combine two words that don't normally go together.	honey	airhoney

In addition to these guidelines and those that might be required by your organization, Windows requires that your new password differ from your three previous ones.

Windows keeps track of all files and folders that you create while you're logged on. If someone tries to use your computer after you have logged off, they won't be able to access any of the files and folders that you have created. Similarly, if you log on to a Windows computer that another person uses, you won't be able to access any files or folders that are password protected or not set up as shared.

The Windows password authorizes access to files and folders stored on a computer. The network password, on the other hand, authorizes access to computers on the network. The Windows password might be the same as the network password, but it doesn't have to be the same. If you need to enter two passwords to work on your computer, the following exercise will change only one of them. Consult your network administrator for help changing the other.

2000 New!

The Windows password also controls access to the My Documents folder.

> **tip**
>
> The Windows password also controls access to the **My Documents** folder—the default folder on your hard disk for storing documents that you create. Each user who logs on to a particular computer will see only the files that he or she has saved.

In this exercise, you change your Windows password to ensure the security of the files and folders that you create on your computer.

Alternatively, click the Start button, point to Settings, and then click Control Panel. Double-click the Users And Passwords icon, and click the desired user name.

1 Hold down Ctrl and Alt, and tap Delete.

The Windows Security dialog box appears.

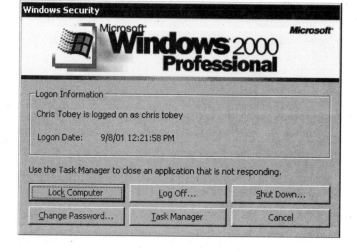

2000 New!

Windows Security dialog box

2 Click the Change Password button.

The Change Password dialog box appears.

Because passwords are case sensitive, note whether the Caps Lock is turned on when you enter your password.

3 In the Old Password box, type your current password, and then press Tab.

The insertion point moves to the New Password box.

4   In the New Password box, type your new password exactly as you want to enter it when you log on to Windows, and press Tab.

To help ensure that you haven't made a mistake in typing your new password, you must type it again.

5   In the Confirm New Password box, retype your new password.

The dialog box should look similar to the following.

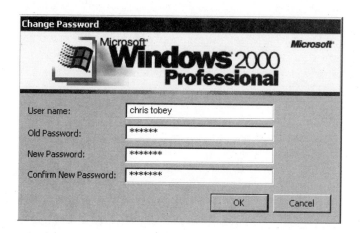

6   If you don't want to change your password now, click the Cancel button. Otherwise, click OK twice.

The Windows Security dialog box reappears.

7   Click the Log Off button.

The Log Off Windows dialog box appears.

8   Click Yes.

If the Welcome To Windows dialog box appears, follow the instructions before logging on.

Windows hides the desktop, and the Log On To Windows dialog box appears.

9   Type your new password, and press Enter.

Windows identifies your password as the correct one for your user name, and it restarts.

tip
You can use the Windows Security dialog box for more than just changing your password. For instance, you can click the Lock Computer button to hide the desktop. With the desktop hidden, it won't be possible to use Windows on this computer until someone types the correct password and presses Enter or clicks OK. Locking the desktop does not log a user off the computer; it only makes the desktop unavailable to anyone who doesn't know the password for the current user. You can also use the Windows Security dialog box to open Task Manager. Click the Task Manager button. The Applications tab in this window lists the programs that are running. You can close a program from the Task Manager by clicking it in the Applications list and clicking the End Task button. However, you should use this approach only if a program stops running correctly.

Setting Up a User

In the Multimedia folder on the Microsoft Windows Professional 2000 Step by Step CD-ROM, double-click the New User icon for a demonstration of how to create a user account.

After completing the previous exercise, you might wonder how your original password was created—if there was one. A network administrator or another person who previously used your computer probably created your user account in Windows. If you upgrade to Windows 2000 (from Windows 95, Windows 98, or Windows NT) on a computer that already had a user account, Windows 2000 will keep this account information when it is installed.

Even if you aren't connected to a network, you might have users who share a computer. Each user needs a user name and a Windows password. When you create an account, you set the user's access level in addition to creating the user's name and password. An access level identifies the actions each user is authorized to perform in files, folders, and other user accounts on that machine. There are three basic access levels:

- **Administrator** Administrators have full access. Among other things, they can create and remove other user accounts.

- **Standard** Standard users can control their own environments, but they cannot perform actions that might adversely affect other users—such as adding or removing hardware and removing software.

- **Restricted** Restricted users have limited privileges and can be assigned to one of the predefined Windows user groups: Users, Backup Operators, Guests, or Replicators. Each group has a different set of privileges.

In this exercise, you add a user account to the system, and you assign the user Standard access. You must be logged on as a user with Administrator access to complete this exercise.

1   Click the Start button, point to Settings, and then click Control Panel.
    Control Panel appears.

Users And Passwords icon

You might see different users displayed in the Users And Passwords dialog box on your computer.

2   Scroll to the bottom of the window, if necessary, and double-click the Users And Passwords icon.
    The Users And Passwords dialog box appears.

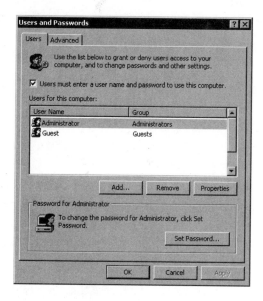

3   Click the Add button.
    The Add New User dialog box appears.

4   In the User Name box, type **SBS User**, and click the Next button.
    You are prompted to type and confirm a password for SBS User.

5   In the Password box, type **testing**, and press Tab. In the Confirm Password box, type **testing** again, and then click the Next button.
    You are prompted to assign access rights.

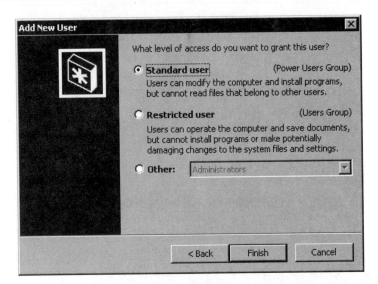

6   Verify that the Standard User option is selected, and click the Finish button.

SBS User is added to the Users list.

7   In the Users And Passwords dialog box, click OK.

The dialog box closes.

Close

8   Click the Close button in the top-right corner of Control Panel.

Control Panel closes.

9   On the Start menu, click Shut Down.

The Shut Down Windows dialog box appears.

10   In the Shut Down Windows dialog box, click the arrow, click Log Off <user name>, and then click OK.

If the Welcome To Windows dialog box appears, follow the instructions before logging on.

After a pause, you are logged off Windows, and the Log On To Windows dialog box appears.

tip

Make a note of your user name, which appears in the Log On To Windows dialog box. You will need it to log back on as yourself, after you log on as SBS User.

11   In the User Name box, select your user name, and type **SBS User**. Press Tab, type **testing**, and then click OK.

You are logged on as SBS User. Windows should look as it did the first time you started it, without any of the changes you might have made since then.

12   Repeat steps 9 through 11, modifying the steps so that you log back on using your user name and password.

The desktop appears exactly as you left it.

Sharing a Folder

Ordinarily, other people do not have access to the disks that are directly connected to your computer. For example, if you store a file in a folder that you've created on your hard disk, that file can be accessed only from your computer when you are logged on to Windows. To allow others to see the folder or work with its files from their computers, you need to specify the folder as shared.

When you set sharing options, you can also set permissions for the level of access you want to provide to other users on the network. You can allow or deny three types of access:

- **Full** A user has the same access to the folder as you do. She or he can even delete it.
- **Change** A user can add files to and remove files from the folder. Unless the user also has Read access, however, he or she cannot see what's already in the folder.
- **Read** A user can examine the contents of a folder. Unless the user also has Change access, however, she or he cannot modify the contents.

In the Share Name box, you can change the folder name that appears to other users on the network. You can also add a comment in the Comment box to provide more folder information.

In this exercise, you share the Windows 2000 Practice folder so that everyone on the network can make changes to it. To help others connect to the folder you've shared, tell them the name of your computer and the share name you give the folder.

tip
To find out the network name of your computer, open Control Panel, and double-click System. In the System Properties dialog box, click the Network Identification tab. Your computer's network identity appears to the right of Full Computer Name.

1   On the desktop, double-click the My Computer icon.

The My Computer window appears.

2   In the My Computer window, double-click Local Disk. (If you've renamed Local Disk, or if you have more than one hard disk, double-click the disk labeled drive C.)

The files and folders stored on the disk appear.

3   Scroll through the list of folders, if necessary, until Windows 2000 Practice is visible. Right-click the Windows 2000 Practice folder.

A shortcut menu appears.

4   On the shortcut menu, click Sharing.

The Windows 2000 Practice Properties dialog box appears, and the Sharing tab is displayed.

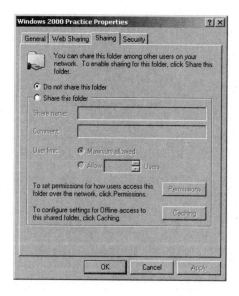

5   On the Sharing tab, click the Share This Folder option.

All options in the dialog box are now available for selection.

6   Click the Permissions button.

The Permissions For Windows 2000 Practice dialog box appears.

7   Select the Deny check box for Full Control, and select the Allow check boxes for Change and Read.

The dialog box should look similar to the following.

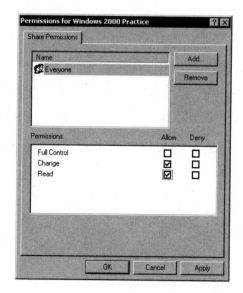

8 Click OK.

A Security dialog box appears, asking if you want to continue.

9 Click Yes.

The Security dialog box closes.

10 In the Windows 2000 Practice Properties dialog box, click OK.

The dialog box closes. After a brief pause, the folder icon for Windows 2000 Practice in the Local Disk window changes to indicate that the folder is shared.

11 Click the Close button in the top-right corner of the Local Disk window.

Close

The Local Disk window closes.

---

tip

To stop sharing a folder, right-click the folder, and click Sharing on the shortcut menu. On the Sharing tab in the Properties dialog box, click the Do Not Share This Folder option, and then click OK. The icon for the folder will change to indicate that the folder is no longer shared.

Mapping a Network Drive

Disk drives on your computer are named using letters of the alphabet followed by colons, starting with *A*: for the floppy disk (and *B*: for a second floppy disk, if you have one). Your primary hard disk is usually named *C*:. Other drives that are physically attached to your computer are assigned the succeeding letters (*D*:, *E*:, and so on). These drives can include additional hard disks, CD-ROM drives, and removable-storage drives (such as Zip, Jaz, and Orb drives).

After all the drives that are physically attached to your computer are named, many letters of the alphabet will remain unassigned. These drive letters can be assigned, or **mapped**, to folders on your network, to provide easier access to those folders. A mapped folder is treated like other disk drives; it is given a drive letter and appears near the top of the Folders pane in Windows Explorer or as a resource in the My Computer window.

For instance, the marketing assistant at Impact Public Relations (IPR) is collaborating with other IPR employees on advertising a charity event to be held at Lakewood Mountains Resort (LMR). Each employee assigned to the project saves his or her work in the same shared folder on the network. Each time the marketing assistant wants to open or save a file for the charity event, he can open My Network Places, double-click the computer where the Charity folder is stored, and then navigate through a series of folders to finally open the Charity folder. To avoid this time-consuming process, the marketing assistant has mapped the Charity folder to one of the unused drive letters on his computer. Now, he can open the Charity folder by double-clicking its shortcut in the My Computer window or from the top of the Folders pane in Windows Explorer.

tip
Another way to access a shared folder quickly is to make it a favorite and open it from the Favorites menu in Windows Explorer or My Computer. In the Folders pane, navigate to the desired folder, and click it. On the Favorites menu, click Add To Favorites. In the Add Favorite dialog box, click OK. The next time you want to access the folder, click the desired folder name on the Favorites menu.

In this exercise, you map a folder to a drive letter.

1   On the desktop, double-click the My Computer icon.

The My Computer window opens.

2 On the Tools menu, click Map Network Drive.

The Map Network Drive dialog box appears, and the first unassigned drive letter is selected in the Drive box.

The Map Network Drive dialog box has been expanded and provides more helpful information.

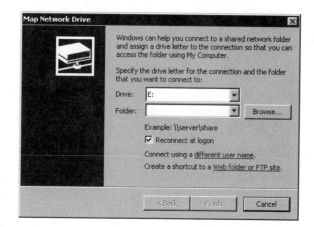

3 Click the Browse button.

The Browse For Folder window appears.

4 Click the plus sign to the left of Computers Near Me.

The networked computers in your domain or workgroup are listed.

5 Double-click one of the computer names.

The shared folders on that computer are listed.

6 Click the name of any folder in the list, and click OK.

In the Map Network Drive dialog box, the full network address of the folder appears in the Folder box.

7 Click the Finish button.

A new window appears, displaying the folders and files for the network folder you just mapped.

tip

If you want to remove mapping from a folder, you cannot delete the icon like you would for any other file or folder. Instead, you disconnect from the folder by clicking Disconnect Network Drive on the Tools menu in Windows Explorer or My Computer. In the Disconnect Network Drive dialog box, click the drive letter you want to remove, and then click OK.

Close

8 Click the Close button in the top-right corner of the networked folder's window.

The window closes, and the My Computer window reappears.

Close

9 Click the Close button in the top-right corner of the My Computer window.
The My Computer window closes.

Lesson Wrap-Up

In this lesson, you examined the contents of your network and directly connected two computers. Then you explored the implications of networking computers, such as the need to change passwords, the benefits of sharing files and mapping drives, and the possibility of adding user accounts.

To return all Windows components to their previous settings:

1 On the desktop, double-click My Network Places, click the Microsoft Files icon, and then press Delete. Click Yes to confirm the deletion.

2 In My Network Places, click the link to Network And Dial-Up Connections. Click the Incoming Connections icon, and press Delete. On the guest computer in the direct connection, double-click My Network Places. Click the link to Network And Dial-Up Connections, click the Networking Practice icon, and then press Delete. Close the Network And Dial-Up Connections window.

3 Click the Start button, point to Settings, and then click Control Panel. In Control Panel, double-click the Users And Passwords icon. In the Users For This Computer list, click SBS User. Click the Remove button, and click Yes to confirm the deletion. Close the Users And Passwords dialog box, and close Control Panel.

4 On the desktop, double-click the My Computer icon. Double-click Local Disk. Right-click the Windows 2000 Practice folder, and click Sharing. Click the Do Not Share This Folder option, and click OK.

5 On the Windows Explorer menu bar, click Tools, and click Disconnect Network Drive. If you are prompted to disconnect, click the Disconnect Now button. Click the drive for the folder you mapped in the last exercise, and click OK.

If you are continuing to other lessons:

● Close all open windows. The desktop should be displayed.

If you are not continuing to other lessons:

1 Close all open windows, and click the Start button on the taskbar.

2 Click Shut Down on the Start menu. If necessary, click the arrow in the Windows Shut Down dialog box, and click Shut Down in the list. Then click OK.

3 After Windows has shut down, turn off the computer and, if necessary, all other hardware devices.

Glossary

direct network *See* peer-to-peer network.

File Transfer Protocol (FTP) A collection of networking rules that computers follow when sending and receiving files to and from servers on the Internet.

local area network (LAN) A network in which computers in a building or several buildings in nearby proximity (such as a university campus or an office complex) are connected via cables or phone lines.

mapping drives Providing shortcuts to network folders by assigning drive letters to folders, which can then be accessed by clicking the drive letters in My Computer or Windows Explorer.

My Documents The default folder on your hard disk for storing documents you create.

network interface card (NIC) A circuit board that can be connected to one of the internal slots on the main circuit board of your computer. The NIC controls the communication of all data received from other computers and sent by your computer to other computers on the network.

parallel port A connector to the main circuit board of a computer that allows two-way communication simultaneously.

password A string of letters and/or numbers that you enter when logging on to gain access to resources. Requiring a password prevents unauthorized individuals from accessing information on your computer or on a network.

Glossary

peer-to-peer network A connection between computers that's also known as a direct network because no server is used to control access to files or to the networked computers. Instead, the computers are cabled directly to each other.

port A connector, usually containing a series of pins or a series of openings where pins from a cable can be connected. A port connects a cable to the main circuit board of your computer.

serial port A connector to the main circuit board of a computer that allows two-way communication, but data can travel in only one direction at a time.

wide area network (WAN) A collection of local area networks that are connected. A WAN can span hundreds or thousands of miles.

Quick Reference

To open a folder on the network

1   On the desktop, double-click the My Network Places icon.

2   Double-click the Computers Near Me icon.

3   Double-click the desired computer name.

4   Navigate to the desired folder.

To directly connect two computers

1   Shut down both computers. Connect the DirectParallel or serial cable to both computers, and start the two computers.

2   In the My Network Places window on one of the computers, click the Network And Dial-Up Connections link, and double-click Make New Connection.

3   Click the Next button, click Connect Directly To Another Computer, and then click the Next button again.

4   Verify that the Host option is selected, and click the Next button.

5   Follow the remaining steps in the Network Connection Wizard, clicking the Next button to move through the steps. Click the Finish button to complete the connection on the host computer.

6   Run the Network Connection Wizard on the guest computer. When you reach the Host Or Guest step, click the Guest option.

Quick Reference

To directly connect two computers (*continued*)

7   Click the Finish button to complete the connection on the guest computer.

8   If prompted, enter your Windows password, and click the Connect button to establish the connection.

To change your Windows password

1   Hold down Ctrl and Alt, and tap Delete.

2   Click the Change Password button.

3   In the Old Password box, type your current password, and press Tab.

4   In the New Password box, type your new password, and press Tab. In the Confirm New Password box, retype your new password, and click OK.

5   In the Windows Security dialog box, click the Cancel button.

To set up a user

1   Click the Start button, point to Settings, and then click Control Panel.

2   In Control Panel, double-click Users And Passwords.

3   Click the Add button.

4   In the User Name box, type a name for the new user, and then click the Next button.

5   In the Password box, type a password for the new user. Press Tab, type the password again, and then click the Next button.

6   Set the access rights for the new user, and click the Finish button.

7   Close the Users And Passwords dialog box, and close Control Panel.

To share a folder

1   On the desktop, double-click the My Computer icon.

        In My Computer window, double-click the disk that contains the folder to be shared.

3   Navigate to the desired folder, and right-click it.

4   On the shortcut menu, click Sharing, and then click the Share This Folder option.

5   Click the Permissions button, set the desired permissions, and then click OK.

6   Close the My Computer window.

Quick Reference

To map a network drive

1   On the desktop, double-click the My Computer icon.

2   On the menu bar, click Tools, and click Map Network Drive.

3   Click the Browse button.

4   Navigate to the desired folder.

5   Click the folder, and click OK.

6   Click the Finish button, and close the My Computer window.

Accessing and Browsing the Internet

ESTIMATED TIME
30 min.

After completing this lesson, you will be able to:

✔ *Connect to the Internet.*

✔ *Display Web pages using links.*

✔ *Display Web pages using the Address bar.*

✔ *Find information on the Web.*

✔ *Revisit Web pages using the Favorites and History lists.*

✔ *Read newsgroup messages.*

In the previous lesson, you learned that a network is a group of computers that are connected so that they can share information. The **Internet** is a network made up of many thousands of computers all over the world, connected by the same kinds of cables used by telephone and cable TV companies. The Internet was actually begun as a project by the U.S. Department of Defense in coordination with universities located throughout the world. The goal of the ARPANET project was to link large computers throughout the world so that the networked computers were independent. For instance, if one of these large computers were to be destroyed, the other computers could still exchange information. Breaking one link in the network would not sever the links between other computers on the network.

Eventually, the Department of Defense abandoned ARPANET as a formal project. However, the network structure that was created remained in place. In fact, this network structure was so effective that universities and other organizations around the world continued to link to it. This elaborate network soon became known as the Internet. So the Internet is a technology, not a physical place or an organization. The Internet is not "owned" by any one government, company, or individual. It continues to exist and evolve because it is in the mutual interest of computer users worldwide.

The **World Wide Web** (or simply the **Web**) is essentially a multimeda interface to the Internet. In the early days of the Internet, information was exchanged in text format only. Advances in hardware and software technologies allowed the Internet to offer graphics, sound, and other multimedia capabilities. Sites on the Internet that are capable of providing content in this multimedia format are called **Web sites**. Collectively, all Web sites are called the World Wide Web. So you can think of the Web as a multimedia extension of the Internet.

Today, most people access the information on the Internet via the Web. As part of the Internet, the Web isn't a physical place; it's the collection of millions of Web pages stored on Internet servers around the world. You access these Web sites using a Web **browser** such as Microsoft Internet Explorer. A browser can display text and graphics on the same page. With a Web browser, you can also watch videos and listen to sound files. Two popular uses of the Internet are to find information and to exchange messages with other people using e-mail and newsgroups.

In this lesson, you will learn how to set up an Internet connection. Then you will access the Web using Internet Explorer. Finally, you will learn about **newsgroups** using Microsoft Outlook Express. A newsgroup is a forum on the Internet where people who share an interest can exchange ideas and information. Newsgroups exist for just about every possible topic—from automobiles to zebrafish.

Connecting to the Internet

The Internet community can be divided into three basic parts: end users (such as yourself), **Internet service providers** (**ISPs**), and the **Internet backbone**. As an end user, you connect to the Internet backbone through a **modem** or an organization's network. Most networks connect computers that are in close proximity, such as those in a building or a campus of buildings. These networks are called **local area networks** (**LANs**). A **modem** converts computer signals (which are pulses of electrical current) into audio waves that can travel through phone lines.

The audio waves travel through your phone line or another cable directly to your ISP's computer. This computer is called a **server** because it serves the requests of many users at a time. Your ISP typically leases fiber optic cables from a long-distance carrier. These connections form the Internet backbone. So after you've connected to your ISP's server, you have fast access to all other Internet-connected computers around the world. An ISP can be a commercial service to which you sub-scribe, just like cable television, or it can be an organization that provides Internet access free to its employees or members over a local area network.

Some ISPs send their new subscribers software that sets up the Internet connec-tion automatically. Setting up the connection yourself, however, is fairly easy to do using the Internet Connection Wizard, as you'll learn in the following exer-cise. Your ISP can provide you with all the information you'll need:

- The local telephone number of your ISP.
- The user name and password that uniquely identify you to the ISP.
- Your Internet e-mail address, if you want to send and receive e-mail messages or join newsgroups.
- The types and names of the servers that handle your incoming and out-going e-mail messages. (Even if your ISP's installation software supplies this information automatically to Windows, you should always ask your ISP for the addresses of these servers. You don't necessarily need to know what the addresses do, but you might have to type them into your browser or e-mail program at a later time.)
- The name of your ISP's **news server**. The news server is the computer that connects you to any of the thousands of newsgroups available on the Internet.

important

After you have completed all of the steps in the Internet Connection Wizard, the Connect To The Internet icon will disappear from the desktop. If the icon is miss-ing, you probably already have a connection. Try double-clicking the Internet Explorer icon on the desktop. If a message such as "The page cannot be displayed" appears, you are not connected. If you are not connected and the Connect To The Internet icon is missing, start the Internet Connection Wizard by clicking the Start button. Point to Programs, Accessories, and Communications, and then click Internet Connection Wizard.

In this exercise, you use the Internet Connection Wizard to manually set up a dial-up connection to the Internet. You need the information listed on the previous page to complete the exercise, and you need to connect your computer's modem to a telephone line.

important

This exercise demonstrates how to set up a dial-up connection. If you want to set up a network connection instead, in step 3, click the I Connect Through A Local Area Network (LAN) option, click the Next button twice, and skip to step 9.

1   On the desktop, double-click the Connect To The Internet icon.

The Internet Connection Wizard appears.

If you have not already chosen an ISP, you can accept the default option on the welcome screen. The Internet Connection Wizard will search for an ISP for you.

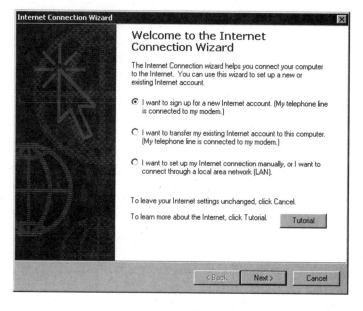

If you have information about logon scripts, IP addresses, or DNS servers, click the Advanced button, and enter the information on the appropriate tabs before continuing to step 5.

2   Click the I Want To Set Up My Internet Connection Manually, Or I Want To Connect Through A Local Area Network (LAN) option, and click the Next button.

3   Verify that the I Connect Through A Phone Line And A Modem option is selected, and click the Next button.

4   Type the appropriate number in the Telephone Number box, and click the Next button.

You are prompted to type your Internet account logon information.

5 Type your user name in the User Name box, and press Tab.

The insertion point moves to the Password box.

6 Type your password.

For security reasons, the password appears as a series of asterisks.

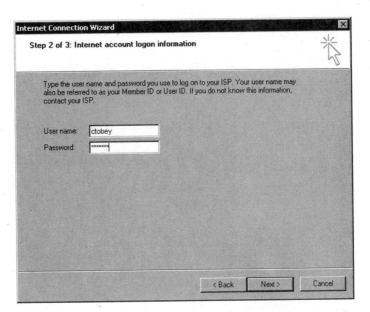

7 Click the Next button.

Because you might have more than one Internet connection, you are prompted to name this one.

8 In the Connection Name box, type **SBS Connection**, and click the Next button.

You will need an e-mail address to complete the newsgroup exercise later in this lesson, so you will set up an Internet e-mail account now.

9 Verify that the Yes option is selected, and click the Next button.

10 If you already have an Internet e-mail account, click the Use An Existing Internet Mail Account option, click the Next button twice, and skip to step 15. Otherwise, verify that the Create A New Internet Mail Account option is selected, and click the Next button.

11 Type your name in the Display Name box, and click the Next button.

This name will appear on all of the messages you send via the Internet.

12 Type your e-mail address in the E-Mail Address box, and click the Next button.

For the next two steps, refer to the information you received from your ISP.

Most incoming mail servers are POP3. If your ISP uses IMAP or HTTP, click the correct choice on the Server list before pressing the Next button.

13   In the Incoming Mail (POP3, IMAP, Or HTTP) Server box, type the name of the ISP computer that will transfer e-mail messages to you. Press Tab, and in the Outgoing Mail (SMTP) Server box, type the name of the ISP computer that will transfer e-mail messages from you. Click the Next button.

Sometimes, the user name and password required to collect your e-mail messages are different from the user name and password required to connect to the Internet, so the next step asks for your Internet e-mail logon information.

14   If necessary, type your user name for e-mail in the Account Name box, and press Tab. In the Password box, type your password for e-mail. Click the Next button.

The final screen of the Internet Connection Wizard appears.

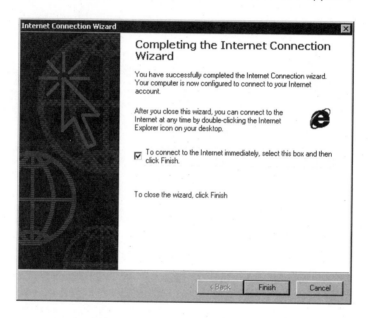

15   Click the Finish button.

Your default browser starts in order to test the connection, and the Dial-Up Connection dialog box appears.

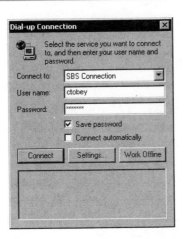

16   If necessary, in the Dial-Up Connection dialog box, click the Connect button.

When you are connected, the dialog box closes. A Connection To dialog box appears briefly in the bottom-right corner of the screen, and text and pictures appear in the Internet Explorer window.

Close

17   Click the Close button in the top-right corner of the Internet Explorer window.

You will learn more about Internet Explorer in the next few exercises in this lesson. For now, it's enough to know that the connection to the Internet works. The Auto Disconnect dialog box appears.

18   If necessary, click the Disconnect Now button.

You are disconnected from the Internet.

Navigating the Web

A Web site is a collection of related files called **Web pages,** and it is operated by a particular person or organization. Each page is represented by a **hyperlink** within other pages. When you navigate on the Web, you can click hyperlinks (or simply **links**) that display different pages on the same Web site, or you can click hyperlinks that take you to sites in other parts of the world. A hyperlink can be a word, a phrase, or even a picture. The important point is that clicking hyperlinks takes you to different pages, or places, on the Web.

When you connect to the Internet using Internet Explorer, the first page the browser displays is your **home page**. This page is the starting point for your Web travels. The default home page in Internet Explorer is MSN, the Microsoft Network, although you might have a different home page, such as one for the company where you work. If you installed software provided to you by your ISP, your ISP's Web site might be your home page.

> ### tip
>
> The phrase *home page* actually has two meanings. The meanings are similar but different enough to be confusing. The page that displays each time you start your Web browser is the home page for *your* computer. You can think of this as your "personal" home page. The main page on every Web site is also called a home page. You can think of this as the home page for that person or organization.

From your home page, you move to another page either by clicking a link to it or by typing its address. A **Web address** (also called a **URL**, which is an acronym for Uniform Resource Locator) provides a way to locate a particular Web page, just like a street address provides a way to locate a particular house. If you know a Web page's address, you can display the page by typing its address in the Address bar, which is located below the Standard Buttons toolbar in the Internet Explorer window.

Only a few links in this example are pointed out.

Standard Buttons toolbar

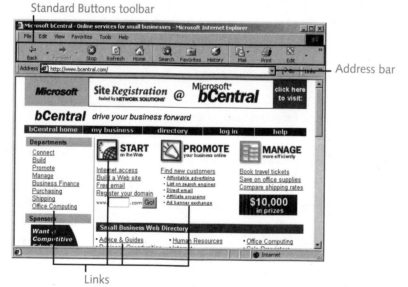

Address bar

Links

The page that you display probably has links of its own. You can click one of these links or type another Web address in the Address bar to display yet another page, which probably has its own links as well. Displaying Web page after Web page is called surfing the Web.

As you surf, you can go back and forth between the pages you've visited by clicking the Back and Forward buttons on the Standard Buttons toolbar—like flipping through pages in a book. If you start to feel lost, you can display your home page by clicking the Home button on the Standard Buttons toolbar.

In this exercise, you visit the Lakewood Mountains Resort Web site by typing its Web address in the Address bar. Then you display different Web pages by clicking links and the buttons on the Standard Buttons toolbar.

You can also start Internet Explorer by clicking its button on the Quick Launch bar.

1   On the desktop, double-click the Internet Explorer icon.

The Internet Explorer window appears. The Dial-Up Connection dialog box also appears if you're accessing the Internet through a dial-up connection.

2   If necessary, connect to the Internet using the Dial-Up Connection dialog box.

When you are connected, the dialog box closes, a Connection To message appears briefly in the bottom-right corner of the screen (as shown below), and your home page appears in Internet Explorer.

3   Click in the Address bar.

4   Select the address in the Address bar, if necessary.

5   Type **mspress.microsoft.com/mspress/products/1349/default1.htm**, and press Enter.

The Lakewood Mountains Resort home page appears. The left frame displays links to other pages in the site, and the right frame displays general information about the resort.

Browsing the Internet

5

The Go button is new in Internet Explorer 5.

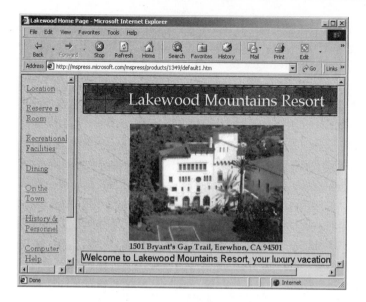

6 In the left frame, click the Location link.

The left frame remains the same, but information about the resort's location appears in the right frame.

7 In the left frame, click the Dining link.

Information about the resort's restaurant appears in the right frame.

Home

You can click the Back button repeatedly to retrace your path through the Web pages you've visited during your current session on the Web.

8 On the Standard Buttons toolbar, click the Home button.

Your home page reappears.

9 On the Standard Buttons toolbar, click the Back button.

You return to the page you visited most recently, the one that displayed information about the restaurant at Lakewood Mountains Resort.

10 On the Standard Buttons toolbar, click the Forward button.

Your home page reappears. Note that you can't use the Forward button now. That's because you haven't navigated to any new pages after returning to your home page.

Keep this Web page open for the next exercise.

Refresh

Browsing the Internet 5

tip

To update a Web page that you've been looking at for a while, click the Refresh button on the Standard Buttons toolbar. Clicking the Refresh button causes Internet Explorer to reload the information for the current Web page. This can be particularly helpful for stock quotes, news headlines, and other information that changes frequently. The Refresh button is also useful for correcting a page that is displayed only partially or incorrectly (usually due to network congestion).

Finding What You Need on the Web

You might enjoy surfing the Web for its own sake, but you might, at some point, want to find specific information on the Web as quickly as possible. One method for finding information on the Web is to use a **search engine**. Search engines are programs that look for information on the Web that relates to words that you specify. Although some search engines charge a fee to perform a search, most search engines are free. Many of the free engines are comparable in quality; however, each engine has a slightly different user interface and provides different features. When you perform a search using Internet Explorer, it uses several search engines at once.

In this exercise, you search for a Web page that provides information about the weather at Lakewood Mountains Resort, which is near Santa Barbara, California.

1   In the Internet Explorer window, click the Search button on the Standard Buttons toolbar.

A Search pane appears in the left side of the Internet Explorer window.

If you want to find all words in your search text in the same order you typed them, enclose the text in quotation marks. The search engine ignores any occurrences that don't exactly match what you typed.

2   In the Find A Web Page Containing box, type **Santa Barbara weather**, and click the Search button in the Search pane.

Links to Web sites that contain information about the weather in Santa Barbara appear in the Search pane.

Internet Explorer changes the order in which search engines are used each time you perform a search. Therefore, you might get different results if you perform the same search at different times.

3   Click the first link in the list.

    The Web page appears in the right pane of the window.

4   Click the Close button in the top-right corner of the Search pane.

    Keep Internet Explorer open for the next exercise.

Close

You can also close the Search pane by again clicking the Search button on the Standard Buttons toolbar.

Keeping Track of Web Sites

You will probably find that you want to frequently revisit certain Web pages. Instead of typing a Web address or clicking a series of links each time you want to view a particular Web page, you can use Internet Explorer's Favorites or History lists to go directly to the page.

The **Favorites list** is like the set of speed dial buttons on a telephone. After you add a Web address to the list, you can return to the page it represents using a single click. The **History list** is like the redial button on a telephone, except instead of displaying only the last page you've visited, it displays a list of all of the pages you've visited recently.

In this exercise, you use the Internet Explorer History list to revisit a Web page. Then you add the page to your Favorites list.

1   On the Standard Buttons toolbar in the Internet Explorer window, click the History button.

    The History pane appears in the left side of the Internet Explorer window.

2   In the History pane, below the Today icon, click the folder named
     Mspress.Microsoft.

     The Lakewood Mountains Resort Web pages you visited are listed.

tip

To sort the History list in ways other than chronological, click the View
button in the History pane, and click the type of sort you want (such as By
Most Visited).

3   Click Lakewood Home Page.

     The Lakewood Mountains Resort home page appears in the right pane of
     the window.

4   On the Standard Buttons toolbar, click the Favorites button.

     The Favorites pane replaces the History pane in the left side of the Internet
     Explorer window.

*You can
also add a page
to the Favorites
list by clicking
Add To
Favorites on the
Favorites menu.*

5   In the Favorites pane, click the Add button.

     The Add Favorite dialog box appears.

6   Click OK.

     The Add Favorite dialog box disappears, and the Lakewood home page
     is added to the Favorites list.

Close

Home

7   Click the Close button in the top-right corner of the Favorites pane.

Closing the Favorites pane makes more room for the Web page.

8   On the Standard Buttons toolbar, click the Home button.

Your home page appears.

9   On the Favorites menu, click Lakewood Home Page.

The Lakewood Mountains Resort home page appears.

Keep Internet Explorer open for the next exercise.

> **tip**
>
> To remove a Web page from the Favorites list, click Organize on the Favorites menu. In the Organize Favorites dialog box, click the name of the page you want to delete, and click the Delete button. Click Yes to verify the deletion, and click the Close button to close the dialog box.

Subscribing to a Newsgroup

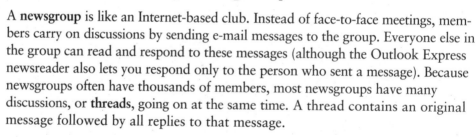

In the Multimedia folder on the Microsoft Windows Professional 2000 Step by Step CD-ROM, double-click the Newsgroup icon for a demonstration of how to subscribe to a newsgroup.

A **newsgroup** is like an Internet-based club. Instead of face-to-face meetings, members carry on discussions by sending e-mail messages to the group. Everyone else in the group can read and respond to these messages (although the Outlook Express newsreader also lets you respond only to the person who sent a message). Because newsgroups often have thousands of members, most newsgroups have many discussions, or **threads,** going on at the same time. A thread contains an original message followed by all replies to that message.

You join a newsgroup by **subscribing** to it. Subscribing identifies you to the newsgroup and tells the newsgroup's administrator that you want to view its messages (also called **posts**). After you have subscribed, you can read and respond to posts sent by other members of the group. If you have a question or topic that is not currently being discussed in the group, you can send a post to start a new thread.

Subscriptions to newsgroups are free.

Think of a newsgroup as a type of party. Everyone's in the same room, but various people are involved in different conversations. Each conversation comprises comments, replies, and opinions relating to a particular topic. These exchanges are like threads. In the Outlook Express newsreader, threads are denoted by plus and minus signs appearing next to the headers of the original messages. Clicking a plus sign expands the thread so that you can see all of the replies. When you expand a thread, message replies are indented below the original message. Clicking a minus sign collapses the thread.

Newsgroup   Expanded thread

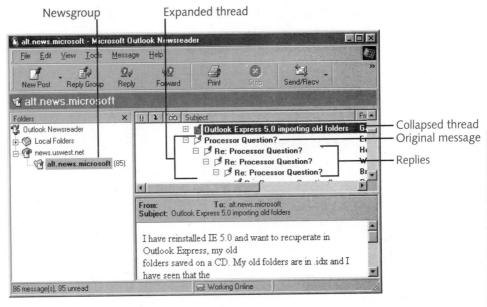

Collapsed thread
Original message
Replies

important

If you use the Internet at work, check your company's policy on newsgroups. Some companies prohibit employee access to newsgroups.

In this exercise, you subscribe to a newsgroup about all-inclusive vacation resorts. This exercise assumes that you have not set up a connection to a news server. You need to know the name of your news server to complete this exercise. Contact your ISP for this information, if necessary.

Mail

1   On the Standard Buttons toolbar, click the Mail button, and then click Read News.

If a connection to a news server is not set up, the Internet Connection Wizard appears. If a connection to a news server is set up, Outlook Express starts, and you can skip to step 7.

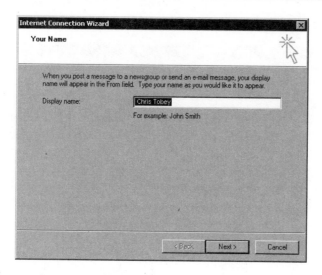

2   In the Internet Connection Wizard, click the Next button, verify that your e-mail address appears, and then click the Next button.

3   In the News (NNTP) Server box, type the name of your news server (for example, news.domain.net), and click the Next button.

4   Click the Finish button.

Outlook Express, which manages your access to e-mail and newsgroups, starts. (You will learn more about e-mail in Lesson 6, "Communicating With Others.")

5   If a dialog box appears with the message "A Dial-Up Networking Connection Is Already Established," click the Try To Locate The Server On The Current Connection option, and then click OK.

Unless you have already subscribed to a newsgroup, a dialog box appears, asking if you want to view a list of available newsgroups.

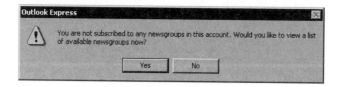

6   Click Yes to view available newsgroups.

After a short pause, the Newsgroup Subscriptions dialog box appears.

If necessary, in the All tab, double-click the line that divides the Newsgroup and Description column headings so that the Newsgroup column is expanded.

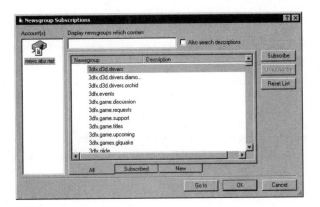

7 In the Display Newsgroups Which Contain box, type **resort**.

   On the All tab, a list of newsgroups with names that contain the word *resort* appears.

8 Double-click Rec.Travel.Resorts.All-Inclusive.

   An icon appears to the left of the newsgroup's name, indicating that you are now subscribed to the group.

Newsgroup Subscribed

9 Click the Go To button.

   The Newsgroup Subscriptions dialog box closes, and the most recent messages from the group appear in Outlook Express.

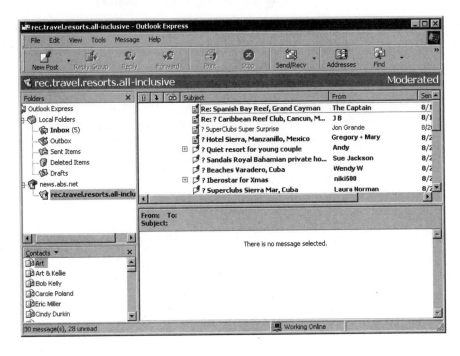

10   In the top-right pane, click the first message.

The message appears in the bottom-right pane in the Outlook Express window.

> ## tip
>
> To cancel your subscription to a newsgroup, right-click the newsgroup's name in the Folder List in the Outlook Express window. Then click Unsubscribe on the shortcut menu.

☒

Close

11   Click the Close button in the top-right corner of the Outlook Express window.

The Outlook Express window closes, and the Internet Explorer window reappears.

☒

Close

12   Click the Close button in the top-right corner of the Internet Explorer window.

The Internet Explorer window closes. If you have a dial-up connection, the Auto Disconnect dialog box appears.

13   If necessary, click the Disconnect Now button.

You are no longer connected to the Internet.

> ## tip
>
> If the Auto Disconnect dialog box doesn't appear when it should, or if you want to disconnect from the Internet without closing Internet Explorer, click the connection icon on the taskbar, to the left of the time. If you have more than one connection icon, click the one that displays a pop-up description with the name of the Internet connection (SBS Connection, in this lesson). In the dialog box that appears, click the Disconnect button.

Computer Viruses, Privacy, and the Internet

Computer **viruses** are programs that are designed to damage or destroy data and other programs on your hard disk. Viruses are transmitted most often when you install software that hasn't been thoroughly checked for viruses—typically software that has been downloaded from the Internet. Therefore, many organizations have implemented policies that require software to be tested by computer-support personnel before it is installed. Check with your supervisor or network administrator about your organization's policy.

The open nature of the Internet makes privacy a concern for some Internet users, especially those who send valuable information, like credit-card numbers, over the Internet. The following precautions can help minimize your risk of contracting a computer virus and having your Internet privacy invaded.

- Watch for security alerts from Internet Explorer, which are displayed when you attempt an action that might threaten the security of your information. Be sure you understand the alert (using the Windows 2000 help system if necessary) before you take any action.

- Follow your organization's security procedures, if any, for using the Internet.

- Install virus-checking software, and use and update it regularly. (For information on installing software, see Lesson 9, "Working with Software and Hardware.")

- Do not open files that are attached to newsgroup or e-mail messages.

- On the Internet Explorer menu bar, click Tools, and click Internet Options. Click the Security tab, and review the settings. Make any necessary changes, and click OK.

- Be selective about the information you send over the Internet. If you are prompted by a Web site to send valuable information, make sure the site is secure. The addresses of secure Web sites start with *https*, which stands for *hypertext transfer protocol secure server*. Also, a small lock appears on the Status bar in the Internet Explorer window when you visit a secure site.

Secure site

Browsing the Internet

5

Lesson Wrap-Up

In this lesson, you learned how to set up an Internet connection, surf the Web, set up a newsgroup account, and subscribe to a newsgroup. You also learned how to track Web sites you visit using the Favorites and History lists.

To return all Windows components to their previous settings:

1   On the desktop, double-click the Internet Explorer icon, and if necessary, connect to the Internet.

2   On the Internet Explorer menu bar, click Favorites, and click Organize Favorites. In the Organize Favorites dialog box, click Lakewood Home Page, and click the Delete button. Click Yes to verify the deletion, and close the Organize Favorites dialog box.

3   On the Standard Buttons toolbar, click the Mail button, and then click Read News. If necessary, click the Try To Locate The Server On The Current Connection option, and click OK. In the Folders pane in the Outlook Express window, right-click Rec.Travel.Resorts.All-Inclusive. Click Unsubscribe on the shortcut menu, and click OK.

4   Close Outlook Express and Internet Explorer. If you are prompted to disconnect, click the Disconnect Now button.

5   Click the Start button on the taskbar, click Settings, and then point to Network And Dial-Up Connections. On the Network And Dial-Up Connections submenu, right-click SBS Connection. On the shortcut menu, click Delete. Click Yes to verify the deletion.

If you are continuing to another lesson:

●   Close all open windows. The desktop should be displayed.

If you are not continuing to another lesson:

1   Close all open windows, and click the Start button on the taskbar.

2   Click Shut Down on the Start menu. If necessary, click the arrow in the Windows Shut Down dialog box, and click Shut Down in the list. Then click OK.

3   After Windows has shut down, turn off the computer and, if necessary, all other hardware devices.

Glossary

browser A program that displays HTML text, graphics, and multimedia stored on Web servers.

Favorites list A feature that stores addresses for Web sites you specify. You can return to any of these sites by clicking the name of the site in the list.

History list A feature that stores addresses for Web sites you have visited recently.

home page The first page your Web browser displays when you connect to the Internet; it's also the starting page at a Web site.

hyperlink A word, phrase, or picture that displays a Web page or site when clicked.

Internet A network made up of millions of computers worldwide. The computers are connected via phone lines or other cables, and they follow the same communication rules.

Internet backbone A collection of fiber optic cables that connect high-capacity servers around the world.

Internet service provider (ISP) A commercial service that provides Internet access for personal computer users.

link *See* hyperlink.

local area network (LAN) A system that connects computers that are typically in close proximity—such as in the same office building or a campus of buildings.

modem A device that converts computer signals (which are pulses of electrical current) into audio waves that can travel through phone lines. Modems also convert the waves back into digital signals recognized by the receiving computer.

newsgroup A forum on the Internet where people who share a similar interest can exchange ideas and information.

news server A computer that connects you to any of the thousands of newsgroups available on the Internet.

posts Messages sent to a newsgroup.

search engine A service that looks for information on the Web based on the text that you specify.

Glossary

server A computer that can process requests for files, programs, or Web pages from hundreds of computers simultaneously.

subscribing In a newsreader program, specifying which newsgroups you access frequently. Subscribing to a newsgroup provides an easy way to track and download new messages.

thread In a newsgroup, an original message, followed by all of the replies to that message. Visual connections (usually lines) show how messages between different senders and respondents relate.

URL (Uniform Resource Locator) *See* Web address.

virus A program that is designed to damage or destroy data and other programs on your hard disk.

Web address A sequence of characters that identify a particular Web page. A Web address can comprise several parts including a domain, a folder path, and a file name. Also called a URL.

Web pages The files that constitute a Web site.

Web site A collection of related files, called Web pages, capable of providing multimedia content. A Web site is operated by a particular person or organization.

World Wide Web (or simply the Web) A graphical, multimedia interface to the Internet. You access Web pages using a Web browser such as Microsoft Internet Explorer.

Quick Reference

To set up an Internet connection

1   On the desktop, double-click the Connect To The Internet icon.

2   Enter the necessary information in the Internet Connection Wizard, clicking the Next button to move from one step to the next.

3   Click the Finish button to start Internet Explorer.

4   If necessary, in the Dial-Up Connection dialog box, click the Connect button.

Quick Reference

To display a Web page in Internet Explorer

1   On the desktop, double-click the Internet Explorer icon.

2   If necessary, connect to the Internet.

3   In Internet Explorer, type an address in the Address bar or click a link on your home page.

4   Use the Back and Forward buttons to display recently visited Web pages.

5   Use the Home button to display your home page.

To find information on the Web

1   On the Standard Buttons toolbar in Internet Explorer, click the Search button.

2   In the Find A Web Page Containing box in the Search pane, type the word or words to search for, and then click the Search button.

3   In the Search pane, click the desired link.

To display a page using the History list

1   On the Standard Buttons toolbar in Internet Explorer, click the History button.

2   In the History pane, click the name of the Web page.

3   Click the Close button in the top-right corner of the History pane.

To add a page to the Favorites list

1   On the Standard Buttons toolbar in Internet Explorer, click Favorites.

2   In the Favorites pane, click the Add button.

3   Click OK.

4   Click the Close button in the top-right corner of the Favorites pane.

Browsing the Internet

5

Quick Reference

To subscribe to a newsgroup

1   On the Internet Explorer Standard Buttons toolbar, click the Mail button.

2   On the Mail menu, click Read News.

3   If necessary, follow the steps in the Internet Connection Wizard, clicking the Next button to move through the steps. Then click the Finish button.

4   If necessary, click the Try To Locate The Server On The Current Connection option, and click OK.

5   Click Yes to view available newsgroups.

6   In the Display Newsgroups Which Contain box, type a word to search for.

7   Double-click the name of the desired newsgroup to subscribe to it.

8   Click the Go To button to access the newsgroup.

9   Click the Close button in the top-right corner of the Outlook Express window after you finish accessing the newsgroup.

LESSON

6

Communicating with Others

ESTIMATED TIME
40 min.

After completing this lesson, you will be able to:

✔ *Send and receive e-mail messages.*

✔ *Add contacts to the Address Book.*

✔ *Organize e-mail messages.*

✔ *Use the Send Fax Wizard.*

Electronic mail, or e-mail, is probably the most popular way to communicate and share information with others via computer. E-mail refers to the process of sending a message from a computer to one or more other computers via a telephone line or other cable. Microsoft Windows 2000 Professional provides extensive e-mail capabilities. Windows also includes tools to help you share and exchange information by fax or via the Internet.

In this lesson, you will learn how to send, receive, and organize e-mail messages in Microsoft Outlook Express. An **e-mail message** can contain text (such as a memo or a letter), a picture, or a combination of both. E-mail messages can even include recorded sound or video clips. To keep track of your collection of e-mail addresses, telephone numbers, and fax numbers, you will also learn how to use the Address Book in Outlook Express. In addition, you will learn how to send faxes.

Managing E-Mail Messages with Outlook Express

E-mail provides people with an alternative to mailing documents through a post office or an overnight courier service. E-mail is less expensive, it is easily accessible, and messages are received within minutes of being sent.

Folder List   Reply   Selected message

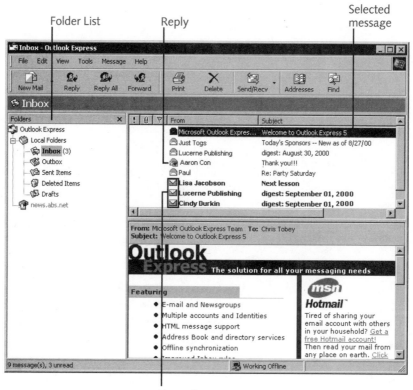

Unread messages

To send an e-mail message, you must know the recipient's **e-mail address**. An e-mail address is a unique identifier for a person on a network, just as a street address uniquely identifies a building's location in a particular city. If you send messages to others on your organization's network, the addresses follow the rules determined by your organization. When a person is hired, he or she is assigned an e-mail address. One typical approach is to use a person's first name and last initial as an e-mail address, such as *mariannek*.

If you send a message to someone outside of your organization, the message will be routed via the Internet to its destination. Therefore, the address will follow the rules set forth by InterNIC (the U. S. Department of Commerce organization that establishes Internet standards), such as *mariannek@JustTogs.com*. The *JustTogs.com* part of the address is called a **domain name,** which identifies the particular computer that *mariannek's* Internet service provider (ISP) uses to host her e-mail service.

For information on Internet service providers and connecting to the Internet, see Lesson 5, "Accessing and Browsing the Internet."

Consider a letter that you send to a friend. You drop the letter into the nearest mailbox, which is then sent to the nearest post office, which in turn sends the letter to the nearest delivery post office. From there, a postal carrier delivers the letter to the recipient. Similarly, an e-mail message must be routed from the sender's computer to his or her ISP's server, which in turns sends it to the recipient's ISP server (identified by *JustTogs.com*). The message resides on this server until the recipient (*mariannek*) checks her e-mail. She uses an e-mail program to connect her computer to her ISP's server so that she can retrieve her e-mail messages.

In this exercise, you use an e-mail program called Outlook Express to send and receive messages via the Internet. You will need to be connected to the Internet to complete this exercise.

When you start Outlook Express for the first time, there's a message from Outlook Express in the Inbox.

1   On the Quick Launch bar, click the Launch Outlook Express button.

The Outlook Express window opens.

important

If you haven't set up Outlook Express yet, the Internet Connection Wizard appears. Refer to steps 11-15 in the "Connecting to the Internet" exercise in Lesson 5, "Accessing and Browsing the Internet," to work through the wizard. Then click Finish.

2   If you receive a message that a "Dial-Up Networking connection is already established," click the Try To Locate The Server On The Current Connection option, and click OK.

3   If you receive a message that Outlook Express is not your default e-mail client, click No.

4   If the Inbox is not visible in the Folder List, click the plus sign to the left of Local Folders.

Local Folders expands to display folders for Inbox, Outbox, Sent Items, Deleted Items, and Drafts.

5 On the Outlook Express toolbar, click the New Mail button.

The New Message window appears.

If you want to send copies of a message to other recipients, type the additional e-mail addresses in the Cc box, separated by commas or semicolons.

6 In the To box, type **someone@microsoft.com**, and press Tab twice.

The e-mail address you typed in the To box is a valid address. It was created specifically for receiving messages from users completing exercises like this one.

7 In the Subject box, type **Test**, and press Tab.

The insertion point moves to the message box.

8 In the message box, type **This is a test of my e-mail system**.

The window should look similar to the following. The subject of the message appears in the window's title bar, so the window is now named *Test* instead of *New Message*.

Formatting Bar

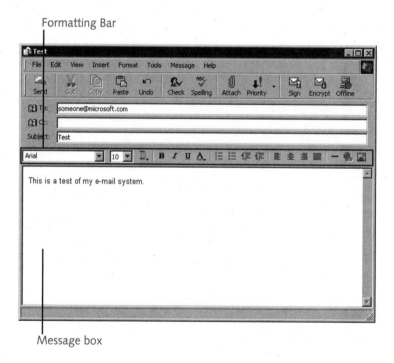

Message box

9 On the Standard Buttons toolbar, click the Send button.

The Test window closes, and the Outlook Express window reappears. In the Folder List, the number 1 appears in parentheses next to the Outbox. This number indicates the number of messages waiting to be sent.

tip

If you are not yet ready to send a message because you want to work on it later, you can save it in the Drafts folder. To do that, click Save on the File menu, and click OK in the Saved Message dialog box. To modify or send a message in your Drafts folder, click Drafts in the Folder List, and then double-click the desired message. In the message window, modify the message, if necessary, and click the Send button on the Standard Buttons toolbar.

10   In the Folder List in the Outlook Express window, click Sent Items.

A list of e-mail messages you've sent appears in the top-right pane.

11   On the Outlook Express toolbar, click the Send And Receive All button.

Clicking the Send And Receive All button causes Outlook Express to search for any new messages to or from you. You should get a response to the message you sent in step 9. When a message is received, you hear a chime if your computer has sound capabilities. The Inbox in the Folder List appears in bold, with the number of unread messages in parentheses next to it. If you don't see or hear these clues that you have incoming mail, wait one minute, and click the Send And Receive All button again.

12   In the Folder List, click Inbox.

A list of e-mail messages you've received appears in the top-right pane. You should see a response from Microsoft.

Keep Outlook Express open for the next exercise.

Communicating

Enhancing your messages

The Formatting Bar (located between the Subject box and the message box) contains buttons for changing the appearance of text in your message. You can change the font style, font size, and font color of the text you type. You can also change the way paragraphs are formatted and add pictures to your message.

Another way to enhance your message is to use stationery, which combines decorative backgrounds, borders, colors, and text to convey a theme. Before you create a message, you can choose stationery for it by clicking the arrow to the right of the New Mail button and clicking a stationery design, such as Clear Day. While you are creating your message, you can apply different stationery by clicking Apply Stationery on the Format menu.

Keep in mind, however, that your recipients might not see enhancements like text colors and stationery if they use e-mail programs other than Microsoft Outlook (an e-mail program that is sold with Microsoft Office and separately) or Outlook Express. Also, messages with enhancements take longer to send and receive than those that contain plain text.

Keeping Track of Contacts

The **Address Book** in Outlook Express functions like a Rolodex, storing important information about your contacts. If you store e-mail addresses in the Address Book, you can insert them from the Address Book when creating messages. You can also store information in the Address Book that can be used by other programs. For example, a fax number you type in the Address Book can be used in the Send Fax Wizard (discussed later in this lesson).

In this exercise, you add information about two of your contacts to the Outlook Express Address Book. Before beginning the exercise, make sure the Inbox in Outlook Express is displayed, with the header for the message from someone@microsoft.com (sent by Example E-Mail Account) clicked.

1   If the Contacts pane (which lists the people in the Address Book) is not open below the Folder List, click Layout on the View menu. Select the Contacts check box, and click OK.

    The Contacts pane appears.

2   In the top-right pane of the Outlook Express window, right-click Example E-Mail Account.

    The following shortcut menu appears.

You can also add a contact to the Address Book by dragging the contact's name from the From column to the Contacts pane.

3 On the shortcut menu, click Add Sender To Address Book.

The Contacts pane now includes Example E-Mail Account, which sent the response to your message to someone@microsoft.com. (You might need to scroll the Contacts pane to see the new address.)

4 On the Outlook Express toolbar, click the Addresses button.

The Address Book appears. It should look similar to the following, although you will have a different list of contacts.

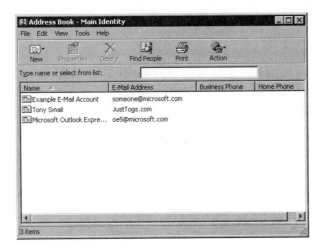

5   On the Address Book toolbar, click the New button, and then click New Contact on the menu.

The Properties dialog box for a new contact appears.

6   In the First box, type **Arlene**, and press Tab twice. In the Last box, type **Huff**.

By default, the first and last names of the contact are shown in the Display box as they would appear in your Contacts list. Also, the name of the dialog box has changed from *Properties* to *Arlene Huff Properties*.

7   Click in the E-Mail Addresses box, type **Arlene@JustTogs.com**, and then click the Add button.

The e-mail address for Arlene Huff appears in the Address box.

8   Click the Business tab.

The Business tab appears, and the insertion point is positioned in the Company box.

9   Type **Lakewood Mountains Resort**.

10   Click in the Phone box, and type **8005550412**. Press Tab, and in the Fax box, type **8005550413**. (You do not need to type hyphens or spaces to separate the numbers.) Click OK.

The contact information for Arlene Huff is added to the Address Book.

tip

When entering contact information, you should not need to type a 1 before long-distance numbers. Windows inserts your area code based on the information entered when your modem or network was set up, and it dials long-distance numbers based on its dialing rules. To view these rules, click the Start button, and click Control Panel on the Settings menu. Double-click the Phone And Modem Options icon. If your connections are set up, click the Edit button. If your phone or modem connections are not yet set up, follow the steps in the Location Information wizard that appears. When you've completed the wizard, double-click the Phone And Modem Options icon again, and click the Edit button. After viewing the dialing rules, click OK twice to close the Edit Location dialog box and the Phone And Modem Options dialog box. Then click the Close button in the top-right corner of Control Panel.

11   Click the Close button in the top-right corner of the Address Book.

The Address Book closes, and the Outlook Express window reappears with the Inbox displayed in the top-right pane.

Keep Outlook Express open for the next exercise.

Organizing Your Messages

In the Multimedia folder on the Microsoft Windows Professional 2000 Step by Step CD-ROM, double-click the Filters icon for a demonstration of how to create a message rule.

When you receive mail that is delivered by the post office, you probably sort through it. Some of it you throw away, and the rest you might organize into categories: bills, catalogs, and personal letters. You can arrange your e-mail messages in Outlook Express in the same way.

In fact, Outlook Express can organize your incoming mail for you, if you set up **message rules**, which let you tell Outlook Express what to do with certain types of messages. For example, the marketing director at Impact Public Relations frequently receives e-mail messages from the sales manager at Lakewood Mountains Resort. She has used the message rules feature to automatically move all incoming messages from the sales manager into a folder named *Clients* which can be seen in the Outlook Express Folder List.

You can organize the following types of messages in Outlook Express:

- From a sender or account you specify.
- With a subject line or message body that contains words you specify.
- To a recipient or recipients you specify.
- Marked with a priority level you specify.
- With a size bigger, smaller, or equal to one you specify.
- With an attachment.
- With security features.

For any of the types of messages above, you can select the following actions for your rule:

- Move or copy the message to a folder you specify.
- Delete the message.
- Forward the message to a recipient (or recipients) you specify.
- Reply to the message.
- Highlight the message with color or a flag.
- Mark the message as read, a watched conversation, or an ignored conversation.

Communicating

6

If you specify Watch Conversation on the Message menu, Outlook Express marks this message with an eyeglass icon, and the message headers for all responses to this message appear in red. The recipients of a watched message will also see the text *This message is being Watched* near the top of the message window. If you specify Ignore Conversation, Outlook Express hides all responses to the message.

In this exercise, you delete the reply from someone@microsoft.com. Then you create a message rule so that messages from someone@microsoft.com are automatically placed in a folder named *Test*. Finally, using the Address Book, you create another message to send to someone@microsoft.com so that you can observe how the message rule works.

You can also click the Delete button on the Outlook Express toolbar to delete a selected message.

1   In the top-right pane in the Outlook Express window, click the message header with *Example E-Mail Account* in the From column, if necessary, and press Delete.

The message no longer appears in the Inbox.

2   In the Folder List, click Deleted Items.

The message from Example E-Mail Account appears in the top-right pane.

3   On the Tools menu, point to Message Rules, and then click Mail.

The New Mail Rule dialog box appears.

4   In the Select Conditions For Your Rule list, select the Where The From Line Contains People check box.

The information in the Rule Description box changes to reflect the selection you made.

5   In the Select The Actions For Your Rule list, select the Move It To The Specified Folder check box.

The information in the Rule Description box changes again.

6   In the Rule Description box, click the link for Contains People.

The Select People dialog box appears.

Alternatively, in the Select People dialog box, click the Address Book button. Click the desired name, click the From button, and then click OK.

7   In the Type One Name At A Time And Click Add box, type **someone@microsoft.com**. Click the Add button, and then click OK.

8   In the Rule Description box, click the link for Specified.

The Move dialog box appears.

9   Click the New Folder button, type **Test**, and then click OK.

The Test folder is added to the Folder List.

10   Click OK to close the Move dialog box. In the New Mail Rule dialog box, select the text in the Name Of The Rule box, type **SBS Test**, and click OK. The New Mail Rule dialog box closes, and the Message Rules dialog box appears.

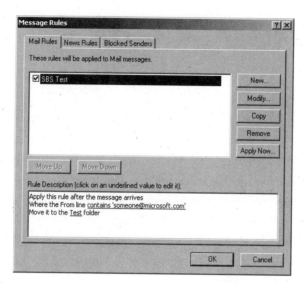

6

Communicating

tip

The Blocked Senders tab in the Message Rules dialog box provides a reliable way to automatically delete messages from particular people or organizations. To block a sender, click the Add button on the Blocked Senders tab, and type the sender's address. You can also block a sender by clicking a message from that sender and clicking Block Sender on the Messages menu. Blocking is helpful if you receive a lot of **junk e-mail** (unwanted or unsolicited mail) or if you subscribe to a newsgroup that has members whose messages you don't want to read.

11   Click OK.

The Message Rules dialog box closes, and the Outlook Express window reappears.

12   On the Outlook Express toolbar, click the New Mail button.

The New Message window appears.

13   Click the To button.

The Select Recipients dialog box appears, listing contacts in your Address Book.

> ## tip
> If you're connected to a network, note the box with Main Identity's Contacts listed. You are the *Main Identity*. You can create additional identities for other people who use your computer. You might also note that a Shared Contacts Address Book is also available so that you can create addresses that other users on your network can view.

14   Click Example E-Mail Account in the Name list, click the To button, and then click OK.

The Select Recipients dialog box closes, and the e-mail address you selected appears in the To box in the New Message window.

15   Press Tab twice, and type **Rules** in the Subject box. Press Tab, and type **This is a test of message rules**.

The message is created.

16   On the Rules toolbar, click the Send button. (If necessary, click the Send And Receive All button to deliver the message.)

The message is sent. Wait one or two minutes for Microsoft to respond.

17   On the Outlook Express toolbar, click the Send And Receive All button to receive the response.

In the Folder List, the Test folder appears in bold, with the number 1 in parentheses to the right of it.

18   In the Folder List, click Test.

The message from Example E-Mail Account was moved to the Test folder.

19   Click the Close button in the top-right corner of the Outlook Express window, and if necessary, disconnect from the Internet.

Close

The Outlook Express window closes.

Using the Send Fax Wizard

Faxing directly from Windows is easier and faster than using a regular fax machine because you don't have to leave your desk or supply paper. You don't even have to dial a number if you are faxing to someone who is already in your Address Book. However, Windows must detect that you have a modem in your computer and that your computer has fax capabilities. (See Lesson 5, "Accessing and Browsing the Internet," for more information about modems.)

In this exercise, you write a short note in WordPad. You then prepare to fax it to Arlene Huff, whose contact information you entered two exercises prior to this one. (Because the fax number for Arlene is fictitious, you won't actually send the fax.)

1   Click the Start button, point to Programs, and then point to Accessories.

   The Accessories submenu appears.

2   On the Accessories submenu, click WordPad.

   The WordPad window opens, and the insertion point is located at the beginning of the document.

3   Type **Please fax a copy of the contract to me as soon as possible. Thanks!**

tip

You can send a short note like this one on a cover page directly from the Send Fax Wizard, without creating a file in WordPad. To send just a cover page from the Send Fax Wizard, click the Start button, and open the Programs, Accessories, Communications, and Fax submenus. On the Fax submenu, click Send Cover Page Fax. Follow the steps in the Send Fax Wizard, clicking the Next button to move from one step to the next. Click the Finish button to send the fax.

4   On the File menu, click Print.

   The Print dialog box appears. If your computer has fax capabilities, a Fax icon appears in the Select Printer box on the General tab.

5   Click the Fax icon, and click the Print button.

   Instead of printing, Windows starts the Send Fax Wizard. If this is the first time you have used this wizard, you are prompted to edit or keep the user information.

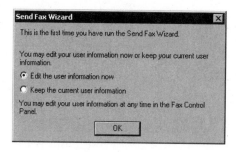

6 Click the Keep The Current User Information option, and click OK.

The dialog box closes, and the Send Fax Wizard appears.

7 Click the Next button.

The wizard prompts you for information about the fax recipient.

If you know someone who won't mind getting a test fax from you, use his or her name and fax number instead of Arlene Huff's.

8 Click the Address Book button.

The Address Book appears.

9 Verify that Main Identity's Contacts appears in the second box. If it doesn't, click the arrow. On the list, click Main Identity's Contacts.

10 Click Arlene Huff in the Name column, and click the To button.

Arlene Huff is added to the Message Recipients list.

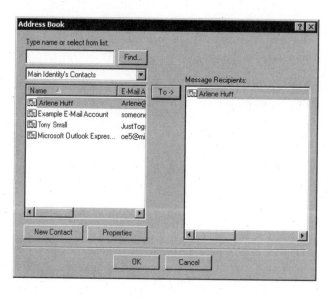

11 Click OK.

Arlene Huff's contact information appears in the Type Each Recipient's Information Above And Then Click Add box.

12 Click the Next button.

The next two steps of the Send Fax Wizard enable you to add a cover page and schedule a particular delivery time. You do not need to modify these settings for this exercise.

13 Click the Next button twice.

The final screen of the Send Fax Wizard summarizes the choices you have made.

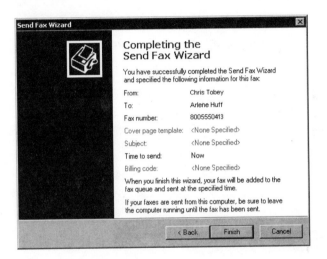

If you used a valid fax number, click the Finish button to display the Fax Monitor dialog box, which lets you control the faxing process.

14 Click the Cancel button.

The Send Fax Wizard closes.

15 Click the Close button in the top-right corner of the WordPad window, and click No when you are prompted to save changes.

The WordPad window closes.

Setting Up a NetMeeting

NetMeeting is a Windows program that takes **teleconferencing** to the next level, enabling you to attend online meetings with anyone in the world. In addition to communicating by voice and video, you can use NetMeeting to exchange files with other meeting participants, share programs, send secure messages, and even collaborate on diagrams and sketches. All participants must have NetMeeting installed on their computers. They also need a connection to the same local network or to the Internet and a way to call the other participants. You can call participants by finding their contact information in one of the directories that is available from NetMeeting when you are online or by typing their **IP addresses**. An IP address is a set of numbers (such as 192.168.0.1) that identifies a particular computer on the Internet or on a local area network.

To set up a NetMeeting, follow the steps below:

1   Contact all participants to arrange a time because everyone must be online and have NetMeeting running.

2   Make sure all participants know how to log on to the meeting, either by typing the IP addresses of other members or by finding their contact information in a directory. To find your IP address, click the Start button, point to Programs, and then click Accessories. On the Accessories menu, click Command Prompt. In the Command Prompt window, type **ipconfig**. You can find the IP address in the displayed information. It should be eight digits, separated by periods, such as 192.168.0.1.

3   At the appointed time, start NetMeeting. From the Start menu, point to Programs, Accessories, and then Communications. On the Communications menu, click NetMeeting. If this is the first time you have run the program, a wizard will guide you in setting it up.

4   For each participant, click NetMeeting's Call button. In the To box, type the participant's IP address or computer name.

5   Conduct the meeting. Use NetMeeting's tools to share programs, chat, draw on the whiteboard, or transfer files, as necessary.

6   When you are ready to leave the meeting, click the Disconnect button.

Lesson Wrap-Up

In this lesson, you were introduced to Outlook Express and the Send Fax Wizard. Using Outlook Express, you learned how to send and receive messages. You also learned how to add contact information to the Address Book, and you learned how to create message rules to store messages in a new folder. Using the Send Fax Wizard, you learned how to send a fax via your computer.

To return all Windows components to their previous settings:

1   On the Quick Launch bar, click the Launch Outlook Express button.

2   In the Contacts pane in the Outlook Express window, click Arlene Huff, press Delete, and then click Yes. Repeat the process for Example E-Mail Account. (If the Contacts pane is not visible, click the Address Book button, and delete the contacts from the Address Book.)

3   In the Folder List in the Outlook Express window, click Test, and then press Delete.

4   On the Outlook Express menu bar, click Tools, point to Message Rules, and then click Mail. Click the SBS Test rule, click the Remove button, and then click Yes. Close the Message Rules dialog box.

5   Close Outlook Express. If you are prompted to disconnect, click the Disconnect Now button.

If you are continuing to other lessons:

●   Close all open windows. The desktop should be displayed.

If you are not continuing to other lessons:

1   Close all open windows, and click the Start button on the taskbar.

2   Click Shut Down on the Start menu. If necessary, click the arrow in the Windows Shut Down dialog box, and click Shut Down in the list. Then click OK.

3   After Windows has shut down, turn off the computer and, if necessary, all other hardware devices.

Glossary

Address Book A window that functions like an electronic Rolodex, storing information about your contacts—such as names, postal addresses, phone numbers, and e-mail addresses.

domain name A portion of a Web address or e-mail address that uniquely identifies a server or a group of servers so that it can be located by other servers anywhere in the world.

e-mail address A unique identifier for a person on a network, just as a street address uniquely identifies a person's location in a particular city.

e-mail message Any message sent from an individual's computer to one or more other personal computers and transmitted as electronic impulses over a telephone line or other cable. An e-mail message can be text (such as a memo or letter), a picture, or a combination of both.

IP address A set of numbers (such as 192.168.0.1) that identifies a computer on the Internet or on a local area network.

junk e-mail Unsolicited and unwanted e-mail messages.

message rules Guidelines that tell Outlook Express what action to take when messages that are received meet the criteria you specify.

teleconference A meeting conducted via computers, in which audio, pictures, files, video, and other information can be sent and received immediately by multiple people.

Quick Reference

To send an e-mail message

1   On the Quick Launch bar, click the Launch Outlook Express button.

2   On the Outlook Express toolbar, click the New Mail button.

3   In the To box, type an e-mail address, or click the To button, and then select an address from the Address Book.

4   In the Subject box, type the word or phrase that best describes the content of the message.

5   In the message box, type the body of the message.

6   On the Standard Buttons toolbar, click the Send button and, if necessary, click the Send And Receive All button.

Quick Reference

To read an e-mail message

1   On the Outlook Express toolbar, click the Send And Receive All button, if necessary, to retrieve new messages.

2   In the Folder List, click Inbox.

3   In the Inbox, double-click the message header of the desired message.

To add a contact to the Address Book

1   In the Folder List in the Outlook Express window, click Inbox, if necessary.

2   In the top-right pane, right-click the desired sender's name.

3   On the shortcut menu, click Add Sender To Address Book.

To delete an e-mail message

1   In the Folder List in the Outlook Express window, click Inbox, if necessary.

2   Click the header of the message you want to delete, and press Delete.

To create a rule for automatically handling certain types of e-mail messages

1   On the Outlook Express menu bar, click Tools, point to Message Rules, and then click Mail to display the New Mail Rule dialog box.

2   In the Select The Conditions For Your Rule list, select the desired check box.

3   In the Select The Actions For Your Rule list, select the desired check box.

4   In the Rule Description box, click the links to describe the people, words, folders, or other criteria that define the rule.

5   After you finish describing all the criteria in the Rule Description box and you click OK, select the text in the Name Of The Rule box. Type a new name for the rule, and click OK.

To fax a document

1   Create or open the document you want to fax.

2   On the menu bar of the program with which the document was created, click File.

3   On the File menu, click Print.

4   In the Print dialog box, click the Fax icon, and then click the Print button.

5   Follow the steps in the Send Fax Wizard, clicking the Next button to move through the steps.

6   Click the Finish button to send the fax.

Communicating

6

2

Review & Practice

You will review and practice how to:

**ESTIMATED
TIME
20 min.**

✔ *Add a user to the system.*
✔ *Change the new user's password.*
✔ *Share folders with others on a network.*
✔ *Map a network drive.*
✔ *Use the Internet to view Web sites and send e-mail.*
✔ *Send a fax from Windows.*

Review & Practice

Before you move on to Unit 3, you can practice the skills you learned in Unit 2 by working through this Review & Practice. In this section, you will add a user to your computer and change the user's password. Then you will change sharing options for a folder and map a folder. Next you will use Internet Explorer to view Web sites, and you'll use Outlook Express to send e-mail messages. Finally, you will practice using the Send Fax Wizard. You will need a connection to the Internet, an e-mail account, and fax capabilities on your computer to complete all the steps in this review.

Scenario

A new copywriter, Mark Lee, needs to be added to the Impact Public Relations computer network. The company policy is to change passwords when a user logs on for the first time and every 90 days after that. The copywriter needs to be able to share information with others and to complete market research on the Web.

Step 1:   Add a User and Change His Password

Add Mark Lee to the system. Immediately after adding him to the system, change his password.

1   Open Control Panel, and open the Users And Passwords dialog box.

2   Add Mark Lee to the system with the user name **mlee**. Type his name in the Full Name box, but skip the Description box. His initial password is **wake1fit**.

3   Assign him Standard User access.

4   Log off, and log back on as **mlee**.

5   Change Mark Lee's password to **tall.city**.

6   Log off as Mark Lee, and log back on as yourself.

For more information about	See
Setting up a user	Lesson 4
Changing passwords	Lesson 4

Step 2:   Share and Map a Folder

Create a folder on your primary hard disk. This folder will store files created by Mark Lee and other employees at Impact Public Relations. Share the folder with everyone on the network, and then map the folder to a drive letter.

1   Using Windows Explorer, create a subfolder named **IPR Copy** on your hard disk.

2   Allow everyone on the network full access to this folder.

3   Map the IPR Copy folder to an available drive letter.

4   Close all open windows.

5   Open My Computer, note the icon for the mapped drive, and then close My Computer.

For more information about	See
Creating folders	Lesson 3
Sharing folders	Lesson 4
Mapping a network drive	Lesson 4

Step 3:   Browse the Web

Give Mark a quick tour of some sites on the Web. Visit the Lakewood Mountains Resort Web site and the United Nations Web site.

1   Start Internet Explorer, and open an Internet connection, if necessary.

2   Go to Lakewood Mountains Resort's home page, using the address **mspress.microsoft.com/mspress/products/1349/default1.htm**.

3   Use the links to display pages on the Lakewood Mountains Resort Web site.

4   Using the Search Assistant, search for the UN's Web site.

5   Close Internet Explorer, but leave the connection to the Internet open for the next step.

For more information about	See
Connecting to the Internet	Lesson 5
Navigating the Web	Lesson 5
Using the Search Assistant in Internet Explorer	Lesson 5

Step 4:   Send an E-Mail Message

To show Mark how to create an e-mail message, send a test message over the Internet.

1   In Outlook Express, send an e-mail to **someone@microsoft.com**, typing any subject and message you want.

2   After a couple of minutes, look for a response.

3   Delete the response.

4   Close Outlook Express, and disconnect from the Internet, if necessary.

For more information about	See
Using Outlook Express	Lesson 6
Sending and receiving e-mail messages	Lesson 6
Disconnecting from the Internet	Lesson 5

Step 5:   **Send a Fax**

Show Mark how to use the Send Fax Wizard.

1   Start WordPad.

2   Open a new blank document, and type **Hello. This is a test**.

3   Start the Send Fax Wizard.

4   If you have a contact in the Address Book who won't mind getting a test fax, use that person's information to send a fax. Otherwise, enter a dummy name and telephone number.

5   Do not include a cover page, and schedule the fax to be sent now.

6   Exit WordPad without saving the sample document.

For more information about	See
Using the Send Fax Wizard	Lesson 6
Keeping track of contacts	Lesson 6

Finish the Review & Practice

1   Remove the *mlee* user account.

2   Disconnect the mapped drive for the IPR Copy folder.

3   Delete the shared IPR Copy folder from your hard disk.

UNIT 3

Getting The Most From Windows 2000 Professional

7

Customizing Your Desktop

ESTIMATED TIME
50 min.

After completing this lesson, you will be able to:

✔ *Create shortcut icons on the desktop.*

✔ *Arrange icons on the desktop.*

✔ *Change the desktop's background and colors.*

✔ *Use screen savers.*

✔ *Add Active Desktop items.*

✔ *Change the way the mouse works.*

✔ *Change the appearance of the Start menu.*

✔ *Customize the taskbar.*

When a new employee starts work at Impact Public Relations, he or she is assigned a desk that has a computer, a telephone, and some basic office supplies. One of the first things the new employee invariably does is start personalizing this workspace—moving the phone to a more accessible location, displaying family photographs, and organizing the office supplies. Similarly, the Windows desktop can be customized in many ways to suit your unique needs and preferences.

In this lesson, you will make the Windows environment more comfortable and attractive by changing the appearance and functionality of the desktop, the taskbar, the Start menu, and the mouse.

Sample files for the lesson To complete the Adding Shortcut Icons to the Desktop exercise in this lesson, you will need to access the IPR Clients file located in the Windows 2000 Practice folder.

Creating Shortcut Icons on the Desktop

As you continue to work with Windows, you'll find yourself repeatedly using certain programs, folders, devices, or files. Accessing these items can become time-consuming if you constantly have to navigate through multiple menus or folders. The Personalized Menus option (discussed later in this lesson) addresses this problem to a certain extent by hiding menu items you rarely use, but the fastest and easiest way to access a program, folder, file, or device is to create a shortcut icon for it on the desktop.

For additional information on how to find, open, or save a file, see Lesson 3, "Managing Files and Folders."

When you install programs, files for the programs can be stored in any number of folders on your hard disk. You usually don't need to know where the programs are stored because the name of each program is added to your Start menu when the program is installed. The name of a program that appears on the Start menu is a kind of shortcut. That is, the program name that's stored in the Start menu also contains hidden information that includes the location of the file that actually starts the program.

Other kinds of shortcuts appear as icons. They work just like the program names that appear on the Start menu, except the hidden information that is used to start the program is represented by an icon that can be placed in any folder on your hard disk—or even on your desktop. In fact, when Windows is installed, it adds several of these shortcut icons to your desktop so that you can start widely-used programs by double-clicking the shortcut icon. You can also add shortcut icons to the desktop yourself.

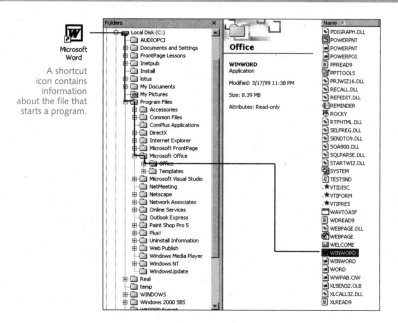

Microsoft
Word

A shortcut
icon contains
information
about the file that
starts a program.

Shortcut icons can also be used to help new Windows users feel less intimidated. For example, the marketing director at Impact Public Relations has hired a new graphic artist. The artist isn't very familiar with Windows, but he needs to begin working on his deadline-driven projects immediately. To help him, the marketing director has created desktop shortcuts to the files, programs, and hardware devices that the artist will use the most. Because the tools the artist needs are easily accessible on the desktop, he can become productive immediately.

2000 New!

Customize
This Folder
Command

tip

To add a shortcut icon to the desktop, hold down the right mouse button, and drag the item from the folder or menu where it is stored onto the desktop. Dragging by using the right mouse button copies an item, whereas dragging by using the left mouse button moves an item.

In this exercise, you create a shortcut icon on the desktop for Character Map (a program for inserting special characters—such as accented letters—into documents). Then you create a shortcut icon to **Windows Explorer** (a window that you can use to navigate through folders and copy, move, delete, and open files) and another to the IPR Clients document.

1   Click the Start button, point to Programs, and then point to Accessories.

The Accessories submenu appears.

You can distinguish a shortcut icon that has been added to the desktop from other desktop components by the small, curved arrow in the bottom-left corner of the icon.

2   On the Accessories submenu, point to System Tools.

The System Tools submenu appears.

3   Point to Character Map, hold down the right mouse button, and drag Character Map from the System Tools submenu onto the desktop, away from the existing desktop icons, and then release the right mouse button.

The following shortcut menu appears, and all other menus close.

4   On the shortcut menu, click Create Shortcut(s) Here.

A shortcut icon to Character Map appears on the desktop.

Character Map

5   Repeat step 1, and on the Accessories submenu, point to Windows Explorer.

6   Hold down the right mouse button, and drag Windows Explorer from the Accessories submenu onto the desktop, near the Character Map shortcut icon.

7   Release the right mouse button, and on the shortcut menu, click Create Shortcut(s) Here.

A shortcut icon to Windows Explorer appears on the desktop.

Windows Explorer

Restore Down

8   Double-click the Windows Explorer shortcut icon.

The Windows Explorer window appears.

9   If necessary, click the Restore Down button so that some of the desktop is visible behind the Windows Explorer window.

10   In the Folders Pane, click Local Disk. (If you have renamed the disk, or if you have more than one hard disk, click the disk with (C:) at the end of the name.)

The contents of the Local Disk appear in the right pane.

Don't worry that the icons are not lined up with everything else on the desktop. You will fix that in the next exercise.

11   Double-click the Windows 2000 Practice folder.

The contents of the folder are displayed in the right pane of the window.

12   Point to the IPR Clients file. Hold down the right mouse button, and drag IPR Clients from the Windows 2000 Practice folder onto the desktop, near the Windows Explorer icon.

13   Release the right mouse button, and on the shortcut menu, click Create Shortcut(s) Here.

A shortcut icon to the IPR Clients file appears on the desktop.

Minimize

14   Click the Minimize button in the top-right corner of the Windows 2000 Practice window.

The window appears as only a button on the taskbar.

> **tip**
> By default, shortcut icons that you create from Windows Explorer are named *Shortcut to* followed by the original file, folder, or device name. For example, the IPR Clients shortcut icon is named *Shortcut To IPR Clients*. Shortcut icons that you create from the Programs menu are not named *Shortcut To*, so the Character Map shortcut icon is named simply *Character Map*. To change a shortcut icon's name, right-click it, click Rename on the shortcut menu, type the new name, and then press Enter.

15   Double-click the Character Map shortcut icon.
The Character Map dialog box appears.

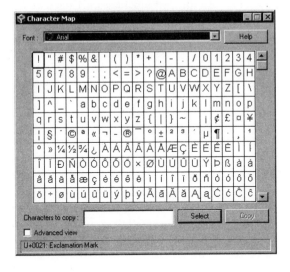

Close

16   Click the Close button in the top-right corner of the Character Map dialog box.
The dialog box closes.

17   Click the Windows 2000 Practice button on the taskbar.
The IPR Clients file is still in the Windows 2000 Practice folder. The icon on the desktop merely contains information about the file's location so that it can be opened quickly.

Close

18   Click the Close button in the top-right corner of the Windows 2000 Practice window.

The Windows 2000 Practice window closes.

Arranging Icons on the Desktop

Lesson 1, "Touring Microsoft Windows 2000 Professional," mentions that you can right-click a blank area on the desktop to display a shortcut menu that includes ways to organize icons. In that lesson, you use Line Up Icons on the shortcut menu to align icons on the desktop.

Now that you have added items to the desktop, you might want to do more than align icons. For instance, you might want to use the options on the Arrange Icons menu to organize your desktop icons.

Option	What It Does
By Name	Icons on the desktop are arranged alphabetically.
By Type	Icons are arranged so that all folders are grouped together, all programs are grouped together, all shortcut icons are grouped together, and so on. Within each group, the icons are sorted alphabetically, so if you have only short cut icons on the desktop, this option provides the same results as By Name.
By Size	Icons are arranged from smallest to largest. In the case of shortcut icons, the size is the number of bytes needed to store the shortcut icon on the disk, not the size of the file, folder, program, or device to which the shortcut icon points.
By Date	Icons are arranged from oldest to newest. In the case of shortcut icons, the date represents when the shortcut icon was made, not the date of the file, folder, program, or device to which the shortcut icon points.
Auto Arrange	Auto Arrange aligns icons on the left side of the screen. With Auto Arrange turned on, icon placement is static; the icons can't be moved around on the desktop. Unlike the other options for arranging icons, Auto Arrange is a **toggle**, meaning that it stays turned on until you click it again to turn it off.

When you no longer need a particular shortcut icon, simply drag it to the Recycle Bin. This procedure deletes the shortcut icon from the desktop; it does not delete the file, folder, program, or device that the icon represented.

In this exercise, you examine the options for arranging icons on the desktop.

At the start of this exercise, Auto Arrange on the Arrange Icons menu should not have a checkmark next to it. If it does, click Auto Arrange, and repeat steps 1 and 2.

1 Right-click a blank area on the desktop.

A shortcut menu offering choices for organizing the desktop appears.

2 On the shortcut menu, point to Arrange Icons, and then click By Name.

Shortcut icons that you've added, including the ones you created in the previous exercise, are placed in alphabetical order after the Windows icons on the left side of the screen.

Depending on what programs you have installed, your screen might differ from the one shown here.

3 Right-click a blank area on the desktop, point to Arrange Icons on the shortcut menu, and then click Auto Arrange to select it.

Although there is no apparent change, the icons are now locked into an invisible grid of rows and columns on the desktop.

Customizing Your Desktop

If Auto Arrange is on when you shut down Windows, it will be on when you restart Windows.

4   Drag the IPR Clients icon to a blank area on the desktop.

The icon snaps back to the invisible grid.

5   Right-click a blank area on the desktop. On the shortcut menu, point to Arrange Icons, and then click Auto Arrange.

Auto Arrange is toggled off, and the icons can once again be moved around on the desktop.

6   Right-click a blank area on the desktop, point to Arrange Icons on the shortcut menu, and then click By Size.

The IPR Clients shortcut icon is placed before the Character Map shortcut icon because the IPR Clients file takes up less storage space.

7   Drag the IPR Clients shortcut icon to the Recycle Bin.

The IPR Clients shortcut icon is removed from the desktop.

8   Double-click the Windows Explorer shortcut icon on the desktop. In the Folders pane, navigate to the Local Disk folder, and double-click the Windows 2000 Practice folder.

The IPR Clients file appears. Its shortcut icon on the desktop was deleted, but the file still exists.

Close

9   Click the Close button in the top-right corner of the Windows 2000 Practice window.

The Windows 2000 Practice window closes.

Changing the Appearance of the Desktop

There are many ways to customize the desktop in addition to arranging the icons on it. For example, you can change the color scheme used for the Windows components, and you can select a background picture (also called **wallpaper**) to display on the desktop.

Changing the color scheme can have a purpose beyond simply making the screen more attractive. Color schemes labeled *high contrast*, *large*, and *extra large* can make the display easier to see for people with visual impairments.

> ## tip
> You can also change the background of a particular folder in Windows Explorer by clicking Customize This Folder on the View menu. Follow the steps in the Customize This Folder wizard, verifying that the Modify Background Picture And File Name Appearance check box is selected.

In this exercise, you customize the appearance of the desktop by changing the color scheme and adding a background picture.

1 Right-click a blank area on the desktop.

A shortcut menu appears.

You can also access the Display Properties dialog box by clicking the Start button, clicking Control Panel on the Settings menu, and then double-clicking Display in Control Panel.

2 On the shortcut menu, click Properties.

The Display Properties dialog box appears.

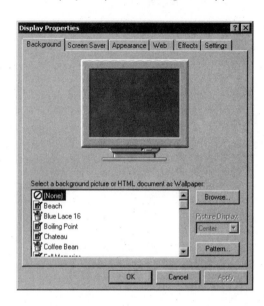

New!

Dozens of new background pictures are available in Windows 2000.

3 Click the Appearance tab, and click the Scheme arrow.

The Scheme list appears. The schemes are listed in alphabetical order.

The term VGA after a color scheme name indicates that the colors will look good even on a monitor that is set to show only 256 colors.

4 Click Red, White, and Blue (VGA).

The color scheme appears in the preview screen in the top-half of the Appearance tab.

5 Click Apply.

The new color scheme is applied to the desktop.

Customizing Your Desktop

7

> **tip**
> To create a custom scheme, click an option in the Item list on the Appearance tab. Depending on the item you choose, you might be able to change the size, color, or font. Repeat this step for any other items you want to change. When your custom scheme is complete, click the Save As button. In the Save Scheme dialog box, type a name in the Save This Color Scheme As box, and click OK.

Some background pictures are small and tiled (repeated over and over). Others are large and centered (displayed once in the middle of the desktop) or stretched (to cover the desktop).

6 Click the Background tab, and on the Select A Background Picture Or HTML Document As Wallpaper list, click Chateau.

The picture appears in the preview screen.

> **tip**
> Any picture that can be displayed as a **thumbnail** in Windows Explorer can be used as a background for the desktop. To add a picture to the list in the Background tab, move or copy the picture to the My Pictures subfolder in the My Documents folder.

7 Click the Picture Display arrow, click Stretch, and then click Apply.

The Chateau background is applied to the desktop.

Keep the Display Properties dialog box open for the next exercise.

Applying a Screen Saver

Originally, screen savers were used to prevent a problem with monitors called **burn-in**. Burn-in is the "ghost" of an image that has remained static on a screen for too long. In effect, the image becomes permanently etched into the phosphor that coats the computer screen. The result is like trying to look "through" one image in order to see another—making the monitor just about worthless. A **screen saver,** which displays an animated image on the screen after the computer has remained idle for a few minutes, was used to solve the burn-in problem.

Modern manufacturing has eliminated the problem of burn-in for most monitors, but screen savers continue to be popular for two reasons. First, they're fun. Second, and more importantly, a screen saver can provide a measure of security by locking an idle computer. Only someone who knows the password can access the desktop.

In this exercise, you modify a screen saver to display a message when you are away from your computer. Then, you password-protect the screen saver.

1   If necessary, open the Display Properties dialog box by right-clicking a blank area on the desktop and clicking Properties on the shortcut menu.

2   Click the Screen Saver tab.

3   Click the Screen Saver arrow.

    The Screen Saver list appears. (None) is selected. It's the default. The remaining items follow in alphabetical order.

4   Click 3D Text (OpenGL).

    An animated, 3D phrase bounces around the preview screen. Note whether the animation is too fast or too slow for your taste.

5   Click the Settings button.

    The 3D Text Setup dialog box appears.

6   If necessary, drag the Speed slider left to decrease the speed of the animated text or right to increase its speed.

You can type up to 16 characters in the Text box.

7   In the Display section, select the text in the Text box, type **Back Soon**, and click OK.

8   Click the Preview button, and take your hand off the mouse. The screen saver will run until you move the mouse or press a key on the keyboard.

9   Move the mouse.

    The desktop appears, just as you left it.

10 Select the Password Protected check box.

    A checkmark appears in the Password Protected check box.

11 Select the number in the Wait box, and type **1**. (You could also use the Wait arrows to increase or decrease the Wait time.)

For the purpose of this exercise, you will set the Wait to its fastest setting: one minute. A more practical Wait time, however, would be 10 or 15 minutes.

12 Click the Apply button, and wait until the screen saver appears.

13 Move your mouse.

    The Unlock Computer dialog box appears.

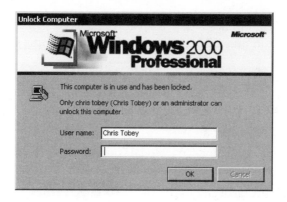

14   Type your password, and press Enter.

The computer is unlocked, and the Windows desktop appears as you left it.

*Password pro-
tecting the
screen saver
does not pre-
vent someone
from turning
the computer
off and on and
logging on as a
different user.*

15   Clear the Password Protected check box, click the Screen Saver arrow, and click (None). Then click Apply.

The screen saver is turned off. Keep the Display Properties dialog box open for the next exercise.

Adding Active Desktop Items

Active Desktop

An **Active Desktop** includes items whose content comes from the Internet. This content is automatically updated when you are connected to the Internet. Then it's stored on your hard disk so you can view it even when you are not connected to the Internet.

An Active Desktop item runs in its own window, such as Microsoft Investor Ticker, shown below. Other Active Desktop items include weather maps, sports scores, and entertainment news, to name a few. Active Desktop items can be acquired from the Active Desktop Gallery on Microsoft's Web site.

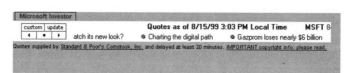

For more information about the Internet, see Lesson 5, "Accessing and Browsing the Internet."

In this exercise, you add Investor Ticker to your Active Desktop. Before you start this exercise, you must be connected to the Internet.

1   Click the Web tab in the Display Properties dialog box, and if necessary, select the Show Web Content On My Active Desktop check box. (If necessary, clear the My Current Home Page check box.)

2   Click the New button.

The New Active Desktop Item dialog box appears.

You can also open the New Active Desktop Item dialog box by right-clicking a blank area on the desktop, pointing to Active Desktop, and then clicking New Desktop Item.

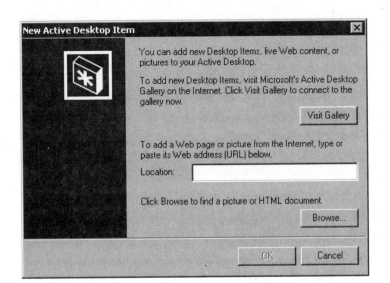

3   Click the Visit Gallery button, and if a security dialog box appears, click Yes.

The Active Desktop Gallery window appears in your default browser. Because Web pages are often updated, the page you see in your browser might look different from the following.

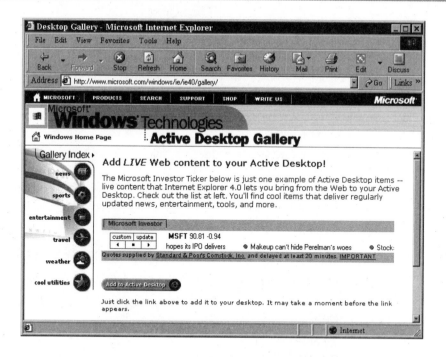

You won't
receive the
warning if
you have
downloaded
Investor Ticker
before, if your
security is set
to trust
Microsoft
content, or
if the item is
no longer on
the Active
Desktop Gallery
home page.

4   If Investor Ticker appears on the page, skip to step 5. Otherwise, click News, click Microsoft Investor Ticker, and click Yes if a security warning appears.

The Investor Ticker appears.

5   Click the Add To Active Desktop button, and click Yes to confirm the addition of the Active Desktop item.

The Add Item To Active Desktop dialog box appears. This dialog box offers options for customizing how much information the Active Desktop item displays and how often the item is updated.

6   Click OK.

The Active Desktop item is added to the desktop.

7   Click the Close button in the top-right corner of the browser window.

The browser closes, and the Active Desktop item (the Investor Ticker) appears on the screen.

8   Point anywhere in the top area of Microsoft Investor Ticker.

A bar similar to a title bar is added to the top of the Investor Ticker window. In the right corner of the bar are buttons for resizing and closing the window.

Close

*If the Investor
Ticker isn't
completely
visible, click
its title bar,
and drag it to
the middle of
the desktop.*

Cover
Desktop button

Split Desktop
With Icons button

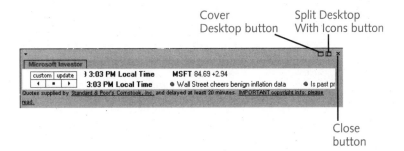

Close
button

9 Click the Split Desktop With Icons button on the bar.

The Investor Ticker window is enlarged so it covers most of the screen, like a background, except for a strip on the left side to show the desktop icons.

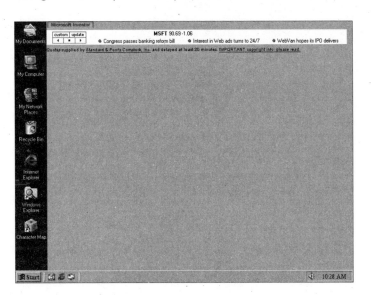

10 Point anywhere in the top area of the Investor Ticker to display the bar, and click the Close button.

The Investor Ticker window closes, and the desktop reappears. Note that the Display Properties dialog box also closes.

tip

To permanently delete an Active Desktop item, right-click a blank area on the desktop, click Properties, and click the Web tab. In the list at the bottom of the tab, click the name of the item to delete, and then click Delete.

Changing Mouse Properties

A computer mouse is like a car; all models have the same basic functions, but each is designed differently, and it takes a little time to get accustomed to a new one. Unlike a car, though, you can enhance a mouse's performance easily. To customize a mouse, use the Mouse Properties dialog box, which is accessed from Control Panel.

The option to single-click or double-click an item is new in Windows 2000.

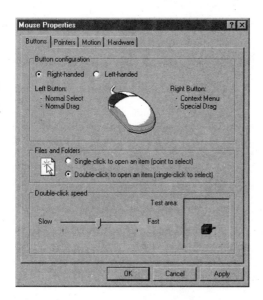

Mouse Properties Tabs

Tab	Used to
Buttons	Swap the functions of the left and right mouse buttons so that the mouse can be more easily used by a left-handed person. This tab can also be used to change the mouse behavior so that single-clicking, rather than double-clicking, opens a selected item.
Pointers	Choose and customize sets of mouse pointers to display. Each pointer displays a small graphical representation of the action that's being performed.
Motion	Fine-tune the way the mouse moves.
Hardware	Install a mouse or troubleshoot a mouse that's not working properly.

In this exercise, you change the double-click speed, pointer scheme, and movement of the mouse.

1   Click the Start button, point to Settings, and then click Control Panel.

Control Panel appears.

2   In Control Panel, double-click the Mouse icon, and in the Mouse Properties dialog box, verify that the Buttons tab is displayed.

> ## tip
> To swap the actions of the mouse buttons, click the Left-Handed option in the Button Configuration section. The right button will be used to make selections and run programs, and the left button will be used to display shortcut menus. Swapping mouse buttons is convenient for users who are left-handed.

Setting the speed to Slow can make a "touchy" mouse easier to use because you have more time to double-click.

3   Drag the Double-Click Speed slider all the way to the left (toward Slow), and click the Pointers tab.

The Pointers tab appears.

4   Click the Scheme arrow.

The Scheme list appears.

5   Click Conductor (System Scheme).

The pointers available in this scheme appear in the Customize section.

If the mouse feels sluggish or out of control, you can adjust its speed on the Motion tab, in the Acceleration section.

6   Click the Motion tab. In the Snap To Default section, select the Move Pointer To The Default Button In Dialog Boxes check box, and click OK.

The Mouse Properties dialog box closes, and the new mouse settings are applied. The mouse pointer now appears as a pointing hand.

7   Slowly double-click Display in Control Panel, pausing briefly between the clicks.

You should find that you can double-click more slowly than usual. Also, you should see the mouse pointer change to a beating drum as Windows determines your display settings.

Drum pointer

8   In the Display Properties dialog box, click the Cancel button.

The Display Properties dialog box closes.

9   Click the Start button on the taskbar, and click Shut Down.

The Shut Down Windows dialog box appears. Notice that the mouse pointer automatically points to the OK button.

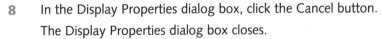

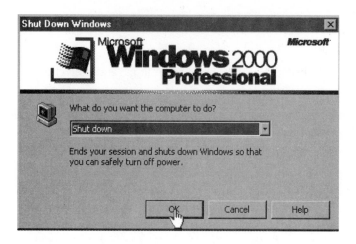

10   Click the Cancel button.

The Shut Down Windows dialog box closes.

11   Double-click the Mouse icon in Control Panel.

The Mouse Properties dialog box appears.

12   On the Buttons tab, drag the Double-Click Speed slider back to the middle. On the Pointers tab, display the Scheme list and click (None). On the Motion tab, clear the Move Pointer To The Default Button In Dialog Boxes check box, and then click OK.

The original settings for the mouse are reapplied, and the Mouse Properties dialog box closes.

Close

13   Click the Close button in the top-right corner of Control Panel.

Control Panel closes.

Customizing the Start Menu

Depending on your needs, you might want to customize the Start menu—perhaps you would prefer the menu to be smaller or offer additional commands. For instance, the reservations manager at Lakewood Mountains Resort reduced the size of each Start menu command and personalized the menus for each reservations agent. Because the reservations computers are never turned off, she also added a Log Off command to the Start menu on each computer in order to help the agents remember to log off at the end of their shifts.

In this exercise, you modify the Start menu, including adding a command for logging off the computer.

1   Click the Start button, point to Settings, and then click Taskbar & Start Menu.

        The Taskbar And Start Menu Properties dialog box appears, and the General tab is displayed. The dialog box should look similar to the following. If it doesn't, select and clear the necessary check boxes so that the tabs match before continuing to step 2.

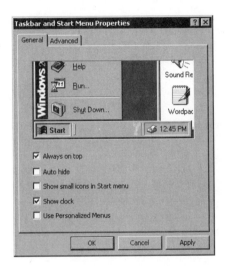

2   Select the Show Small Icons In Start Menu check box.

        The modified Start menu appears in the preview screen.

3   Select the Use Personalized Menus check box.

        This option customizes menus so that only the menu commands you use most often are initially displayed.

4   Click the Advanced tab.

        The Advanced tab appears.

5   In the Start Menu Settings section, select the Display Logoff check box, if necessary.

        A command for logging off the computer is added to the Start menu.

?

Help

> **tip**
> To learn about the other options in the Start Menu Settings list, click the Help button in the top-right corner of the Taskbar And Start Menu Properties dialog box, and click an option in the list. To close the pop-up window, click inside of it.

6   Click the Apply button.

The new settings are applied.

7   Click the Start button. The Start menu is noticeably smaller, and it displays the Log Off command near the bottom of the menu.

8   Point to Programs.

The Programs menu shows only the commands you use most often.

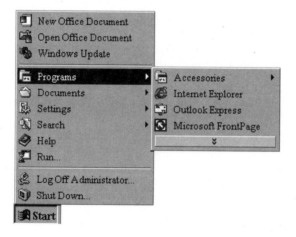

9   Click the double-arrow at the bottom of the Programs submenu.

All menu commands appear. Menu commands that were initially hidden appear "indented."

10 · Click Log Off <user name>.

The Log Off Windows dialog box appears.

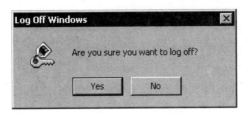

11 Click No to cancel the logoff process.

Keep the Taskbar And Start Menu Properties dialog box open for the next exercise.

Customizing the Taskbar

You can customize the taskbar by adding or deleting the toolbars it displays. By default, the Quick Launch bar appears. By right-clicking the taskbar, you can choose to display any of the following toolbars instead of (or in addition to) the Quick Launch bar.

2000 New!

Adding these three bars to the taskbar.

- **Address bar** Adds a box to the taskbar in which you can type a Web address. When you press Enter, your Web browser starts. If you are connected to the Internet, the Web page opens.

- **Links toolbar** Provides links to particular Web sites. You can add your own links to this toolbar.

- **Desktop toolbar** Displays icons for My Documents, My Computer, and the other standard desktop icons.

In the Multimedia folder on the Microsoft Windows 2000 Professional Step by Step CD-ROM, double-click the Custom Taskbar icon for a demonstration of how to customize the taskbar and the Start menu.

You can also use the Taskbar And Start Menu Properties dialog box to make the taskbar disappear under certain circumstances, so that you have more room for your windows.

In this exercise, you customize the desktop by hiding the desktop icons and adding them to the taskbar instead. Then you change the display options for the taskbar so that the taskbar is hidden unless you point to the bottom of the screen.

1 Right-click a blank area on the desktop.

A shortcut menu appears.

2 On the shortcut menu, point to Active Desktop, and then click Show Desktop Icons.

The desktop icons no longer appear.

You can right-click any blank area on the taskbar to display its shortcut menu, but the time makes a convenient target to aim for.

3   In the right corner of the taskbar, right-click the time.

A shortcut menu appears.

4   On the shortcut menu, point to Toolbars, and then click Desktop.

The Desktop toolbar is added to the taskbar. Only the first few buttons fit on the taskbar, however.

Move pointer

> **tip**
> To resize a toolbar on the taskbar, point to the double vertical lines on the left side of the desired toolbar. When the move pointer appears, drag left or right.

Double Arrow

5   On the right side of the Desktop toolbar, click the right-pointing double-arrow.

A menu displaying the remaining shortcuts appears.

The menu on your computer might differ from the menu here, depending on what icons you have on your desktop.

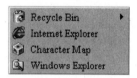

6   Click Character Map.

The Character Map window appears just as it would if you had double-clicked its shortcut icon on the desktop.

☒

Close

7   Click the Close button in the top-right corner of the Character Map window.

The Character Map window closes.

8   Click the General tab in the Taskbar And Start Menu Properties dialog box, and select the Auto Hide check box.

In the preview screen, the desktop appears without the taskbar.

9   Click the Apply button.

The taskbar disappears, except for a thin strip at the bottom of the screen.

10   Point to the strip at the bottom of the screen.

The taskbar reappears.

11   Point to the middle of the screen.

The taskbar is hidden again.

Lesson Wrap-Up

In this lesson, you learned how to add and manage shortcut icons on the desktop, and you learned how to change the appearance of the desktop. You also learned how a screen saver can become a security device if you are away from your computer while it is running. In addition, you learned how to add an Active Desktop item that can provide up-to-the-minute information. Finally, you learned how to customize the mouse, the Start menu, and the taskbar.

To return all Windows components to their previous settings:

1   Right-click a blank area on the desktop, point to Active Desktop on the shortcut menu, and then click Show Desktop Icons.

2   Drag the Character Map shortcut icon to the Recycle Bin.

3   Right-click a blank area on the desktop, and click Properties on the shortcut menu. In the Display Properties dialog box, click the Background tab, and set the Background back to (None). Click the Appearance tab, and set the Scheme back to Windows Standard. Click the Web tab, delete Microsoft Investor Ticker, click Yes, and then click OK.

4   In the Taskbar And Start Menu Properties dialog box, clear all check boxes except the Always On Top and Show Clock check boxes. Click the Advanced tab, clear the Display Logoff check box, and then click OK.

5   Right-click the time on the taskbar, point to Toolbars on the shortcut menu, and then click Desktop.

If you are continuing to other lessons:

●   Close all open windows. The desktop should be displayed.

If you are not continuing to other lessons:

1   Close all open windows, and click the Start button on the taskbar.

2   Click Shut Down on the Start menu. If necessary, click the arrow in the Windows Shut Down dialog box, and click Shut Down in the list. Then click OK.

3   After Windows has shut down, turn off the computer and, if necessary, all other hardware devices.

Customizing Your Desktop

Glossary

active desktop A feature that extends how you can display screen objects and folders.

Address bar A bar that can be added to the taskbar in which you can type a Web address. When you press Enter, your Web browser starts. If you're connected to the Internet, the Web page opens.

burn-in The "ghost" of an image that has remained static on a screen for too long. Burn-in is not a problem on modern color monitors.

Desktop toolbar A toolbar that can appear on the taskbar and display the icons on your desktop. The Desktop toolbar makes it easy to select a desktop item without having to minimize open windows.

Links toolbar A toolbar that provides icons that link to frequently used Web sites. You can add your own links to this toolbar.

screen saver A feature that displays an animated image on the screen after the computer has remained idle for a specified time.

thumbnail A small representation of a picture, Web page, or video that appears in the Image Preview area of the My Computer or Windows Explorer window when you click the name of a graphic, Web page (HTML file), or video.

toggle An option or button that acts as an on/off switch so that clicking the option or button each time reverses the settings.

wallpaper A background picture on your desktop.

Windows Explorer A window that you can use to navigate through folders and copy, move, delete, and open files.

Quick Reference

To add a shortcut to the desktop

1   Open the folder or menu that contains the item for which you want to create a shortcut icon.

2   Hold down the right mouse button, and drag the item onto the desktop.

3   On the shortcut menu, click Create Shortcut(s) Here.

Quick Reference

To arrange icons on the desktop

- Right-click a blank area on the desktop, point to Arrange Icons on the shortcut menu, and then click By Name, By Type, By Size, or By Date.

To lock icons on the desktop

- Right-click a blank area on the desktop, point to Arrange Icons on the shortcut menu, and then click Auto Arrange.

To remove a shortcut icon from the desktop

- Drag the shortcut icon you want to delete to the Recycle Bin.

To change the Windows color scheme

1   Right-click a blank area on the desktop, and click Properties on the shortcut menu.

2   Click the Appearance tab, click the desired color scheme in the Scheme list, and then click Apply or OK.

To add a background to the desktop

1   Right-click a blank area on the desktop, and click Properties on the shortcut menu.

2   Click the Background tab, click the desired picture, and if necessary, change the Picture Display to Center, Tile, or Stretch.

3   Click Apply or OK.

To turn on a screen saver

1   Right-click a blank area on the desktop, and click Properties on the shortcut menu.

2   Click the Screen Saver tab, click the desired screen saver in the Screen Saver list, and then type the desired amount of idle time in the Wait box.

3   If necessary, click the Settings button, make the desired changes, and then click OK.

4   If necessary, select the Password Protected check box, and click Apply or OK.

To add an Active Desktop item

1   Connect to the Internet, if necessary.

2   Right-click a blank area on the desktop, and click Properties on the shortcut menu.

Customizing Your Desktop 7

Quick Reference

To add an Active Desktop item (*continued*)

3   Click the Web tab, and click the New button.

4   Click the Visit Gallery button, and click Yes in any warning boxes.

5   On the Desktop Gallery page in your Web browser, find the item you want, and click the Add To Active Desktop button.

6   Click Yes, and click OK. After the item is added, click the Close button in the top-right corner of the Web browser window.

7   Disconnect from the Internet, if necessary.

To resize an Active Desktop item

1   Point inside the item's window until a bar appears at the top.

2   On the bar, click the Cover Desktop button or the Split Desktop With Icons button.

To customize the mouse

1   Click the Start button.

2   Point to Settings, and click Control Panel.

3   Double-click the Mouse icon. Make the desired changes using the Buttons, Pointers, Motion, and Hardware tabs.

4   Click Apply or OK.

To modify the Start menu or taskbar

1   Click the Start button, point to Settings, and click Taskbar & Start Menu.

2   Click the General tab, if necessary, and select and clear the desired check boxes.

To change the content on the Start menu

1   Click the Start button, point to Settings, and click Taskbar & Start Menu.

2   In the Taskbar And Start Menu Properties dialog box, click the Advanced tab.

3   Click the Add or Remove buttons to create or delete a menu item, or select and clear check boxes in the Start Menu Settings section, as desired.

To add or remove a toolbar on the taskbar

●   Right-click a blank area on the taskbar, point to Toolbars on the shortcut menu, and then click the desired toolbar.

8

Using Windows on the Go

**ESTIMATED
TIME
60 min.**

After completing this lesson, you will be able to:

✔ *Manage power usage.*

✔ *Connect to a network through a phone line.*

✔ *View Web pages when you're not connected to a network.*

✔ *Synchronize offline files.*

✔ *Set file and folder security options.*

Many people use more than one computer. For instance, a business person might use a stand-alone desktop computer at home, a networked desktop computer at the office, and a laptop for travel. Windows provides tools that support the capabilities and requirements of each type of computer, including how it consumes power and connects to a network. Windows also lets you protect files from unauthorized users and keep files current between two computers.

In this lesson, you will use power schemes to manage power usage, and you will use **dial-up** connectivity to connect to a network from a remote location. Dial-up means that you use a standard phone line to make a connection between your computer and a network. You will also keep your work up-to-date both on the road and in the office by working offline and using the Synchronization Manager. Finally, you will set permissions for files and folders.

Using Power Schemes

Power schemes

Before the president of Impact Public Relations types a memo on her laptop during a business flight, she sets options in Windows to conserve as much power as possible. Before she uses the laptop in her hotel room, she plugs the laptop into a wall socket. Then she sets the options to allow the computer to consume more power.

You might want to set the power options on your desktop or laptop computer. For example, you can set an option called **Stand By**. This feature turns off the monitor when the computer has been idle for a while.

In this exercise, you create a Windows power scheme based on the Max Battery scheme. (This scheme maximizes the life of the battery for a laptop, but you can also use it with a desktop computer.) You modify the scheme so that if the computer is idle for more than one minute, it goes on Stand By.

1   Click the Start button, point to Settings, and then click Control Panel.

Control Panel appears.

2   Double-click the Power Options icon.

The Power Options Properties dialog box appears. Note the current power scheme; you will need to return to it later in this exercise.

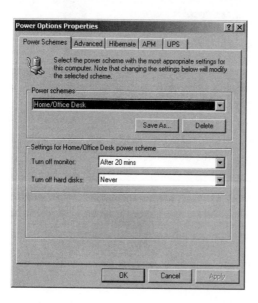

Normally, you would choose a longer time span before Stand By takes effect.

3 Click the Power Schemes arrow, and click Max Battery. Click the Turn Off Monitor arrow, click After 1 Min, and then click the Save As button.

The Save Scheme dialog box appears.

Hibernation

> ## tip
>
> If you have a Hibernate tab in the Power Options Properties dialog box, your computer supports hibernation in addition to Stand By. Hibernation is similar to Stand By except it saves all open files, and it stores your desktop settings before reducing power consumption. If you want to use hibernation, click the Hibernate tab, and select the Enable Hibernate Support check box. Then click the Apply button.

If you change a power scheme and don't save it with a new name, the changes made to the existing scheme are permanent.

4 Type **Power Practice**, and click OK twice.

The dialog boxes close, and the new power scheme is enabled.

5 Save any open files, and do not use your keyboard or mouse for at least one minute.

After one minute, the computer switches to Stand By mode, appearing to shut down. Actually, the monitor is turned off, but the computer is still running. If power is cut off, you will lose unsaved work.

6 Move the mouse. (On a laptop, move a finger over the trackpad or other mouse device.)

The desktop reappears.

7 In Control Panel, double-click the Power Options icon.

The Power Options Properties dialog box appears.

8 Click the Power Schemes arrow, and click the default scheme for your computer. (You noted the default in step 2; it's probably Home/Office Desk.) Then click OK.

The options in the dialog box are reset, the dialog box closes, and the default power scheme is restored.

9 Click the Close button in the top-right corner of Control Panel.
Control Panel closes.

Close

Creating a Dial-Up Network Connection

*Network Con-
nection Wizard*

The president of Impact Public Relations wants to read her e-mail messages from the company's network server while she travels. To do this, she uses a dial-up connection from her laptop to the network.

In a dial-up connection, your computer dials a phone number for a computer that is directly connected to a network. (Lesson 5, "Accessing and Browsing the Internet," also explains dial-up connections. However, in that lesson, you connect to the Internet rather than to a private network.) The computer on the network connects your computer to the network. The network treats the remote computer as though it were directly attached, even if the two are thousands of miles apart.

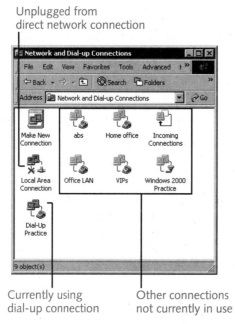

Unplugged from
direct network connection

Currently using
dial-up connection

Other connections
not currently in use

To create a dial-up connection, whether to a private network or to the Internet, you use the Network Connection Wizard. You will need the following information to use the wizard:

- The phone number that connects you to a server on the network.

- The user name and password that identify you as an authorized user on the network.

- Any protocols, clients, scripts, or services you might need to exchange information over the network. (Your network administrator should provide these files.)

In this exercise, you create and test a dial-up connection to a network. To complete this exercise, your computer must have a modem, which must be connected to a phone line.

Alternatively, click the My Network Places icon on the desktop, click the Network And Dial-Up Connections link, and then double-click Make New Connection.

1 Click the Start button, point to Settings, point to Network And Dial-Up Connections, and then click Make New Connection.

The Network Connection Wizard appears.

2 Click the Next button.

The wizard prompts you for the type of connection you want to create.

3 Verify that the Dial-Up To Private Network option is selected, and click the Next button. (If you have more than one dial-up device on your computer, select one when prompted, and click the Next button.)

You are prompted to type the phone number of the computer or network to which you want to connect.

4 If you need to follow certain rules to make a phone call—such as including the area code—select the Use Dialing Rules check box.

tip

If you are not sure whether the dialing rules on your computer are appropriate for the location from which you are dialing, you can clear the Use Dialing Rules check box. Then you can type the entire number, including any prefix and area code, in the Phone Number box. Suppose your dial-up number is 8005550412, and the hotel where you are staying requires you to enter *11 to get an outside line. You would clear the Use Dialing Rules check box, and type *11,8005550412 in the Phone Number box. (The comma inserts a one-second pause while the hotel's telephone system switches you to an outside line.)

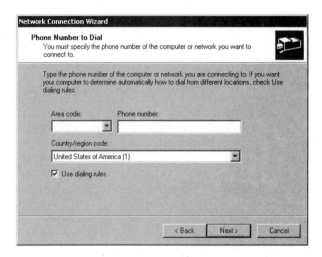

*If you don't
have the
number for
a real dial-up
server, type
your own
home or work
number in
the Phone
Number box.*

5   If necessary, enter an area code in the Area Code box. Then type a number in the Phone Number box, and click the Next button.

You are prompted to specify whether to give other users on your system access to this dial-up connection.

6   Click the Only For Myself option, and click the Next button.

The final wizard dialog box appears. You are prompted to type the name you want to use for the connection you just created.

7   Type **Dial-Up Practice**, and click the Finish button.

The Connect Dial-Up Practice dialog box appears.

8   If you are not actually connecting to a remote network server, click the Cancel button, and continue to the next section in this lesson. If you are connecting, enter the user name and the password for this connection. (They are probably different from your Windows user name and password.) Click the Dial button.

When you click the Dial button, the Connecting dialog box appears. You might see other messages as well, depending on the scripts and programs that run when you connect. Eventually, the Connection Complete dialog box and a pop-up window appear.

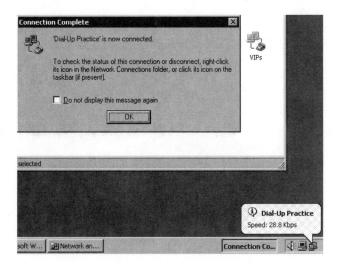

9   In the Connection Complete dialog box, click OK.

You can now send and receive information to and from the network.

tip

Error messages that appear when you use a dial-up connection usually indicate a problem with the dial-up properties. To identify the problem, point to Settings on the Start menu. Point to Network And Dial-Up Connections, and click the name of the connection you are trying to use (Dial-Up Practice, in this exercise). In the Connect Dial-Up Practice dialog box, click the Properties button, and then click the Networking tab. Note the settings that appear there. Then compare them with settings recommended by your network administrator to make sure all protocols, clients, and services on the tab are configured correctly.

10   In the Network And Dial-Up Connections window, double-click the Dial-Up Practice icon.

The Dial-Up Practice Status dialog box appears.

11   Click the Disconnect button.

Your computer is disconnected from the network.

Close

12   Click the Close button in the top-right corner of the Network And Dial-Up Connection window.

The window closes.

Understanding VPN Connections

Virtual Private Network

VPN stands for **virtual private network,** a type of dial-up connection that lets you access a network without having to dial it directly. It's similar to calling someone using directory assistance instead of dialing the number yourself. You connect to the Internet, which acts as the operator. Then you provide information about the private network to which you want to connect—specifically, a **host name** or **IP** (Internet protocol) **address.** Host names and IP addresses are two ways of uniquely identifying a private network.

A VPN prevents anyone who is not part of the VPN from viewing data that is traveling across the Internet. A VPN also can provide a cheaper alternative to dialing into a network directly. Rather than dialing a long-distance number to access the network, you can use a local Internet number. To create a VPN, you need the following:

- Windows 2000 running on all computers that will connect to the VPN.

- Internet access for all computers that will connect to the VPN.

- The host name or IP address of the private network. Host names are words or abbreviations separated by periods, such as host1.JustTogs.com. IP addresses are four numbers separated by periods, such as 192.168.0.12.

- A user name and a password the private network recognizes.

- A VPN connection. (Run the Network Connection Wizard, click the Connect To A Private Network Through The Internet option, and follow the steps in the wizard.)

Using Web Files Offline

At times, you might want to view Internet sites or work with files on a local area network (LAN) even though you're not connected to the Internet or to the network. Windows provides an easy way to do this. You can save files, folders, Web pages—even entire Web sites—for offline use. Because these files and folders are typically available only when you're online, saving them for offline use also makes them available when you're not connected to a network. When you use the Make Available Offline menu command, Windows copies specified files and folders to your hard disk while you're connected to the Internet or your LAN. You can then view or work with the files and folders even when you aren't connected.

For more information about the Favorites list in Internet Explorer, see Lesson 5, "Accessing and Browsing the Internet."

To make a Web page available offline, you need to add it to your Favorites list in Internet Explorer. To save a network file or folder for offline access, you simply right-click it in Windows Explorer, and click Make Available Offline on the shortcut menu that appears.

tip
If you no longer need a file or folder while you're offline, right-click it, and click Make Available Offline on the shortcut menu again to clear its checkmark. If you no longer need a Web page while you're offline, start Internet Explorer, click Favorites on the menu bar, and click Organize Favorites. Click the desired page in the Favorites list, and click Make Available Offline to clear its checkmark.

In this exercise, you make a Web page available for use offline. You must have an Internet connection to complete this exercise.

You can also start Internet Explorer by clicking its button on the Quick Launch bar.

1   On the desktop, double-click the Internet Explorer icon.

The Internet Explorer window appears. The Dial-Up Connection dialog box might also appear if you are not currently connected to the Internet.

For more information on connecting to the Internet, refer to Lesson 5, "Accessing and Browsing the Internet."

2   If necessary, use the Dial-Up Connection dialog box to connect to the Internet.

When you are connected through a dial-up connection, a Connection To message is briefly displayed in the bottom-right corner of the screen, and your home page appears in Internet Explorer.

3   Click in the Address bar, type **mspress.microsoft.com/mspress/products/ 1349/default1.htm**, and then press Enter.

The home page for Lakewood Mountains Resort appears.

Windows on the Go   8

You can also access your Favorites list from the My Computer or Windows Explorer windows.

4   On the Internet Explorer menu bar, click Favorites, and then click Add To Favorites.

The Add Favorite dialog box appears.

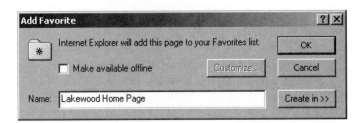

5   In the Add Favorite dialog box, select the Make Available Offline check box, and click OK.

The Synchronizing dialog box appears briefly while the page is copied to a folder on your hard disk.

> ## tip
> To make an existing favorite page available offline, click Organize Favorites on the Internet Explorer Favorites menu. Click the desired page in the Organize Favorites dialog box, select the Make Available Offline check box, and then click Close.

Working Offline

Internet Explorer retrieves offline files from a folder on your hard disk rather than from the Internet.

6   On the Internet Explorer menu bar, click File, and then click Work Offline.

A small icon appears on the Internet Explorer Status bar to indicate that you are working offline.

Keep Internet Explorer open in preparation for the next exercise.

Using the Synchronization Manager

Synchronization Manager

When you make files available for offline reading, it's a good bet that you'll also want to edit those files while you're offline. If you've downloaded a Web file for offline use, you might want to synchronize the offline file with the online version in case it has changed. This can be a tedious process if you have to update several files yourself. Fortunately, the Synchronization Manager handles the entire process for you. You simply indicate which offline files, folders, or Web pages you want to synchronize, and the Synchronization Manager takes care of the rest.

In this exercise, you use the Synchronization Manager to synchronize the offline and online versions of the Lakewood Mountains Resort home page.

In Windows Explorer, you can also click Synchronize on the Tools menu.

1   On the Internet Explorer menu bar, click Tools, and then click Synchronize.

The Items To Synchronize window appears. Each item in the list has a check box to its left. If an item is selected, it will be synchronized when you click the Synchronize button.

2   Select and clear check boxes as necessary until only the Lakewood Home Page is selected.

The window should look similar to the following, although you might have different check boxes to clear.

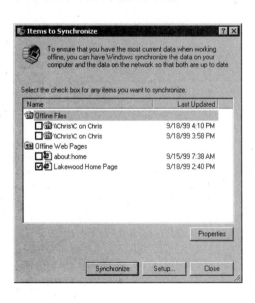

*To cancel syn-
chronization,
click the Stop
button in the
Synchronizing
window.*

3   Click the Synchronize button.

The Synchronizing window appears while the files are made available for offline use. This might take several minutes. Then the Synchronization Complete dialog box appears briefly.

Close

4   Click the Close button in the top-right corner of the Internet Explorer window. If necessary, click the Disconnect Now button.

The Internet Explorer window closes.

---

tip

To specify a particular schedule for synchronizing, click the Setup button in the Items To Synchronize dialog box. Use the options in the Synchronization Settings dialog box to select items to synchronize under various conditions, such as when you log off the network. To schedule synchronization at a particular time (such as once a week at 5 P.M.), click the Scheduled tab, and click the Add button. Then follow the steps in the Scheduled Synchronization Wizard.

Setting File and Folder Security Options

When the president of Impact Public Relations travels, her assistant has access to the president's computer. There are certain folders and files, however, to which the assistant should have limited or no access. By default, all users who have access to your files and folders in Windows can change and delete them. However, you can permit or deny specific types of access for particular files or folders on a user-by-user basis.

There are six levels of permissions for files and folders:

■ **Full Control** User can read and make any changes to a file or a folder, including deleting it.

■ **Modify** User can change the contents of a file, add or delete files to a folder, or rename files or folders.

■ **Write** User can change the contents of a file or add files to a folder.

■ **Read & Execute** User can look at the contents of a file or a folder or double-click a program to start it.

■ **Read** User can look at the contents of a file.

■ **List Folder Contents** User can look at the contents of a folder.

important

To set the security level for a file or folder, display the Security tab in the file or folder's Properties dialog box. You will see this tab if your disk has an NTFS file system. A file system provides a disk's basic structure; it's associated with the operating system installed on the computer. The recommended file system for Windows 2000, as well as Windows NT, is *NTFS* (which stands for *New Technology File System*). However, if your computer is set up to run an operating system in addition to Windows 2000, such as Windows 98, you probably have a different file system, such as *FAT* or *FAT32*. (FAT stands for *File Allocation Table*.) Changing file systems should be done only by experienced Windows users; the process is beyond the scope of this book.

In this exercise, you change the permissions for the Windows 2000 Practice folder so that others can view the folder and the files and subfolders it contains, but they can't modify it or any of its files or subfolders.

In the Multimedia folder on the Microsoft Windows 2000 Professional Step by Step CD-ROM, double-click the Security icon for a demonstration of how to apply security settings to a file.

1   On the desktop, double-click the My Computer icon.

The My Computer window appears.

2   Click the Folders button.

The Folders pane appears in the left side of the window.

3   In the Folders pane, click the plus sign to the left of Local Disk. (Your disk name could be different. If so, click the disk that contains a (C:) at the end of the name.) Click the Windows 2000 Practice folder.

The contents of the Windows 2000 Practice folder appear in the right pane of the window.

4   In the Folders pane, right-click the Windows 2000 Practice folder, and then click Properties on the shortcut menu.

The Windows 2000 Practice Properties dialog box appears.

If you don't see a Security tab in the Properties dialog box, your disk is not NTFS. Close the Properties dialog box, and continue to the next section in this lesson.

5   Click the Security tab, and verify that *Everyone* is selected.

The dialog box should look similar to the following.

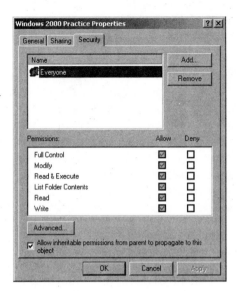

6   In the Permissions section of the dialog box, select the Deny check box for Write.

Write permission is denied.

7   Click OK.

An alert box appears.

8   Click Yes to confirm the permissions you just set.

The write permission for the folder changes.

9   In the right pane of the Windows 2000 Practice window, double-click the To Do List file.

The To Do List opens in Notepad.

10   Click in the last line, after the *d* in *ad*.

The insertion point moves to the right of the *d* in *ad* in the last line.

11   Type **vertising**.

Close

12   Click the Close button in the top-right corner of the Notepad window.

An alert box appears, asking if you want to save the changes.

13   Click Yes.

The Save As dialog box appears.

14   Click the Save button.

An alert box appears, informing you that you don't have permission to complete this action.

Close

15　Click OK. Click the Close button in the top-right corner of the Save As dialog box, and click the Close button in the top-right corner of the Notepad window.

An alert box appears, asking if you want to save the changes.

16　Click No.

The Notepad window closes.

Close

17　Click the Close button in the top-right corner of the Windows 2000 Practice window.

The Windows 2000 Practice window closes.

File and Folder Encryption

Encrypting Files and Folders

Another way to provide additional security is to **encrypt** a file or folder. An encrypted file can be opened only by the user who encrypted it. As is true with file and folder permissions, encryption is available only on NTFS-formatted disks.

To encrypt a file or folder, right-click its name in the Folders pane, and click Properties. On the General tab in the Properties dialog box, click the Advanced button. In the Advanced Attributes dialog box, select the Encrypt Contents To Secure Data check box, and click OK twice.

If you encrypt a file, an Encryption Warning dialog box appears. The dialog box explains the security risks of encrypting a file without encrypting the folder it's in. Click the desired option in the dialog box, and click OK.

If you encrypt a folder, the Confirm Attribute Changes dialog box appears. Click the desired option to encrypt just the folder or to also encrypt the files and subfolders it contains. Then click OK.

To test encryption, log off, and log back on as a different user. When you try to use the encrypted file or folder, you'll see a message that access is denied.

Lesson Wrap-Up

In this lesson, you learned to use power schemes to manage power usage for your personal computer and laptop, and you learned how to create a dial-up connection so that you can connect to a network from a remote location. You also learned how to save and synchronize offline Web files. Finally, you learned how to set security options for files and folders.

Windows on the Go

To return all Windows components to their previous settings:

1   Click the Start button, point to Settings, and click Control Panel. In Control Panel, double-click the Power Options icon. Click Power Practice in the Power Schemes list, and click the Delete button. Click Yes to verify the deletion. Click OK, and close Control Panel.

2   On the desktop, double-click My Network Places, and click the link to Network And Dial-Up Connections. Click the Dial-Up Practice icon, and press Delete. Click Yes to verify the deletion. Close the Network And Dial-Up Connections window.

3   On the desktop, double-click the Internet Explorer icon. On the Favorites menu, click Organize Favorites. In the list of Favorites, click Lakewood Home Page, and then click Delete. Click Yes to verify the deletion, and close the Organize Favorites dialog box. On the File menu, click Work Offline to toggle it off. Close Internet Explorer, and if necessary, disconnect from the Internet.

4   Double-click the Windows Explorer icon on the desktop, and navigate to the Windows 2000 Practice folder in the Folders pane. In the Folders pane, right-click the Windows 2000 Practice folder, and click Properties on the shortcut menu. Click the Security tab, and clear the Deny check box for Write. Click OK. Close the Windows Explorer window.

If you are continuing to other lessons:

●   Close all open windows. The desktop should be displayed.

If you are not continuing to other lessons:

1   Close all open windows, and click the Start button on the taskbar.

2   Click Shut Down on the Start menu. If necessary, click the arrow in the Windows Shut Down dialog box, and click Shut Down in the list. Then click OK.

3   After Windows has shut down, turn off the computer and if necessary, all other hardware devices.

Glossary

dial-up connection The process in which your computer uses a modem to dial a phone number to connect to an Internet service provider's host computer.

encrypting Encoding a file or folder so that only the creator of the file or folder can access it.

host name Words or abbreviations separated by periods, such as host1.JustTogs.com, that identify a computer on the Internet or on a LAN.

Glossary

IP address   A set of numbers (such as 192.168.0.1) that identifies a computer on the Internet or a local area network.

Stand By   A feature that suspends power to the monitor when the computer has been idle for a period of time. Some computers also allow you to suspend power to the hard disk after a period of inactivity.

VPN (virtual private network)   A type of dial-up connection that enables you to access a network without dialing it directly. Instead a VPN establishes a connection to other computers by making private connections through the Internet.

Quick Reference

To apply a power scheme

1   Click the Start button, point to Settings, and click Control Panel.

2   Double-click the Power Options icon.

3   Click a scheme in the Turn Off Monitor (or Power Schemes) list, and click the desired length of time in the System Stand By list.

4   Modify the scheme as necessary, setting options on the various tabs in the dialog box. On the Power Schemes tab, click the Save As button, and rename the modified scheme.

5   Click OK, and close Control panel.

To create a dial-up network connection

1   Click the Start button, point to Settings, point to Network And Dial-Up Connections, and then click Make New Connection.

2   In the Network Connection Wizard, click the Next button, verify that the Dial-Up To Private Network option is selected, and then click the Next button again.

3   Follow the remaining steps in the Network Connection Wizard, clicking the Next button to move through the steps. Click the Finish button to complete the connection.

4   When prompted, enter your user name and password for the connection, and then click the Dial button to establish the connection.

Quick Reference

To make a file or folder available offline

1   On the desktop, double-click the My Network Places icon.

2   Navigate to the desired file or folder on a network computer.

3   Right-click the file or folder, and click Make Available Offline.

To make a Web page available offline

1   On the desktop, double-click the Internet Explorer icon, and if necessary, connect to the Internet.

2   Navigate to the desired Web page.

3   On the Favorites menu, click Add To Favorites. Select the Make Available Offline check box, and click OK.

4   On the File menu, click Work Offline.

5   On the Favorites menu, click the name of the desired Web page.

To synchronize offline files

1   On the Internet Explorer Tools menu, click Synchronize.

2   In the Items To Synchronize window, select and clear check boxes until only the desired files are selected.

3   Click the Synchronize button.

4   On the Internet Explorer menu bar, click File, and then click Work Offline.

To set security permissions for a file or folder

1   On the desktop, double-click the My Computer icon. In the My Computer window, click the Folders button.

2   In the Folders pane, navigate to the desired folder or file, and right-click it.

3   On the shortcut menu, click Properties.

4   In the Properties dialog box, click the Security tab.

5   Click the name of a user or group, or click the Add button, and then click the name of a user or group.

6   In the Permissions section of the dialog box, select and clear the Deny and Access check boxes as desired.

7   Click OK, and click Yes to verify the change in permissions.

LESSON

9

Working with Software and Hardware

ESTIMATED TIME
40 min.

After completing this lesson, you will be able to:

✔ *Add Windows components.*

✔ *Install and remove software.*

✔ *Add a printer driver.*

✔ *Install Plug and Play hardware.*

✔ *Install non-Plug and Play hardware.*

When a new graphic artist started work at Impact Public Relations, her office contained, among other things, a computer that had Microsoft Windows 2000 Professional installed. A printer and a digital camera were already attached to the computer, and a new scanner, still in the box, was on the table next to the printer. On her chair were CD-ROMs for Windows, illustration and design software, and software that would help her control the hardware attached to her computer. Although the digital camera and printer had been physically set up, she still needed to install software for the specific tasks of her job.

You'll find it necessary to install hardware and software on your computer from time to time. During installation, the files for the software are usually copied from a CD-ROM, a floppy disk, or a network drive to a folder on your hard disk. Installing software might also involve changing your computer so that Windows, the new software, and your hardware can work with one another. Most of this process is transparent to you, although you might be prompted to accept the changes made during installation.

In this lesson, you will discover how to add and remove programs that you acquire from other sources. You will also add and remove Microsoft Windows 2000 Professional components that are not part of the default installation. Next you will set up a printer to be shared with others on a network. Finally you will learn about other types of hardware and how to install them.

To complete the "Configuring Windows Components" and "Installing Plug and Play Hardware" exercises in this lesson, you will need to access Windows files (stored on either a CD-ROM or on the network), and you must have Administrator privileges on your computer. You will also need Administrator privileges to complete the "Installing Non-Plug and Play Hardware" exercise.

You will know that you don't have Administrator privileges if you see a message telling you that you aren't authorized to perform the actions described. If you see this message, you need to log off Windows and log back on, typing *Administrator* in the User Name box and typing *password* in the Password box. The Administrator account was created and the password was set when Windows was installed on your computer. The password for the Administrator account is *password* unless whoever installed Windows specified a different password or the password has since been changed. If a network administrator set up Windows on your system, you need to ask him or her for the correct password to use to log on as Administrator.

Sample files for the lesson ➡ To complete this lesson's procedures on installing and removing software, you will need to use a program called Microsoft Pandora's Box, which is located on the Microsoft Windows 2000 Professional Step by Step CD-ROM.

Configuring Windows Components

The typical installation of Windows includes all of its most frequently used components, such as Windows Explorer, the help system, and Control Panel. However, other Windows components will be installed only if you attempt to use them. These *install on first use* programs perform tasks that aren't used frequently or used by many users. Windows prompts you to insert the Microsoft Windows 2000 Professional CD-ROM when you first attempt to use one of these programs.

In this exercise, you add certain components of Internet Information Server that can work with Microsoft FrontPage 2000 to help you manage a Web site. To complete this lesson, you must have Administrator privileges and the Microsoft Windows 2000 Professional CD-ROM.

Start   **1**   Click the Start button, point to Settings, and then click Control Panel.

Control Panel appears.

2 In Control Panel, double-click the Add/Remove Programs icon.

The Add/Remove Programs window appears.

3 In the left side of the window, click the Add/Remove Windows Components icon.

The Windows Components Wizard appears. The available components are listed next to check boxes in the Components list. Any item in the Components list that has a checkmark is already installed. In the following example, the Indexing Service has already been installed on the computer.

Windows Components Wizard

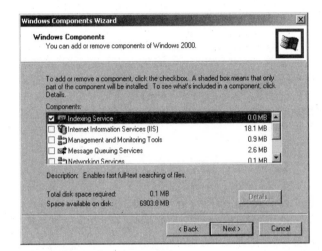

important

If there is already a checkmark to the left of Internet Information Services (IIS) in the Components list, it's already installed on your computer. Don't complete steps 4 through 8, or you will uninstall part of it. Instead, find an item in the Components list that is not checked, select its check box, and continue with step 5.

4 In the Components list, select the Internet Information Services (IIS) check box.

The Description area provides information about the component you have selected.

5 Click the Details button.

The Internet Information Services (IIS) dialog box appears. All subcomponents of Internet Information Services are selected.

The shaded check box next to Internet Information Services (IIS) indicates that only some of its subcomponents will be installed.

6 Clear all check boxes except Common Files, FrontPage 2000 Server Extentions, Internet Information Services Snap-In, and World Wide Web Server, and then click OK.

The Internet Information Services (IIS) dialog box closes, and the Windows Components Wizard reappears.

7 Click the Next button.

Windows begins to install the new component. After a moment, an Insert Disk dialog box appears.

8 Insert the Windows 2000 Professional CD-ROM into your CD-ROM drive, and click OK.

A **progress bar** appears. It shows you what percentage of the software has been installed. After the installation is complete, the Windows Components Wizard reports that installation was successful.

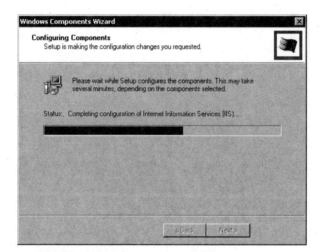

9 Click the Finish button.

The Windows Components Wizard closes.

10 Click the Close button in the Add/Remove Programs window.

The Add/Remove Programs window closes.

11 In Control Panel, double-click the Administrative Tools icon.

The Administrative Tools window appears. Note the Internet Services Manager icon. It provides a shortcut to the subcomponents you just installed.

*Administrative
Tools window*

*The Adminis-
trative Tools
window on
your computer
might look
different from
the one
shown here.*

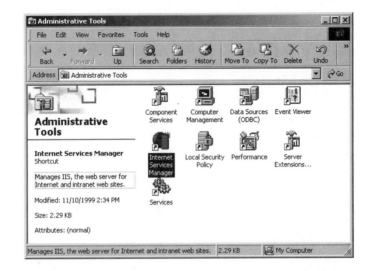

Close

12 Click the Close button in the top-right corner of the Administrative Tools window, and remove the Microsoft Windows 2000 Professional CD-ROM from the CD-ROM drive.

Installing Software

After you acquire software, you need to add, or **install,** it before you can use it. Some programs that are distributed on CD-ROM include an Autorun program. The Autorun program tells Windows to start the installation process as soon as you insert the CD-ROM. A wizard appears and leads you step by step through the installation process.

important

A computer **virus** (a program designed to damage or destroy data and programs on your hard disk) is often transmitted when you install new software that hasn't been thoroughly checked for viruses—typically software that has been downloaded from a site on the Internet. Therefore, many organizations have implemented policies that require software to be tested by computer-support personnel before it's installed. Check with your supervisor or network administrator about the policy in your organization before completing the following exercise.

In this exercise, you install the Microsoft Pandora's Box Trial program.

In the Multimedia folder on the Microsoft Windows Professional 2000 Step by Step CD-ROM, double-click the Install Software icon for a demonstration of how to install software.

1   Click the Start button, point to Settings, and click Control Panel.

Control Panel appears.

2   Double-click the Add/Remove Programs icon.

The Add/Remove Programs window appears.

3   In the left side of the window, click the Add New Programs icon.

You are prompted to add a program from a disk (CD-ROM or floppy) or from the Microsoft Windows Update site on the Web.

If Autorun appears, click the Exit button and proceed with the instructions in this exercise.

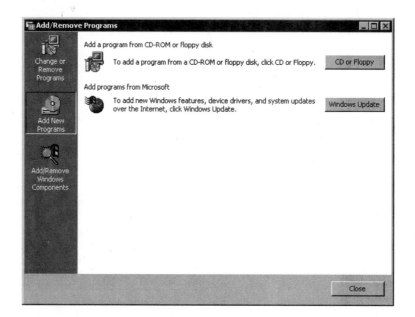

4   Click the CD Or Floppy button.

The Install Program From Floppy Disk Or CD-ROM dialog box appears.

5   Insert the Microsoft Windows 2000 Professional Step by Step CD-ROM for this book, and click the Next button.

Windows looks in the floppy drive and in the CD-ROM drive for a **setup.exe file** (a utility program that installs an application). It's unable to locate the installation program.

6   Click the Browse button.

The Browse dialog box appears.

tip
You can use Windows Explorer to examine the contents of a CD-ROM or floppy disk before you install software from it. If you find a file named Setup, it's usually the installation program.

7   Click the Look In arrow, and click the drive that represents your CD-ROM drive. Click the Files Of Type arrow, and click All Files.

The pandemo file appears in the File list.

8   Double-click the pandemo file name in the file list.

The Run Installation Program dialog box reappears. The setup file (pandemo.exe) appears in the Open box.

9   Click the Finish button.

The setup screen for Microsoft Pandora's Box appears.

Software and Hardware

9

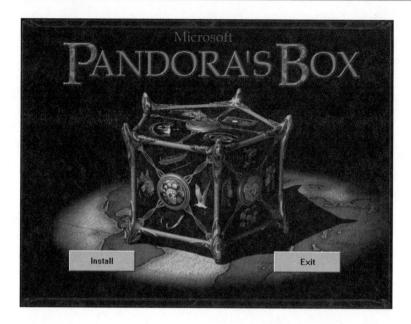

10   Click the Install button.

The End User License Agreement dialog box appears.

11   Read the agreement, and click the Accept button.

The Microsoft Pandora's Box Trial dialog box appears.

12   Click OK.

The File Copy dialog box displays the installation progress. Then an alert box appears, asking if you would like to install an icon on the desktop.

13   Click No.

An alert box appears, informing you that the trial version of Microsoft Pandora's Box has been successfully installed. It also provides instructions for starting the game.

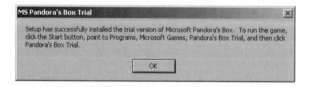

14   Click OK.

The Add/Remove Programs window reappears.

Close

15 Click the Close button in the Add/Remove Programs window, and click the Close button in the top-right corner of Control Panel.

   The Add/Remove Programs window and Control Panel close.

16 Click the Start button, point to Programs, point to Microsoft Games, point to Pandora's Box Trial, and then click Pandora's Box Trial.

   The Microsoft Pandora's Box program starts.

17 Click Esc.

   You are prompted to verify the decision.

18 Click Yes.

   You are prompted to either buy or exit the program.

19 Click Exit.

   The Microsoft Pandora's Box program closes.

20 Remove the CD-ROM from the CD-ROM drive.

Removing Software

When you no longer need a file, you can delete it. When you no longer need a program, you should **uninstall** it. Uninstalling not only deletes the files that were installed, it also removes any Windows settings that were created when the software was installed.

To uninstall most programs, you use the Add/Remove Programs window. However, some programs include an uninstall program when they're installed on the computer. For example, the Microsoft Pandora's Box Trial program that you installed in the previous exercise added an uninstall command on its menu. (To see the uninstall command, click the Start button, point to Programs, point to Microsoft Games, and point to Microsoft Pandora's Box Trial.) Instead of using the Add/Remove Programs window to uninstall Microsoft Pandora's Box Trial, you could navigate to the program's uninstall command from the Start menu, and click it.

In this exercise, you uninstall the Microsoft Pandora's Box program that you installed in the previous exercise. (Even though this program has an uninstall command, you use the Add/Remove Programs window so that you can learn how to uninstall programs that don't have an uninstall command.)

1 Click the Start button, point to Settings, and click Control Panel.

   Control Panel appears.

2   In Control Panel, double-click the Add/Remove Programs icon.

The Change Or Remove Programs button is the default option in the left side of the window, and the list of software that can be uninstalled is listed in the right side of the window.

3   Click MS Pandora's Box Trial Version.

The program name is selected.

The programs listed in the Add/Remove Programs window on your computer will probably be different from the programs listed here.

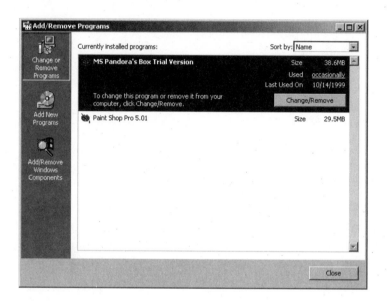

4   Click the Change/Remove button.

An alert box appears, asking you to confirm your decision.

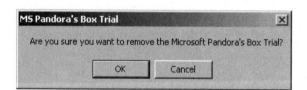

5   Click OK.

An alert box appears, informing you that Pandora's Box Trial has been successfully removed.

6 Click OK.

The Pandora's Box Trial program is removed from the Currently Installed Programs list in the Add/Remove Programs window.

Close

7 Click the Close button in the Add/Remove Programs window, and click the Close button in the top-right corner of Control Panel.

The Add/Remove Programs window and Control Panel close.

Adding a Printer Driver

A printer is the most common type of hardware that people add to their computers. In fact, many people have more than one printer available. You might have a printer attached locally to your computer; that is, the printer and computer are physically connected by means of a cable that plugs into the computer at one end and the printer at the other. You might also have access to printers that are shared on a network.

The art director at Impact Public Relations has access to three printers. His Printers folder is shown on the following page. You can learn information about the printers he uses by noting their icons.

Icon	Name	Description
	JustTogs	A network printer. It is physically connected to the Home computer on the Impact Public Relations network.
	Canon Bubble-Jet BJC-250	A local printer that only the art director can use. The checkmark on the printer's icon indicates that it is the art director's default printer. (This means that his documents will be printed from this printer unless he specifies a different printer.)
	HP Color LaserJet 5	A local printer that the art director shares with other people on the network.

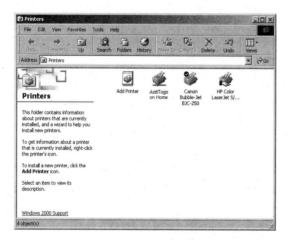

Whether a printer is local or networked, a driver for the printer must be installed on your computer before you can print to it. A driver is a program that Windows uses to operate a hardware device, such as a printer or monitor.

In this exercise, you install an HP Color LaserJet printer, like the one the art director uses. You also specify that the printer can be shared by others.

important

Even if you don't have an HP Color LaserJet printer, you can still complete the following exercise.

Alternatively, from the Control Panel, double-click the Printers icon.

1   Click the Start button, point to Settings, and click Printers.

The Printers window appears, listing the printers you already have installed.

2   Double-click the Add Printer icon.

The Add Printer Wizard appears.

3   Click the Next button, and verify that the Local Printer option is selected. Clear the Automatically Detect And Install My Plug And Play Printer check box, if necessary, and click the Next button.

You are prompted to select the **port** you want your printer to use. The port is the connection on the back of your computer to which the printer cable is attached.

LPT1 is an abbreviation for Line Printer 1.

4   Click LPT1, if necessary, and click the Next button.

You are prompted to specify the manufacturer and model of the printer.

5   In the Manufacturers list, scroll down, and click HP. In the Printers list, scroll down, and click HP Color LaserJet 5/5M PS.

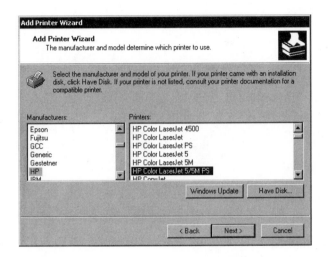

6   Click the Next button. If you are prompted to keep the existing driver, click the Next button again. (You would receive this message if you already have an installed printer that uses one or more of the same driver files as the printer you are installing uses.)

You are prompted to name the printer. As the wizard advises, keep the name short.

To make a printer the default after it is installed, right-click its icon in the Printers folder, and click Set As Default Printer on the shortcut menu.

7   In the Printer Name box, type **HP LJ5**.

8   In response to Do You Want Your Windows-Based Programs To Use This Printer As The Default Printer, click the No option, and then click the Next button.

You are prompted to specify whether you want to share the printer. If you share it, you might want to assign it a unique name that will help identify it to other people on the network.

9   Click the Share As option to select it, and in the Share As box, type **ArtColorLJ**.

Typing a name without spaces is advisable if you share a printer on a network that might also include computers that use a different operating system.

10   Click the Next button.

11   In the Location box, type **Art Department**, press Tab, and in the Comment box, type **Use only for final color proofs.**

This information will be available to other users if they use this printer.

12   Click the Next button, click the No option, and then click the Next button.

The last step in the Add Printer Wizard summarizes the choices you have made.

> ## tip
> When you work through a wizard in Windows and the summary screen appears, consider whether you need to make any changes based on the information displayed. If you decide to make a change, click the Back button until you return to the step where the change should be made. Make the desired changes, and continue to click the Next button until you return to the summary screen.

13   Click the Finish button.

The Add Printer Wizard closes, and an icon for the new printer appears in the Printers folder.

14   Click the HP LJ5 icon.

The information you entered in the wizard appears in the left side of the window.

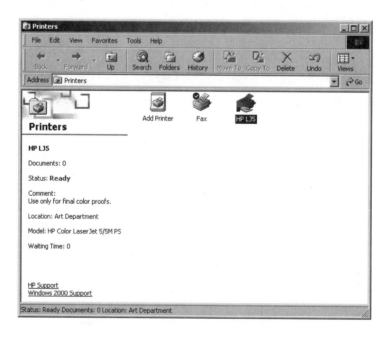

Close

15   Click the Close button in the top-right corner of the Printers window.

The Printers window closes.

Installing Plug and Play Hardware

Plug and Play hardware is a special class of printers, scanners, mice, digital cameras, and other devices that are designed to be automatically recognized by Windows. Plug and Play hardware is easy to install—you just plug it in and follow the steps in the Found New Hardware Wizard, which starts automatically. When computer manufacturers began discussing the creation of an industry-wide Plug and Play standard, the goal was for devices to configure themselves—with no help required from the user. However, in reality, this ideal goal is often not attained. For instance, many printers and monitors that advertise themselves as Plug and Play require the user to install a driver.

Using USB Hardware

If a hardware device is labeled **USB** (for Universal Serial Bus), it can probably take advantage of Plug and Play. A USB port is a small, rectangular opening, usually on the back of a computer, that fits a USB cable.

USB overcomes some of the limitations common with older types of ports (such as parallel and serial ports). You do not need to have a separate port for each piece of hardware you add to your computer. (Instead, you connect the first hardware device to your USB, and you connect other devices to one another.) Also, you can add and remove hardware without having to restart the computer. Most computers manufactured since the mid-1990s include one or more USB ports. USB printers, scanners, mice, digital cameras, disk drives, and other devices are available.

Software and Hardware

— USB ports

In this exercise, you install a Plug and Play scanner. To complete this exercise, you need to have Administrator privileges. You also need an actual piece of Plug and Play hardware. (Although a scanner is used in this exercise, the steps are similar for any Plug and Play device.) In addition, you might need to have the Microsoft Windows 2000 Professional CD-ROM available to complete this exercise.

1   Set up the scanner according to the manufacturer's instructions, and plug its cable into the appropriate port on your computer.

    The Found New Hardware message box briefly appears, and the Found New Hardware Wizard appears.

2   Click the Next button.

    The next step in the Found New Hardware Wizard explains the need to find a device driver for the scanner. The Search For A Suitable Driver For My Device (Recommended) option is selected.

3   Click the Next button.

    You are prompted to tell Windows where to search for the driver files.

4   If necessary, insert the CD-ROM or floppy disk into the appropriate drive. (If the disk you insert starts a setup or installation window, click Cancel.) In the Found New Hardware Wizard, verify that the drive check box is selected, and then click the Next button.

    When the device driver is found, the Found New Hardware Wizard displays a message similar to the following.

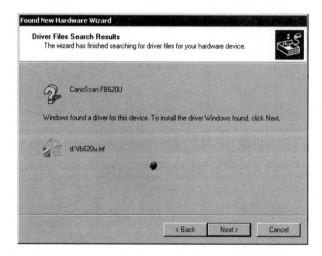

tip
A Digital Signature Not Found dialog box might appear if the driver files you're installing have not been tested by Microsoft. Click Yes to continue the installation.

5   If you're prompted to do so, insert the Windows 2000 Professional CD-ROM, and click the Next button.

Status messages appear briefly while the hardware is set up. Then the final step in the wizard appears, indicating that the hardware setup is complete.

6   Click the Finish button.

The Found New Hardware Wizard closes.

important
After your hardware is installed, additional software might still be needed for it to run. For example, a scanner usually comes with image-processing software. The installation program for that software might start automatically as soon as the Found New Hardware Wizard closes, or you might need to start it yourself. Refer to "Installing Software," explained earlier in this lesson, and the documentation that came with your hardware for more information.

Installing Non-Plug and Play Hardware

Plug and Play makes adding hardware easy, but not all hardware is Plug and Play. For hardware that is not recognized by the Found New Hardware Wizard, the Add/Remove Hardware Wizard walks you through the steps of setting up your equipment.

In this exercise, you install a Nikon CoolPix 900 digital camera using the Add/Remove Hardware Wizard. You don't need the camera to complete the exercise; however, you do need to have Administrator privileges.

1   Click the Start button, point to Settings, and then click Control Panel.

Control Panel appears.

2   In Control Panel, double-click the Add/Remove Hardware icon.

The Add/Remove Hardware Wizard appears.

Software and Hardware

3   Click the Next button.

The Choose A Hardware Task step appears. The default option, Add/Troubleshoot A Device is selected.

4   Click the Next button.

There is a pause while Windows searches for any Plug and Play hardware attached to your computer that hasn't yet been installed. Because there isn't any, it assumes you either want to troubleshoot an existing device or add one that isn't Plug and Play.

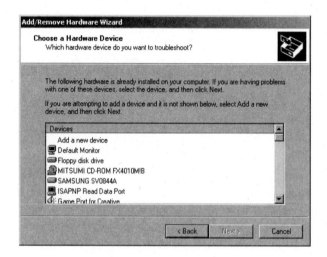

5   In the Devices list, click Add A New Device, and then click the Next button.

The Find New Hardware step appears. Unless the camera is attached to your computer, there's no point in having Windows look for it.

6   Click the No, I Want To Select The Hardware From A List option, and click the Next button.

You are prompted to select the type of hardware you want to install.

7   In the Hardware Types list, click Imaging Devices, and then click the Next button.

There is a pause while Windows searches for imaging device drivers. A list similar to the following appears.

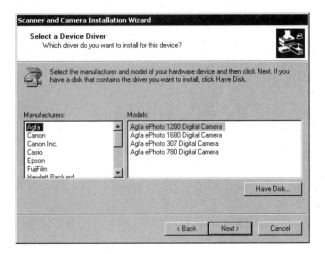

8   In the Manufacturers list, scroll to Nikon, and click it. In the Models list, click Nikon CoolPix 900 Digital Camera, and click the Next button.

The next step appears. In the Available Ports list, Automatic Port Select is selected by default.

> **tip**
>
> Not all equipment is listed in the Manufacturers or Models lists. But if you have a disk or CD-ROM from the manufacturer, the device driver is probably on it. Put the disk or CD-ROM in the drive, and click the Have Disk button. If that doesn't work, check Windows Update (which is explained in Lesson 2, "Getting Help When You Need It"), or contact the manufacturer for an updated device driver.

9   Click the Next button.

The default name for the camera appears in the Device Name box.

10   Click the Next button.

The wizard has all the information it needs to install the camera; it prompts you to click the Finish button.

11   Click the Finish button.

When installation is complete, the Add/Remove Hardware Wizard closes.

12   In Control Panel, double-click the Scanners And Cameras icon.

The Scanners And Camera Properties dialog box appears, and the Nikon CoolPix 900 Digital Camera is listed.

Software and Hardware

13   Click Cancel.

The Scanners And Camera Properties dialog box closes.

Uninstalling Hardware

To uninstall a printer, simply open the Printers folder from the Settings menu, click the printer's icon, click Delete on the Standard Buttons toolbar, and then click Yes to confirm the deletion. Performing these steps does not send the printer driver to the Recycle Bin; it permanently deletes it from your system.

To uninstall other hardware, whether it is Plug and Play or not, run the Add/Remove Hardware Wizard in Control Panel. In the Choose A Hardware Task step, click Uninstall/Unplug A Device, and click the Next button. In the Choose A Removal Task step, click Uninstall A Device, and click the Next button. In the Devices list, click the name of the hardware you want to uninstall, click the Next button, and then click the Yes, I Want To Uninstall This Device option. Click the Next button, and click Finish.

Lesson Wrap-Up

In this lesson, you used several wizards to change the hardware and software on your computer: the Windows Component Wizard, the Add Printer Wizard, the Found New Hardware Wizard, and the Add/Remove Hardware Wizard. You also used the Add/Remove Programs window to practice installing and uninstalling a program you acquired from another source.

To return all Windows components to their previous settings:

1   If necessary, open Control Panel from the Settings menu on the Start menu. In Control Panel, double-click Add/Remove Programs, and then click Add/Remove Windows Components. In the Windows Component Wizard, clear the check box to the left of Internet Information Services (IIS), and then complete the remaining steps in the wizard. Close the Add/Remove Programs window.

2   In Control Panel, double-click the Add/Remove Hardware icon. Click the Next button. In the Choose A Hardware Task step, click Uninstall/Unplug A Device. Click Next twice. In the Installed Devices On Your Computer step, click the Plug and Play hardware you installed (in the exercise, the scanner), and follow the remaining steps to uninstall the hardware.

3   Repeat step 2 for the Nikon CoolPix 900 digital camera installed in the last exercise, and close Control Panel.

4   Open the Printers window from the Settings menu on the Start menu. Click the HP LJ5 icon, press Delete, and then click Yes to confirm the deletion.

If you are continuing to other lessons:

●   Close all open windows. The desktop should be displayed.

If you are not continuing to other lessons:

1   Close all open windows, and click the Start button on the taskbar.

2   Click Shut Down on the Start menu. If necessary, click the arrow in the Windows Shut Down dialog box, and click Shut Down in the list. Then click OK.

3   After Windows has shut down, turn off the computer and, if necessary, all other hardware devices.

Glossary

Autorun A program that tells Windows to start the installation process as soon as you insert the CD-ROM.

driver A program that Windows uses to operate a hardware device, such as a printer or monitor.

install To set up hardware or software to work with a computer, printer, or other hardware. Many programs include a setup utility that does most of the work of setting up the program.

Plug and Play A set of specifications that allows a computer to automatically recognize hardware (such as a printer, scanner, monitor, modem, or mouse) that becomes connected to the computer; the computer configures itself to work with the external hardware. Users can "plug" hardware into a computer, and "play" it without having to install and set up additional software.

port A channel through which data is transferred between the computer's processor and an input device, such as an external disk drive, or an output device, such as a printer. Hardware cables are attached to ports on the back of a computer's central processing unit (CPU).

progress bar A visual representation that tracks the percentage of completion for a task, such as the installation of software.

setup.exe file A utility program that does most of the work of installing software or hardware.

Glossary

uninstall To remove software and all files, components, and Windows settings associated with it from a computer system.

USB An abbreviation for Universal Serial Bus. A port that can connect external hardware, such as a scanner or printer, to a computer system through a single, general-purpose port. A single USB port can support multiple devices that can be connected externally through additional USB ports located on the hardware devices. This approach is sometimes called "daisy chaining."

virus A program that damages or destroys files on a hard disk by inserting copies of itself into those files.

Quick Reference

To add a Windows component

1   Click the Start button, point to Settings, and then click Control Panel.

2   In Control Panel, double-click the Add/Remove Programs icon.

3   Click the Add/Remove Windows Components icon.

4   Follow the steps in the Windows Component Wizard, clicking the Next button to move from one step to the next.

5   Click the Finish button in the last step of the Windows Component Wizard, and close the Add/Remove Programs Window and Control Panel.

To add software

1   Click the Start button, point to Settings, and then click Control Panel.

2   In Control Panel, double-click the Add/Remove Programs icon.

3   Click the Add New Programs icon.

4   Click the CD Or Floppy button, insert the CD-ROM or floppy disk, and click the Next button.

5   If necessary, click the Browse button, and use the Browse dialog box to find the program to install.

6   Click the Finish button, and close Control Panel.

7   Follow the instructions on your screen to complete the set up process.

Quick Reference

To remove software

1   Click the Start button, point to Settings, and then click Control Panel.

2   In Control Panel, double-click the Add/Remove Programs icon.

3   Click the Add/Remove Windows Components icon.

4   In the Currently Installed Programs list, click the program to uninstall, and then click the Change/Remove button.

5   If prompted, insert the program's CD-ROM or follow any specific uninstallation instructions that appear.

6   Click OK, if necessary, to complete the uninstallation, and then close Control Panel.

To add a printer

1   Click the Start button, point to Settings, and then click Printers.

2   In the Printers window, double-click the Add Printer icon.

3   Follow the steps in the Add Printer Wizard, clicking the Next button to move from one step to the next.

4   Click the Finish button in the last step of the Add Printer Wizard.

5   Click the Close button in the top-right corner of the Printers Window.

To install Plug and Play hardware

1   Set up the hardware according to the manufacturer's instructions, and plug its cable into the appropriate port on your computer.

2   Follow the steps in the Found New Hardware Wizard, clicking the Next button to move from one step to the next.

3   Click the Finish button in the last step of the Found New Hardware Wizard.

To install non-Plug and Play hardware

1   Click the Start button, point to Settings, and then click Control Panel.

2   In Control Panel, double-click the Add/Remove Hardware icon.

3   Follow the steps in the Add/Remove Hardware Wizard, clicking the Next button to move from one step to the next.

4   Click the Finish button in the last step of the wizard, and close Control Panel.

Software and Hardware

9

10

Maintaining Peak Performance

**ESTIMATED
TIME**
40 min.

After completing this lesson, you will be able to:

✔ *Reclaim space on a hard disk.*

✔ *Speed up access to your files by defragmenting.*

✔ *Find and fix problems on a hard disk.*

✔ *Back up and restore data.*

✔ *Schedule automatic maintenance.*

Imagine you've just bought your dream house. At first, you're happy just to enjoy the house as it is. After a while, though, you realize it's time to make some repairs and changes. You might need to caulk the windows or fix a leaky pipe. Maybe you need to reorganize a closet to use its space better. Like most home owners, you probably realize that conducting routine maintenance lowers your overall costs and increases your overall satisfaction.

Your computer is like that dream house. A little maintenance now and then with the easy-to-use tools provided by Microsoft Windows 2000 Professional pays big dividends in keeping your system running smoothly.

In this lesson, you will learn how the Disk Cleanup, Disk Defragmenter, and Check Disk tools help keep your hard disk efficient and error-free. You will also learn how the Backup and Restore Wizards help guard against loss of valuable files. Finally, you will use the Scheduled Task Wizard to ensure regularly scheduled maintenance.

To complete the exercises in the "Freeing Up Disk Space" and "Defragmenting A Disk" sections of this lesson, you must have Administrator privileges. You will know that you aren't logged on with Administrator privileges when you see a message on screen telling you that you aren't authorized to perform the specified actions. If you see this message, you need to log off Windows and log back on, typing *Administrator* in the User Name box and typing *password* in the Password box. The Administrator account was created and the password was set when Windows was installed on your computer. The password for the Administrator account is *password* unless whoever installed Windows specified a different password or the password has since been changed. If a network administrator set up Windows on your system, you need to ask him or her for the Administrator password. In the "Backing Up Data" exercise in this lesson, you will back up data in the Windows 2000 Practice folder.

Sample files for the lesson ⇨

Freeing Up Disk Space

It's important to keep your hard disk uncluttered and running smoothly because it's the primary storage location for many programs. Suppose you've cleaned up your hard disk by uninstalling programs you never use, as discussed in the previous lesson. Or perhaps you've deleted old pictures and documents, as discussed in Lesson 3, "Managing Files and Folders." You could still have unnecessary files on your computer. It's not unusual for programs to create "temporary" files that remain on your hard disk long after they're needed.

Web browsers, such as Microsoft Internet Explorer, copy files from the Web sites you visit so that the sites load faster if you revisit them. Similarly, files that you open from a network are sometimes copied to your hard disk for faster access. If you don't revisit those Web sites or use those files from the network, the files are useless, and they can waste a lot of space. Fortunately, Windows provides **Disk Cleanup**, a utility that finds and removes unnecessary files.

Before you use Disk Cleanup or the other tools discussed in this lesson for optimizing a hard disk, you should find out how much space is available on your hard disk. To do this, double-click the My Computer icon on the desktop, and click the Local Disk icon. (If you have more than one hard disk, click the one that you want to check. If you've renamed the hard disk, click the name that ends (C:).) The left side of the My Computer window provides information about the total capacity of your hard disk: how much space is being used and how much space is available. A good rule of thumb is to keep at least 10 percent of your hard disk space available for the temporary files that Windows and programs can create.

tip

To reduce the amount of disk space reserved for temporary Internet files, open Control Panel from the Start menu. Double-click Internet Options, and verify that the General tab in the Internet Properties dialog box is displayed. In the Temporary Internet Files section, click the Settings button. The Settings dialog box appears. In the Amount Of Disk Space To Use section, drag the slider to the left or click the arrows in the MB box to reduce the number of megabytes (MB) devoted to storing temporary Internet files. Click OK to close the Settings dialog box, and click OK to close the Internet Properties dialog box.

In this exercise, you find out how much space is available on your hard disk. Then you use Disk Cleanup to increase the amount of available space and delete temporary Internet files.

1   Double-click the My Computer icon on the desktop.

    The My Computer window appears.

2   Click the Local Disk icon. (If you have more than one hard disk, click the one that you want to check. If you've renamed the hard disk, click the name that ends with (C:).)

    A pie chart appears in the left side of the window. It indicates the amount of free and used space on the disk. The amount of space is measured in either megabytes (MB) or gigabytes (GB), depending on the size of the hard disk.

The pie chart for representing used and free disk space is new in Windows 2000.

A megabyte is about a million characters (or, to be precise, 1,048,576 bytes). A gigabyte is about a billion characters (1,073,741,824 bytes).

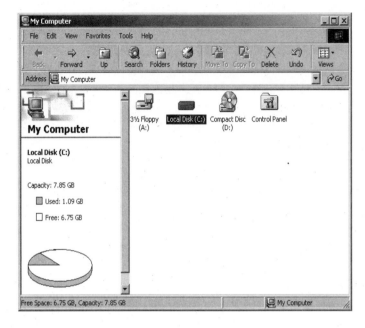

Alternatively, click the Start button, navigate through Programs, Accessories, and System Tools. On the System Tools menu, click Disk Cleanup.

3   Right-click the Local Disk icon.

A shortcut menu appears.

4   On the shortcut menu, click Properties.

The Local Disk Properties dialog box appears, and the General tab is displayed. Note the exact amount of free space, in bytes.

Disk cleanup and drive compression are new in Windows 2000.

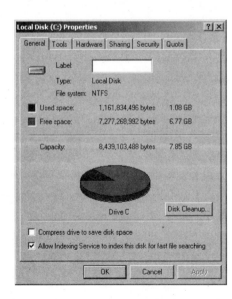

The Disk Cleanup button is available only when you open the Properties dialog box of a disk that is physically attached to your computer, not a disk that you are connecting to over a network.

5   Click the Disk Cleanup button.

A Disk Cleanup alert box appears briefly while Windows analyzes your disk. Then the Disk Cleanup dialog box appears.

6   Clear all check boxes, except the Temporary Internet Files check box.

Temporary Internet Files is the only item selected.

7   Click the name *Temporary Internet Files*. (Be careful not to clear the check box.)

A description of the Temporary Internet Files folder appears in the Description section.

8   Click the View Files button.

A window similar to the following appears.

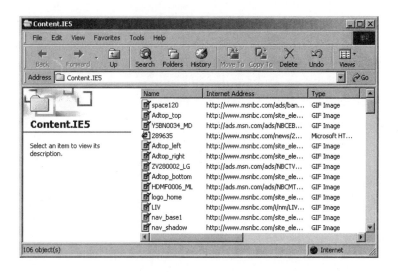

tip
If you find a file you want to keep, note its location in the Address box. Close the Disk Cleanup dialog box, and use Windows Explorer to copy the file from the location you noted to a folder you have created. Disk Cleanup doesn't affect folders that you create.

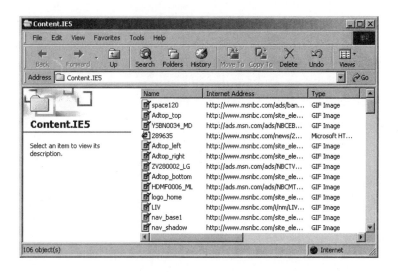

Close

9   Click the Close button in the top-right corner of the window.

The window closes.

10   Click OK in the Disk Cleanup dialog box, and click Yes to confirm your decision. A Disk Cleanup alert box flashes briefly on the screen while the files are deleted, and the Disk Cleanup dialog box closes. The amount of free space should have increased (unless you haven't used the Internet at all, in which case you never had any temporary Internet files).

Keep the Local Disk Properties dialog box open for the next exercise.

Defragmenting a Disk

Files and folders tend to get **fragmented,** or split into pieces to fit in the available spaces on a disk. The more often you save changes and the less disk space you have available, the more fragmented your files and folders will become. Having to pull together all the scattered pieces of a file to open it, as well as splitting the file again to resave it, can cause programs to run slowly.

Defragmenting changes the physical position of a fragmented file or folder on the disk so that it is saved in one continuous chunk of storage space instead of scattered across the hard disk. This process doesn't have any effect on the folder structure you see in the Folders pane.

Because defragmenting involves moving pieces of files and folders throughout your disk, it can take a long time to complete—sometimes several hours. Therefore, Windows analyzes your disk to help you decide whether it's fragmented enough to make defragmenting worth your time.

In this exercise, you use the Disk Defragmenter to analyze the way files and folders are stored on the hard disk. Then you start the process of defragmenting the disk so you can see how it works.

Alternatively, from the Start button, navigate through Programs, Accessories, and System Tools. On the System Tools menu, click Disk Defrag-menter.

1   Click the Tools tab in the Local Disk Properties dialog box, and click the Defragment Now button.

The Disk Defragmenter window appears.

2   Click the Analyze button in the bottom-left corner of the Disk Defragmenter window.

After a short pause, the Analysis Complete dialog box appears and reports whether the disk (referred to here as a **volume**) needs to be defragmented.

3   In the Analysis Complete dialog box, click the View Report button.

The Analysis Report dialog box appears. It provides detailed information about the disk.

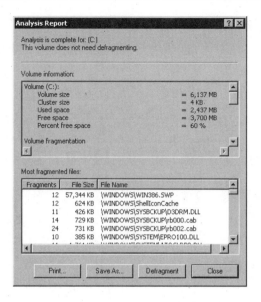

tip
You can print or save the Analysis Report by clicking the Print or Save As buttons in the bottom of the dialog box. All the information in the Analysis Report dialog box is converted to a text file that you can keep for later review.

4 In the Volume Information section, scroll down to view the percentages of volume and file fragmentation.

The Disk Defragmenter can run in the background while you use other programs.

5 In the bottom of the dialog box, click the Defragment button.

The Analysis Report dialog box closes. After a pause, the Defragmentation Analysis box begins to display the progress of the defragmentation.

Maintaining Peak Performance   10

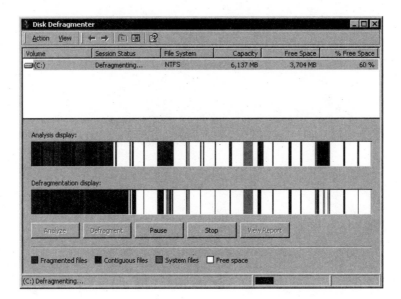

6   After you have run the Disk Defragmenter long enough to see a difference between the Analysis Display and the Defragmentation Display, click the Stop button.

The two display bars return to their original gray color.

Close

7   Click the Close button in the top-right corner of the Disk Defragmenter window.

The Disk Defragmenter window closes.

Keep the Local Disk Properties dialog box open for the next exercise.

Checking a Disk for Errors

Like any other mechanical device, a disk can have flaws that affect its performance. For example, it might have **bad sectors**, which are small areas of the disk that are physically damaged and should be marked by Windows as being unusable. Problems might also develop with the part of the disk that keeps track of where different files are stored (called the **file system**). To help you fix these problems, Windows provides the Check Disk tool.

In this exercise, you run Check Disk to look for bad sectors on a hard disk.

1   On the Tools tab in the Local Disk Properties dialog box, click the Check Now button.

The Check Disk dialog box appears.

2   Select the Scan For And Attempt Recovery Of Bad Sectors check box, and
     click the Start button.

     Windows checks for bad sectors. This process can take several minutes.
     When the process completes, the Checking Disk dialog box appears.

3   Click OK.

     The Checking Disk dialog box closes.

     Keep the Local Disk Properties dialog box open for the next exercise.

important

You can fix problems with a disk's file system only when the disk isn't in use. So
if you select the Automatically Fix File System Errors check box (in the Check
Disk dialog box) for your hard disk, a message appears notifying you that Windows cannot obtain "exclusive access to the drive." Click Yes to schedule Check
Disk the next time the computer starts.

Backing Up Data

Backup Wizard

Backing up your data involves copying important files and storing them in a
separate location. Backing up your data is one of those chores that can save
you an enormous amount of trouble if your hard disk should ever fail.
When you back up data, Windows copies the files to the backup disk or tape
you specify. Then if the data is damaged or accidentally deleted, you can restore
it from the backup.

Maintaining Peak Performance 10

The size and frequency of your backup depends on the way you use your computer. One of the computer systems at Lakewood Mountains Resort, for example, stores all guest information, including critical billing information, in a reservations database. The hard disk in that computer needs to be backed up every day so its contents can be duplicated quickly in the event of an emergency. The hard disk is backed up to a set of removable hard disks, each holding several gigabytes of data. They are stored offsite for added security.

At the other extreme, the president of Impact Public Relations has a laptop she uses primarily for writing reports and giving presentations when she travels. In the course of a trip, she generates about a half-dozen new files, all stored in a folder on the hard disk. She simply backs up this folder to a floppy disk once or twice a week.

important

If your computer is connected to a network, your organization might already have established procedures for backing up your data. Contact your network administrator for more information.

Alternatively, from the Start menu, navigate through Programs, Accessories, and System Tools. On the System Tools menu, click Backup.

In this exercise, you back up the Windows 2000 Practice folder. To keep this exercise simple, you will back up data to your hard disk; however, you should always back up live data to another disk or to a tape.

1   On the Tools tab in the Local Disk Properties dialog box, click the Backup Now button.

   The Backup window appears.

In the Multi-media folder on the Microsoft Windows 2000 Professional Step by Step CD-ROM, double-click the File Backup icon, for a demonstration of how to back up specific files from the Start menu.

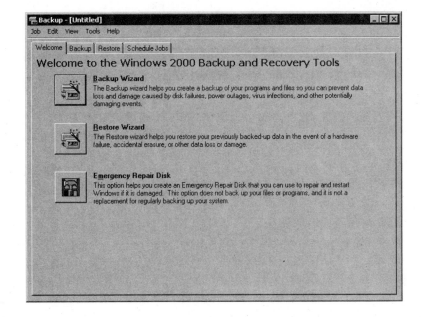

Backup Wizard

2   On the Welcome tab, click the Backup Wizard button.

The Backup Wizard dialog box appears.

3   Click the Next button.

You are prompted to specify what you want to back up.

4   Click the Back Up Selected Files, Drives, Or Network Data option, and click the Next button.

You are prompted to select the desired disk drives, folders, or files to back up. This step looks similar to the Folders pane in Windows Explorer.

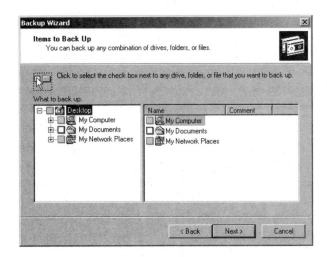

Maintaining Peak Performance **10**

tip

In addition to the plus and minus signs that expand and collapse folders, check boxes are displayed for selecting disk drives, folders, or files to back up. Certain items, such as the desktop, have gray check boxes that cannot be selected; you have to click the plus sign to expand the folder, and navigate to the desired disk drive, folder, or file to be backed up.

5   In the left pane, click the plus sign to the left of My Computer.

The My Computer folder expands.

6   In the left pane, click the plus sign to the left of C: (or the letter that designates your hard disk).

The hard disk folder expands.

If you want to back up only a few files in the Windows 2000 Practice folder, click the Windows 2000 Practice folder in the left pane, and click the check boxes for the desired files in the right pane.

7   In the left pane, select the check box to the left of the Windows 2000 Practice folder.

You have selected all the contents of the Windows 2000 Practice folder, including any subfolders.

tip

After you've performed a few backups, you might want to skip directly to the Backup tab on the Backup window instead of using the Backup Wizard. In the section titled Click To Select The Check Box For Any Drive, Folder, Or File That You Want To Backup, select the resources to back up. In the Backup Destination section, select the desired destination.

8   Click the Next button.

You are prompted to specify the backup storage location.

If you're not sure of the name of the drive or folder where backups are stored, you can search for it by clicking the Browse button in the Backup Wizard dialog box. Then expand the Look In list in the Open dialog box.

important

Ordinarily, you would type the name of the disk or tape drive you are using for backups in the Backup Media Or File Name box. In this exercise, though, you will create a file on the hard disk to store the backed up files.

9   Type **C:\practice backup** (if necessary, substitute the *C* with the appropriate drive letter for the hard disk you want to use), and click the Next button.

The final step in the Backup Wizard summarizes the choices you've made.

10   Click the Finish button.

The Backup Progress dialog box appears.

11   Note the date and time when you created the backup, as well as its location and name.

You will need this information if you create other backups before you begin the next exercise in this lesson.

12   In the Backup Progress dialog box, click the Close button.

The Backup Progress dialog box closes, and the Backup window reappears.

Keep the Backup window open for the next exercise.

Creating an Emergency Repair Disk

An **emergency repair disk** contains files needed to start and run Windows if the Windows files on your hard disk are damaged or accidentally deleted. Some of these files are normally hidden, so they probably wouldn't be included as part of a regular backup.

To create an emergency repair disk from the Welcome tab in the Backup window, click the Emergency Repair Disk button. Select the Also Back Up The Registry To The Repair Directory check box to include information about the way your system is configured. Next put a blank floppy disk in the floppy disk drive, and click OK in the Emergency Repair Diskette dialog box. A progress bar appears in the dialog box, followed by a message reminding you to label the disk and store it in a safe place. Click OK to close the dialog box.

Restoring Data

When everything is working on your computer, backing up data can seem like a nuisance. However, you will be glad you took the time if the day comes when you need that backed-up data. The Restore Wizard simplifies the restoration process for you, so that you can move on to other concerns.

In this exercise, you simulate an emergency in which the Windows 2000 Practice folder is accidentally erased. Then you run the Restore Wizard to solve the problem, using the backup file you created in the previous exercise.

1   Click the Minimize button in the top-right corner of the Backup window.

The Backup window appears as only a button on the taskbar, and the Local Disk Properties dialog box becomes the active window.

2   Click the Cancel button in the Local Disk Properties dialog box.

The Local Disk Properties dialog box closes.

3   Click the Folders button in the My Computer window.

The Folders pane appears in the left side of the window.

4   In the Folders pane, double-click Local Disk.

The Local Disk window appears.

important

Make sure the Windows 2000 Practice folder, and only that folder, is selected before you proceed to step 5. You are going to permanently delete the folder rather than send it to the Recycle Bin. However, if for some reason, you are unable to restore this folder, you can still follow the steps in the "Using the Microsoft Windows 2000 Professional Step by Step CD-ROM" section in the beginning of the book to return the files to your hard disk.

5   In the right pane of the window, click the Windows 2000 Practice folder.

The Windows 2000 Practice folder is selected.

6   Hold down Shift, and press Delete.

The Confirm Folder Delete dialog box appears.

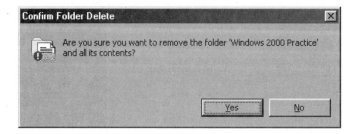

7   Click Yes to confirm the deletion.

The Windows 2000 Practice folder is permanently deleted from your hard disk.

> **tip**
> Holding down Shift and pressing Delete bypasses the Recycle Bin, causing Windows to permanently delete the selected files and folders.

Minimize

8 Click the Minimize button in the top-right corner of the Local Disk window.

The Local Disk window appears as only a button on the taskbar.

9 Click the Backup button on the taskbar.

The Backup window reappears.

10 On the Welcome tab, click the Restore Wizard button.

The Restore Wizard dialog box appears.

Restore Wizard

11 Click the Next button.

You are prompted to specify which backup you want to restore.

Drag the bar that separates the two panes to the right, if necessary, so you can see the date and time for each backup.

12 In the left pane, click the plus sign to the left of *File*.

If you have backed up folders or files before now, there will be several folders listed below File. Otherwise, there will be only one folder—the backup you created in the previous exercise.

13 Click the plus sign to the left of the Media icon that represents the date and time when you created the backup in the previous exercise.

The hard disk folder appears when you expand the Media branch.

14 In the left pane, select the hard disk check box.

A checkmark appears in the check box.

The folder with the question mark to the left of the hard disk folder indicates that one or more specific files or folders were backed up from the hard disk.

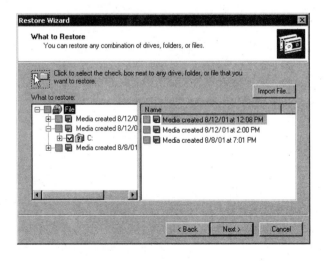

Maintaining Peak Performance 10

15 Click the Next button.

The final step in the Restore Wizard summarizes the choices you've made.

16 Click the Finish button.

The Enter Backup File Name dialog box appears.

17 If necessary, type **c:\practice backup** (substitute the appropriate drive letter for the hard disk you want to use, if it isn't labeled "C:"), and click OK.

The Restore Progress dialog box tracks the result of the restore process. When the restore process finishes, the dialog box should look similar to the following.

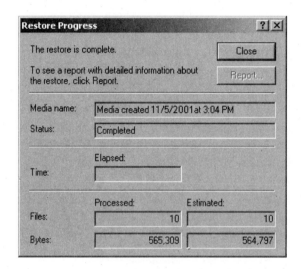

18 Click the Close button in the Restore Progress dialog box, and click the Close button in the top-right corner of the Backup window.

The Restore Progress dialog box and the Backup window close.

19 Click the Local Disk button on the taskbar.

The Local Disk window appears. Note that the Windows 2000 Practice folder has been restored.

20 Click the Close button in the top-right corner of the Local Disk window.

The Local Disk window closes, and the desktop reappears.

Close

Close

Scheduling Maintenance

Scheduling Maintenance

It's one thing to acknowledge that you should run tools like Backup and Disk Defragmenter on a regular basis; it's quite another to actually remember to do it. Fortunately, the Scheduled Task Wizard can automate the backup process for you. You choose the tasks you want to run and how often you want to run them, and Windows handles the rest. For example, the network administrator at Lakewood Mountains Resort schedules system backup to occur every day at 2 A.M., when the computer system is not in high demand.

In this exercise, you schedule Disk Cleanup to run every time you log on to the computer. (Normally, you would not need to run Disk Cleanup this often. For this exercise, you want to see the result of scheduling a task without having to wait or change the Windows calendar to a different day.)

You can also open the Scheduled Tasks folder by clicking the Start button, pointing to Settings, clicking Control Panel, and then double-clicking Scheduled Tasks.

1   Click the Start button, point to Programs, and then point to Accessories.

The Accessories submenu appears.

2   On the Accessories submenu, point to System Tools, and click Scheduled Tasks.

The Scheduled Tasks window appears.

The Windows Critical Update Notification icon is from Windows Update, which is discussed in Lesson 2, "Getting Help When You Need it."

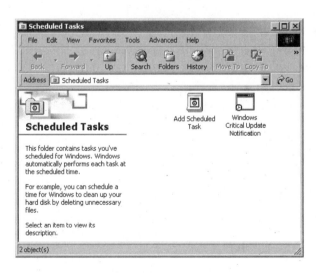

If you were scheduling a task to occur daily, weekly, or monthly, the Scheduled Task Wizard would prompt you to enter information about the time, day, and frequency for the task.

3   Double-click the Add Scheduled Task icon.

The Scheduled Task Wizard dialog box appears.

4   Click the Next button.

You are prompted to click the program you want Windows to run.

5   Scroll down the Application list, and click Disk Cleanup.

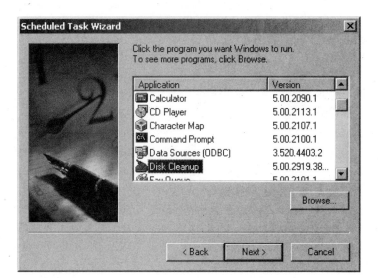

6   Click the Next button.

You are prompted to name the task and choose how often it should be performed.

7   Click the When I Log On option, and click the Next button.

You are prompted to identify yourself to Windows.

8   Click in the Enter The Password box, and type the password you use to log on to Windows. Press Tab to move to the Confirm Password box, and type your password again. (Windows already knows your user name, so you don't need to type it.) Click the Next button.

The final step in the Scheduled Task Wizard summarizes the choices you've made.

9   Click the Finish button.

Disk Cleanup

The Scheduled Task Wizard closes, and an icon for the Disk Cleanup task appears in the Scheduled Tasks window.

10   Click the Minimize button in the top-right corner of the Scheduled Tasks window.

The Scheduled Tasks window appears as only a button on the taskbar.

11   Click the Start button, and click Shut Down.

The Shut Down Windows dialog box appears.

12   Click the arrow, click Log Off in the list, and then click OK.

Windows logs you off. After a pause, the Log On To Windows dialog box appears.

If the Welcome To Windows dialog box appears, follow the instructions before logging on.

13   Type your password, and click OK.

As soon as you log on, the Select Drive dialog box appears. The Scheduled Tasks window also appears (behind the Select Drive dialog box).

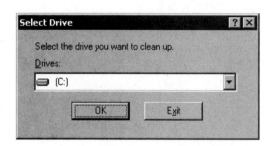

14   In the Select Drive dialog box, click Exit.

The Select Drive dialog box closes.

Delete

15   On the taskbar, click the Scheduled Tasks button, and click the Disk Cleanup icon. Click the Delete button, and click Yes to confirm the decision.

The Disk Cleanup icon is removed from the Scheduled Tasks window.

Close

16   Click the Close button in the top-right corner of the Scheduled Tasks window.

The Scheduled Tasks window closes.

Lesson Wrap-Up

In this lesson, you learned how to use the Windows tools Disk Cleanup, Disk Defragmenter, and Check Disk to keep your computer running in optimal condition. You also learned how to use the Backup and Restore Wizards to prepare for and recover from a situation that permanently damages the data on your computer. Finally, you learned how to simplify these maintenance chores by running them automatically, using the Scheduled Task Wizard.

To return all Windows components to their previous settings:

●   Double-click the My Computer icon on the desktop. Double-click Local Disk, click Practice Backup, and then press Delete. Click Yes to confirm the deletion. Close the Local Disk window.

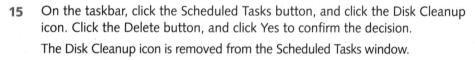

Maintaining Peak Performance 10

If you are continuing to the Review & Practice:

●   Close all open windows. The desktop should be displayed.

If you have finished reading this book:

1   Close all open windows. The desktop should be displayed.

2   Click Shut Down on the Start menu. If necessary, click the arrow in the Windows Shut Down dialog box, and click Shut Down in the list. Then click OK.

3   After Windows has shut down, turn off the computer and, if necessary, all other hardware.

Glossary

bad sectors Small areas of the disk that are physically damaged and should be marked by Windows as being unusable..

backing up Copying important files and storing them in a separate location.

defragmenting Rewriting parts of a file to adjacent sectors of a disk to increase the speed of access and retrieval of the file.

Disk Cleanup A Windows program that searches a disk and lists unnecessary files that you can delete, such as temporary files, Internet cache files, and unused program files.

emergency repair disk Also called a startup disk, a floppy disk that contains the files necessary to start and run Windows in the event that the Windows files on the hard disk are damaged or deleted.

file system The structure in which files are named, stored, and organized.

fragmented A state of a disk in which parts of files are split and scattered over different sectors of a disk so that they fit on the disk.

volume A disk or tape that stores computer data. Another word for disk.

Quick Reference

To clean up wasted disk space on the hard disk

1   Double-click the My Computer icon on the desktop, and click the Local Disk icon.

2   Right-click the Local Disk icon.

3   On the shortcut menu, click Properties, and on the General tab, click the Disk Cleanup button.

Quick Reference

To clean up wasted disk space on the hard disk (*continued*)

4   Make the desired choices in the Disk Cleanup dialog box, and click OK.

5   Click Yes to confirm the cleanup.

To defragment the hard disk

1   Double-click the My Computer icon on the desktop, and click the Local Disk icon.

2   Right-click the Local Disk icon.

3   On the shortcut menu, click Properties, and on the Tools tab, click the Defragment Now button.

4   Click the Analyze button, click the View Report button if necessary, and then click the Defragment button.

5   Click the Close button in the top-right corner of the Disk Defragmenter window when defragmenting finishes.

To check the hard disk for errors

1   Double-click the My Computer icon on the desktop, and right-click the Local Disk icon.

2   Right-click the Local Disk icon.

3   On the shortcut menu, click Properties, and on the Tools tab, click the Check Now button.

4   Make the desired choices in the Check Disk dialog box, and click the Start button.

5   Click OK when the process is complete.

To back up data on the hard disk

1   Double-click the My Computer icon on the desktop, and right-click the Local Disk icon.

2   Right-click the Local Disk icon.

3   On the shortcut menu, click Properties, and on the Tools tab, click the Backup Now button.

4   Click the Backup Wizard button, and follow the steps.

5   Click the Finish button when you are finished.

6   Click the Close button.

Maintaining Peak Performance   10

Quick Reference

To restore data on the hard disk

1   Double-click the My Computer icon on the desktop, and right-click the Local Disk icon.

2   Right-click the Local Disk icon.

3   On the shortcut menu, click Properties. On the Tools tab, click the Backup Now button, click the Restore Wizard button, and then follow the steps.

4   Click the Finish button when you are finished.

5   Click the Close button.

To schedule maintenance to occur automatically

1   Click the Start button, and navigate through the Programs, Accessories, and System Tools menus.

2   On the System Tools menu, click Scheduled Tasks.

3   Double-click the Add Scheduled Task icon, and follow the steps in the Scheduled Task Wizard.

4   Click the Finish button when you are finished.

5   Shut down your computer and log off.

3

Review & Practice

**ESTIMATED
TIME
30 min.**

You will review and practice how to:

✔ *Customize the desktop.*
✔ *Apply a power scheme.*
✔ *Create a dial-up connection.*
✔ *Add a printer driver.*
✔ *Reduce wasted disk space.*
✔ *Back up the contents of a folder.*
✔ *Delete a folder and restore it using the backup.*

Before you complete this book, you can practice the skills you learned in Unit 3 by working through this Review & Practice. In this section, you will customize the desktop, create a dial-up connection to a network, customize a power scheme, and install a printer driver. Finally, you will use Disk Cleanup and the Backup Wizard to maximize the efficiency of your hard disk.

Scenario

The sales director at Impact Public Relations (IPR) travels extensively. He has recently installed Microsoft Windows 2000 Professional on his laptop, and he needs to customize his desktop and update his presentation while on the plane to his next meeting. (In order to meet these goals, he'll need to conserve power on his laptop.) When he arrives at his destination, he'll not only need to dial up to the IPR network, he'll also need to print the notes for his presentation. On the return flight, he plans to clean up the laptop's hard disk.

Review & Practice

Step 1:   Modify the Windows Desktop

Change the desktop background to Paradise, the color scheme to Teal, and the screen saver to 3D Maze. Change the screen saver so that, after one minute, only someone who has the password can access the laptop.

1   Open the Display Properties dialog box.

2   Note the current settings for the display so that you can reset them later.

3   On the Background tab, click the Paradise background, and center it on the desktop.

4   On the Appearance tab, click the Teal scheme.

5   Apply the changes you've made so far.

6   On the Screen Saver tab, click the 3D Maze screen saver. Password protect the screen saver, and have it start when Windows is idle for more than one minute.

7   Click OK, and wait for the screen saver to appear.

8   Stop the screen saver, and log back on to Windows.

For more information about	See
Changing the appearance of the desktop	Lesson 7
Applying a screen saver	Lesson 7

Step 2:   Apply a Power Scheme

Create a power scheme based on the Laptop/Portable scheme that goes on Stand By quickly when the computer is idle.

1   Open the Power Options Properties dialog box.

2   On the Power Schemes tab, note the current power settings so that you can reset them later.

3   Click the Portable/Laptop power scheme, and set Turn Off Monitor to After 1 Minute so that the system goes on Stand By after one minute.

4   Save the modified power scheme using the name **My Laptop**.

5   Apply the scheme, and close all open dialog boxes.

6   Test the scheme by waiting one minute for Stand By.

7   Redisplay the desktop.

For more information about	See
Using power schemes	Lesson 8

Step 3:   Create a Dial-Up Connection

Enable the computer to connect to a network in a remote location by dialing the telephone number of a server on that network.

1   In the Network And Dial-Up Connections folder, start the process of making a new connection.

2   In the Network Connection Wizard, create a dial-up connection to a private network.

3   Complete the remaining steps in the wizard, choosing the options you prefer. For the telephone number, use your own office or home number, or use an actual network number.

4   When you are prompted to dial the network, if you entered a real network number, type your user name and password, and dial the number. Otherwise, close the dialog box.

5   If necessary, disconnect from the network. Close all open dialog boxes.

For more information about	See
Creating a dial-up network connection	Lesson 8

Step 4:   Add a Printer Driver

Use the Add Printer Wizard to install a printer driver on your computer.

1   Open the Printers folder, and note the types of printers installed.

2   Start the Add Printer Wizard.

3   Add a local printer connected to LPT1.

4   Choose any manufacturer and printer you want (other than ones already installed) for this fictional connection.

5   Complete the remaining steps in the wizard, making sure the new printer is not set as the default.

6   Close all dialog boxes and windows.

For more information about	See
Adding a printer driver	Lesson 9

Step 5:   Run Disk Cleanup

Remove the temporary Internet files on your computer to increase available disk space.

1   Start Disk Cleanup.

2   Choose your primary hard disk (probably drive C) for cleanup.

3   Delete temporary Internet files only.

For more information about	See
Freeing up disk space	Lesson 10

Step 6:   Back Up and Restore a Folder

Back up the Windows 2000 Practice folder. Delete the folder, and then restore it using the backup.

1   Start the Backup Wizard.

2   Select the Windows 2000 Practice folder from your hard disk as the folder to back up.

3   Back up the folder to a floppy disk, if possible. Otherwise, use the Browse button in the Backup Wizard to back up the folder to My Documents. Name the backup **Backup Practice**.

4   Complete the remaining steps in the Wizard.

5   When backup is complete, close the Backup Progress dialog box, and minimize the Backup window.

6   Delete the Windows 2000 Practice folder from its original location on your hard disk.

7   Maximize the Backup window, and use the Restore Wizard to return the Windows 2000 Practice folder to its original location on your hard disk.

8   Close all open dialog boxes and windows.

9   Using either Windows Explorer or My Computer, confirm that the Windows 2000 Practice folder was restored, and close the window.

For more information about	See
Backing up data	Lesson 10
Restoring data	Lesson 10

Finish the Review & Practice

1   Reset the background and color scheme settings to their defaults (probably None and Windows Standard, respectively).

2   Turn off the screen saver.

3   Delete the My Laptop power scheme, and reset the power scheme setting to its default (probably Home/Desktop).

4   Delete the new dial-up connection from the Network And Dial-Up Connections folder.

5   Delete the new printer driver from the Printers folder.

A

Matching the Exercises

Because Microsoft Windows 2000 Professional has many options that affect the desktop, dialog box options, and the operation of certain functions, your computer might look and act differently from what the exercises in this book show. In general, these variations will not affect your ability to perform the exercises. When a specific Windows setting or component is required to complete an exercise, the lesson provides information about preparing the setting or component for use in the exercise.

You can ensure that your results correspond as closely as possible with those shown in the exercises by following the steps in this appendix. It isn't essential that you understand the steps in this appendix as you work through them. All steps and settings in this appendix are explained in the lessons and exercises within this book.

Checking Your Access Level

In Windows, each person who uses a computer has a user account. Associated with that account is an access level that groups users according to the tasks they are allowed to perform. Most of the exercises in this book require the user's access level to be set to Standard User, which is the default for most users. Some exercises, however, require Administrator-level access, which is the highest level of access.

To check your access level, follow these steps:

Start

1   Click the Start button, point to Settings, and then click Control Panel.

2   In Control Panel, scroll to the bottom of the window, if necessary, and then double-click the Users And Passwords icon.

3   On the Users tab, find the user name that appears when you log on to Windows. If you are not prompted to log on to Windows, you need to set up a user account. To set up a user account, follow these substeps:

   a   Click the Add button. In the User Name box, type your desired user name, and click the Next button. (Your user name can be your first name, your first name and last initial, or any combination that you choose.)

   b   In the Password box, type your desired password, and press Tab. (Your password should be at least six characters, and it should combine letters with numbers.)

   c   In the Confirm Password box, type your password again, and then click the Next button.

   d   Verify that the Standard User option is selected, and click the Finish button.

4   Note the group in the Group column next to your user name. It should read either Standard User or Administrator. If it doesn't, contact the network administrator in your organization for information about changing your access level.

5   In the Users And Passwords dialog box, click OK. Then click the Close button in the top-right corner of Control Panel.

Close

Checking the Mouse Settings

The instructions in this book are written for right-handed mouse use, and they assume that your mouse is set for double-clicking to open folders and files and to start programs. (These are the default settings.) To match the default mouse settings, follow these steps:

Start

1   Click the Start button, point to Settings, and then click Control Panel.

2   In Control Panel, double-click the Mouse icon.

3   On the Buttons tab in the Mouse Properties dialog box, click the Right-Handed option, click the Double-Click To Open An Item (Single-Click To Select) option, and then click OK.

✕

Close

4   Click the Close button in the top-right corner of Control Panel.

If you prefer to set your mouse for left-handed use, follow these steps:

Start

Start

1   Click the Start button, point to Settings, and then click Control Panel.

2   In Control Panel, double-click the Mouse icon.

3   On the Buttons tab in the Mouse Properties dialog box, click the Left-Handed option, and then click OK.

✕

Close

4   Click the Close button in the top-right corner of Control Panel.

Checking the Button Settings

The Standard Buttons toolbars as displayed in this book appear as large icons with text labels.

If you change the Standard Buttons toolbar settings in My Computer, the changes will also appear in Windows Explorer.

To match the Standard Buttons toolbar settings in the My Computer, Windows Explorer, and Internet Explorer windows, follow these steps:

1   On the desktop, double-click the My Computer icon.

2   On the View menu, point to Toolbars, and click Customize to display the Customize Toolbar dialog box.

3   Click the Text Options arrow, and click Show Text Labels.

4   Click the Icon Options arrow, click Large Icons, and then click Close.

✕

Close

5   Click the Close button in the top-right corner of the My Computer window.

To match the Standard Buttons toolbar settings in the Outlook Express window, follow these steps:

Launch Outlook Express

1   On the Quick Launch toolbar, click the Launch Outlook Express button to start Outlook Express.

2   On the View menu, click Layout to open the Window Layout Properties dialog box.

3   Click the Customize Toolbar button, and click the Reset button.

4   Click the Close button, and in the Window Layout Properties dialog box, click OK.

Close

5   Click the Close button in the top-right corner of the Outlook Express window.

Checking the Desktop Setup

In general, the arrangement of items on the Windows desktop will not affect your ability to complete the exercises. However, if you want to exactly match the look of the desktop shown in the exercises, make sure the following icons are arranged in a column on the desktop, in the order given:

- My Documents (optional)
- My Computer
- My Network Places
- Recycle Bin
- Internet Explorer

If necessary, drag the icons to put them in order. To be able to rearrange the icons, verify that Auto Arrange is toggled off:

1   Right-click a blank area on the desktop, and point to Arrange Icons on the shortcut menu that appears.

2   If there is a checkmark to the left of Auto Arrange, click Auto Arrange to clear it. Otherwise, click a blank area on the desktop to close the shortcut menu.

To match the appearance of your desktop with the appearance of the desktop in the book, follow these steps:

1   Right-click a blank area on the Windows desktop, and click Properties on the shortcut menu that appears.

2   On the Background tab in the Display Properties dialog box, click (None) in the Select A Background Picture Or HTML Document As Wallpaper list.

3   On the Screen Saver tab, click (None) in the Screen Saver list.

4   On the Appearance tab, click Windows Standard in the Scheme list.

5   On the Web tab, verify that the Show Web Content On My Active Desktop
     check box is cleared. All other check boxes on this tab should also be cleared.

6   Click OK to close the Display Properties dialog box.

Checking Taskbar and Start Menu Settings

You might find certain Windows features, such as personalized menus, distracting while you are completing the exercises in this book. For best results with the exercises, follow these steps to turn the appropriate Windows features on or off:

Some of the menus displayed in this book show Personalized Menus to point out when you'll need to click the down arrows at the bottom of a menu to see additional menu commands.

1   Right-click a blank area on the taskbar, and click Properties on the
     shortcut menu.

2   On the General tab in the Taskbar And Start Menu Properties dialog box,
     select the Always On Top and Show Clock check boxes. All other check
     boxes on this tab should be cleared.

3   On the Advanced tab, select the Expand Network And Dial-Up Connections
     check box in the Start Menu Settings list. All other check boxes on this tab
     should be cleared.

4   Click OK.

5   Right-click the taskbar again, and point to Toolbars on the shortcut menu.

6   On the menu that appears, verify whether Quick Launch is the only toolbar
     name with a checkmark to the left of it. If another toolbar name has a
     checkmark, click the name to remove the checkmark.

7   If necessary, repeat steps 5 and 6 until only Quick Launch is selected.

B

Installing
Windows 2000

Microsoft Windows 2000 Professional can be made available on your computer
in one of three ways:

- It can be installed by the computer manufacturer before you receive
  the computer.
- It can be installed by someone else at your organization, such as a
  network administrator.
- It can be installed by you.

If Windows 2000 is already installed on your computer, you don't need to read this
appendix. However, if you need to install Windows 2000 yourself, don't worry. The
developers at Microsoft have worked hard to make installation as easy as possible,
and with the help of this appendix, the process should be quite straightforward.

Before You Install Windows 2000

Before you install Windows 2000, you have a few important tasks to perform:

- Back up copies of your important files to a disk other than the one on which Windows 2000 will be installed. If you are on a network, back up your files to a network disk. If you are not on a network, back up files to floppy disks or to a backup disk or tape.
- Decide which of the two major types of installation you want: upgrade or clean.
- Upgrading replaces an older version of Windows that is already on your computer with Windows 2000. The older version will no longer be available once Windows 2000 is installed, but Windows 2000 will retain the preferences you have specified in the older version of Windows for things like the display settings. Also, you won't need to reinstall all the programs on your computer.
- A clean installation adds Windows 2000 as a completely new operating system instead of basing it on an existing operating system. Computer manufacturers and system administrators often perform clean installations when they install Windows 2000. Performing a clean installation is beyond the scope of this book.

Upgrading an Older Version of Windows

To upgrade Windows 95, Windows 98, or Windows NT to Windows 2000 Professional, follow these steps:

important

The installation process on your computer might differ slightly from the following process, depending on your computer's specific setup. In the case of a difference, follow the prompts that appear on your screen.

1   Start your current Windows operating system.
2   Insert the Microsoft Windows 2000 Professional CD-ROM into the CD-ROM drive, or double-click Setup in the appropriate folder on your network. (If you are performing a network installation, the name of the computer and folder that contains the Windows 2000 setup files should be provided to you by your network administrator.)

3   An alert box appears, stating that the CD-ROM contains a newer version of Windows than the one currently installed, and it asks if you want to continue.

4   Click Yes.

The Microsoft Windows 2000 CD dialog box appears.

5   Click Install Windows 2000.

The first screen in the Windows 2000 Setup wizard appears.

6   Verify that the Upgrade To Windows 2000 (Recommended) option is selected, and click the Next button.

The licensing agreement appears.

7   After reading the agreement, click the I Accept This Agreement option, and click the Next button.

Contact your network administrator for specific information on locating the Windows 2000 Professional setup files on your network.

While the wizard loads the files needed to run the setup process, you might be prompted to change the file system to NTFS. Because you are replacing an older operating system, you won't need any older file systems, so you should probably agree to this. If you think you might want to revert to an older operating system later, such as Windows 98, do not agree to change the file system to NTFS. Converting to NTFS will typically result in additional free space on your hard drive and will speed up access to files and folders stored on your hard drive. If you agree to convert to NTFS, all of your existing programs, folders, and files will be retained. Converting to NTFS adds about 10 minutes to the installation procedure.

8   If necessary, verify that the Yes, Upgrade My Drive option is selected, and click the Next button.

The file system is changed, if necessary. This might take several minutes.

9   The wizard checks that your system meets the basic requirements to run Windows 2000 and prepares for installation. Then it automatically restarts your computer.

After your computer restarts, the Windows 2000 Professional Setup screen appears.

The Setup screen displays messages as it examines the contents of your hard disk to see what to replace and what to save from the previous version of Windows. This might take several minutes, after which the computer automatically restarts again.

The Windows 2000 Professional Setup screen reappears while files are loaded on your computer. This takes several minutes. Your computer automatically restarts again.

The Windows 2000 Startup screen appears. Then the Windows 2000 Setup alert box appears for several minutes.

The Windows 2000 Professional Upgrade dialog box appears while the devices and components that are needed for your system are installed. This takes several minutes.

A message box appears, letting you know that Windows was successfully upgraded.

The computer is automatically restarted for the final time.

Depending on your setup, you might need to supply user information and a password, as well as details that will enable Windows to determine the correct time and language conventions to use.

If necessary, enter your password in the Log On To Windows dialog box, and click OK. If you performed a network installation, you might need to hold down the Ctrl and Alt keys while pressing Delete before you can log on. After you log on, the Windows 2000 desktop appears.

Other Tasks Related to Installation

After you install Windows, you might need to perform some setup procedures, such as installing specific hardware drivers and other software. Detailed steps for performing these tasks are provided in the lessons in this book.

To Do This	See
Install a printer	Lesson 9, "Adding a Printer Driver"
Install other hardware	Lesson 9, "Installing Plug and Play Hardware" and "Installing Non-Plug and Play Hardware"
Install software	Lesson 9, "Installing Software"
Set up network connections	Lesson 8, "Creating a Dial-Up Network Connection"
Set up an Internet connection	Lesson 5, "Connecting to the Internet"

Index

ActiveEducation & Microsoft Press

Microsoft Windows 2000 Professional Step by Step has been created by the professional trainers and writers at ActiveEducation, Inc., to the exacting standards you've come to expect from Microsoft Press. Together, we are pleased to present this self-paced training guide, which you can use individually or as part of a class.

ActiveEducation creates top-quality information technology training content that teaches essential computer skills for today's workplace. ActiveEducation courses are designed to provide the most effective training available and to help people become more productive computer users. Each ActiveEducation course, including this Step by Step book, undergoes rigorous quality control, instructional design, and technical review procedures to ensure that the course is instructionally and technically superior in content and approach. For more information about ActiveEducation, visit the ActiveEducation Web site at *www.activeeducation.com*.

Microsoft Press is the book publishing division of Microsoft Corporation, the leading publisher of information about Microsoft products and services. Microsoft Press is dedicated to providing the highest quality computer books and multimedia training and reference tools that make using Microsoft software easier, more enjoyable, and more productive.

About the Author

Marianne Krcma (pronounced "KERCH-ma") has over 14 years of computer publishing experience, the last six years as a freelance writer and editor. Marianne writes on a wide range of computer topics; recent books have covered HTML, Microsoft Project, Microsoft Word, and Crystal Reports.

In addition to writing and editing, Marianne provides hands-on computer training and consulting. Her clients range from small nonprofit organizations to Fortune 500 companies. Working in person with hundreds of computer users each year gives Marianne an in-depth understanding of their needs and challenges, which she draws on in her writing. With this in mind, she encourages your comments on this book. You can reach her at mkrcma@excite.com. (And in case you were wondering, there are no typos in her last name.)

MICROSOFT LICENSE AGREEMENT
Book Companion CD

IMPORTANT—READ CAREFULLY: This Microsoft End-User License Agreement ("EULA") is a legal agreement between you (either an individual or an entity) and Microsoft Corporation for the Microsoft product identified above, which includes computer software and may include associated media, printed materials, and "online" or electronic documentation ("SOFTWARE PRODUCT"). Any component included within the SOFTWARE PRODUCT that is accompanied by a separate End-User License Agreement shall be governed by such agreement and not the terms set forth below. By installing, copying, or otherwise using the SOFTWARE PRODUCT, you agree to be bound by the terms of this EULA. If you do not agree to the terms of this EULA, you are not authorized to install, copy, or otherwise use the SOFTWARE PRODUCT; you may, however, return the SOFTWARE PRODUCT, along with all printed materials and other items that form a part of the Microsoft product that includes the SOFTWARE PRODUCT, to the place you obtained them for a full refund.

SOFTWARE PRODUCT LICENSE

The SOFTWARE PRODUCT is protected by United States copyright laws and international copyright treaties, as well as other intellectual property laws and treaties. The SOFTWARE PRODUCT is licensed, not sold.

1. **GRANT OF LICENSE.** This EULA grants you the following rights:

   a. **Software Product.** You may install and use one copy of the SOFTWARE PRODUCT on a single computer. The primary user of the computer on which the SOFTWARE PRODUCT is installed may make a second copy for his or her exclusive use on a portable computer.

   b. **Storage/Network Use.** You may also store or install a copy of the SOFTWARE PRODUCT on a storage device, such as a network server, used only to install or run the SOFTWARE PRODUCT on your other computers over an internal network; however, you must acquire and dedicate a license for each separate computer on which the SOFTWARE PRODUCT is installed or run from the storage device. A license for the SOFTWARE PRODUCT may not be shared or used concurrently on different computers.

   c. **License Pak.** If you have acquired this EULA in a Microsoft License Pak, you may make the number of additional copies of the computer software portion of the SOFTWARE PRODUCT authorized on the printed copy of this EULA, and you may use each copy in the manner specified above. You are also entitled to make a corresponding number of secondary copies for portable computer use as specified above.

   d. **Sample Code.** Solely with respect to portions, if any, of the SOFTWARE PRODUCT that are identified within the SOFTWARE PRODUCT as sample code (the "SAMPLE CODE"):

      i. **Use and Modification.** Microsoft grants you the right to use and modify the source code version of the SAMPLE CODE, *provided* you comply with subsection (d)(iii) below. You may not distribute the SAMPLE CODE, or any modified version of the SAMPLE CODE, in source code form.

      ii. **Redistributable Files.** Provided you comply with subsection (d)(iii) below, Microsoft grants you a nonexclusive, royalty-free right to reproduce and distribute the object code version of the SAMPLE CODE and of any modified SAMPLE CODE, other than SAMPLE CODE, or any modified version thereof, designated as not redistributable in the Readme file that forms a part of the SOFTWARE PRODUCT (the "Non-Redistributable Sample Code"). All SAMPLE CODE other than the Non-Redistributable Sample Code is collectively referred to as the "REDISTRIBUTABLES."

      iii. **Redistribution Requirements.** If you redistribute the REDISTRIBUTABLES, you agree to: (i) distribute the REDISTRIBUTABLES in object code form only in conjunction with and as a part of your software application product; (ii) not use Microsoft's name, logo, or trademarks to market your software application product; (iii) include a valid copyright notice on your software application product; (iv) indemnify, hold harmless, and defend Microsoft from and against any claims or lawsuits, including attorney's fees, that arise or result from the use or distribution of your software application product; and (v) not permit further distribution of the REDISTRIBUTABLES by your end user. Contact Microsoft for the applicable royalties due and other licensing terms for all other uses and/or distribution of the REDISTRIBUTABLES.

2. **DESCRIPTION OF OTHER RIGHTS AND LIMITATIONS.**

   - **Limitations on Reverse Engineering, Decompilation, and Disassembly.** You may not reverse engineer, decompile, or disassemble the SOFTWARE PRODUCT, except and only to the extent that such activity is expressly permitted by applicable law notwithstanding this limitation.

   - **Separation of Components.** The SOFTWARE PRODUCT is licensed as a single product. Its component parts may not be separated for use on more than one computer.

   - **Rental.** You may not rent, lease, or lend the SOFTWARE PRODUCT.

   - **Support Services.** Microsoft may, but is not obligated to, provide you with support services related to the SOFTWARE PRODUCT ("Support Services"). Use of Support Services is governed by the Microsoft policies and programs described in the user manual, in "online" documentation, and/or in other Microsoft-provided materials. Any supplemental software code provided to you as part of the Support Services shall be considered part of the SOFTWARE PRODUCT and subject to the terms and conditions of this EULA. With respect to technical information you provide to Microsoft as part of the Support Services, Microsoft may use such information for its business purposes, including for product support and development. Microsoft will not utilize such technical information in a form that personally identifies you.

- **Software Transfer.** You may permanently transfer all of your rights under this EULA, provided you retain no copies, you transfer all of the SOFTWARE PRODUCT (including all component parts, the media and printed materials, any upgrades, this EULA, and, if applicable, the Certificate of Authenticity), **and** the recipient agrees to the terms of this EULA.

- **Termination.** Without prejudice to any other rights, Microsoft may terminate this EULA if you fail to comply with the terms and conditions of this EULA. In such event, you must destroy all copies of the SOFTWARE PRODUCT and all of its component parts.

3. **COPYRIGHT.** All title and copyrights in and to the SOFTWARE PRODUCT (including but not limited to any images, photographs, animations, video, audio, music, text, SAMPLE CODE, REDISTRIBUTABLES, and "applets" incorporated into the SOFTWARE PRODUCT) and any copies of the SOFTWARE PRODUCT are owned by Microsoft or its suppliers. The SOFTWARE PRODUCT is protected by copyright laws and international treaty provisions. Therefore, you must treat the SOFTWARE PRODUCT like any other copyrighted material **except** that you may install the SOFTWARE PRODUCT on a single computer provided you keep the original solely for backup or archival purposes. You may not copy the printed materials accompanying the SOFTWARE PRODUCT.

4. **U.S. GOVERNMENT RESTRICTED RIGHTS.** The SOFTWARE PRODUCT and documentation are provided with RESTRICTED RIGHTS. Use, duplication, or disclosure by the Government is subject to restrictions as set forth in subparagraph (c)(1)(ii) of the Rights in Technical Data and Computer Software clause at DFARS 252.227-7013 or subparagraphs (c)(1) and (2) of the Commercial Computer Software—Restricted Rights at 48 CFR 52.227-19, as applicable. Manufacturer is Microsoft Corporation/One Microsoft Way/Redmond, WA 98052-6399.

5. **EXPORT RESTRICTIONS.** You agree that you will not export or re-export the SOFTWARE PRODUCT, any part thereof, or any process or service that is the direct product of the SOFTWARE PRODUCT (the foregoing collectively referred to as the "Restricted Components"), to any country, person, entity, or end user subject to U.S. export restrictions. You specifically agree not to export or re-export any of the Restricted Components (i) to any country to which the U.S. has embargoed or restricted the export of goods or services, which currently include, but are not necessarily limited to, Cuba, Iran, Iraq, Libya, North Korea, Sudan, and Syria, or to any national of any such country, wherever located, who intends to transmit or transport the Restricted Components back to such country; (ii) to any end user who you know or have reason to know will utilize the Restricted Components in the design, development, or production of nuclear, chemical, or biological weapons; or (iii) to any end user who has been prohibited from participating in U.S. export transactions by any federal agency of the U.S. government. You warrant and represent that neither the BXA nor any other U.S. federal agency has suspended, revoked, or denied your export privileges.

DISCLAIMER OF WARRANTY

NO WARRANTIES OR CONDITIONS. MICROSOFT EXPRESSLY DISCLAIMS ANY WARRANTY OR CONDITION FOR THE SOFTWARE PRODUCT. THE SOFTWARE PRODUCT AND ANY RELATED DOCUMENTATION ARE PROVIDED "AS IS" WITHOUT WARRANTY OR CONDITION OF ANY KIND, EITHER EXPRESS OR IMPLIED, INCLUDING, WITHOUT LIMITATION, THE IMPLIED WARRANTIES OF MERCHANTABILITY, FITNESS FOR A PARTICULAR PURPOSE, OR NONINFRINGEMENT. THE ENTIRE RISK ARISING OUT OF USE OR PERFORMANCE OF THE SOFTWARE PRODUCT REMAINS WITH YOU.

LIMITATION OF LIABILITY. TO THE MAXIMUM EXTENT PERMITTED BY APPLICABLE LAW, IN NO EVENT SHALL MICROSOFT OR ITS SUPPLIERS BE LIABLE FOR ANY SPECIAL, INCIDENTAL, INDIRECT, OR CONSEQUENTIAL DAMAGES WHATSOEVER (INCLUDING, WITHOUT LIMITATION, DAMAGES FOR LOSS OF BUSINESS PROFITS, BUSINESS INTERRUPTION, LOSS OF BUSINESS INFORMATION, OR ANY OTHER PECUNIARY LOSS) ARISING OUT OF THE USE OF OR INABILITY TO USE THE SOFTWARE PRODUCT OR THE PROVISION OF OR FAILURE TO PROVIDE SUPPORT SERVICES, EVEN IF MICROSOFT HAS BEEN ADVISED OF THE POSSIBILITY OF SUCH DAMAGES. IN ANY CASE, MICROSOFT'S ENTIRE LIABILITY UNDER ANY PROVISION OF THIS EULA SHALL BE LIMITED TO THE GREATER OF THE AMOUNT ACTUALLY PAID BY YOU FOR THE SOFTWARE PRODUCT OR US$5.00; PROVIDED, HOWEVER, IF YOU HAVE ENTERED INTO A MICROSOFT SUPPORT SERVICES AGREEMENT, MICROSOFT'S ENTIRE LIABILITY REGARDING SUPPORT SERVICES SHALL BE GOVERNED BY THE TERMS OF THAT AGREEMENT. BECAUSE SOME STATES AND JURISDICTIONS DO NOT ALLOW THE EXCLUSION OR LIMITATION OF LIABILITY, THE ABOVE LIMITATION MAY NOT APPLY TO YOU.

MISCELLANEOUS

This EULA is governed by the laws of the State of Washington USA, except and only to the extent that applicable law mandates governing law of a different jurisdiction.

Should you have any questions concerning this EULA, or if you desire to contact Microsoft for any reason, please contact the Microsoft subsidiary serving your country, or write: Microsoft Sales Information Center/One Microsoft Way/Redmond, WA 98052-6399.

OWNER REGISTRATION CARD

Register Today!

1-57231-847-3

Return the bottom portion of this card to register today.

Microsoft® Windows® 2000 Professional
Step by Step®

FIRST NAME   MIDDLE INITIAL   LAST NAME

INSTITUTION OR COMPANY NAME

ADDRESS

CITY   STATE   ZIP

(   )

E-MAIL ADDRESS   PHONE NUMBER

U.S. and Canada addresses only. Fill in information above and mail postage-free.
Please mail only the bottom half of this page.

**For information about Microsoft Press®
products, visit our Web site at
mspress.microsoft.com**

OWNER REGISTRATION CARD

Register Today!

1-57231-847-3

Return the bottom portion of this card to register today.

Microsoft® Windows® 2000 Professional
Step by Step®

FIRST NAME   **MIDDLE INITIAL**   **LAST NAME**

INSTITUTION OR COMPANY NAME

ADDRESS

CITY   **STATE**   **ZIP**

( )

E-MAIL ADDRESS   **PHONE NUMBER**

U.S. and Canada addresses only. Fill in information above and mail postage-free.
Please mail only the bottom half of this page.

For information about Microsoft Press® products, visit our Web site at

mspress.microsoft.com

Microsoft®